Gates of Fear

BOOKS BY BARNABY CONRAD

The Innocent Villa

Matador

La Fiesta Brava

Gates of Fear

My Life as a Matador
BY CARLOS ARRUZA WITH BARNABY CONRAD

BARNABY CONRAD

Gates of Fear

BONANZA BOOKS • NEW YORK

Designed by EMIL SILVESTRI

LIBRARY OF CONGRESS CATALOG CARD NO. 57-10110

2 3 4 5 6 7 8 9 10

*This edition published by Bonanza Books,
a division of Crown Publishers, Inc.,
by arrangement with Thomas Y. Crowell Co.*

ACKNOWLEDGMENTS

Grateful acknowledgment is made to the following publishers and authors for permission to reprint copyrighted material:

True Bowen for excerpt from a newspaper article, *The Mexico City Daily News*.

Rodney Bright for excerpts from *Toros Without Tears*, published in Mexico.

Herb Caen for "Death of an Atomic Pig" from *San Francisco Examiner* column.

Dodd, Mead & Company, Inc., and Cornelia Otis Skinner for excerpt from *Soap Behind The Ears* by Cornelia Otis Skinner, copyright 1941 by Cornelia Otis Skinner.

Doubleday & Company, Inc. for excerpts from *Juan Belmonte, Killer of Bulls* by Leslie Charteris, copyright 1937 by Doubleday & Company, Inc.

E. V. Durling for excerpt from "On the Side" by E. V. Durling, copyrighted by King Features Syndicate, Inc.

Ediciones Destino for excerpts from *Historia Del Toreo*, by Néstor Luján, copyright 1954, Barcelona, Spain.

Esquire magazine, for excerpt from an article by Sidney Franklin, copyright 1951.

Harcourt, Brace and Company, Inc., for letter quoted in Andre Gide's foreword to *Night Flight* by Antoine de Saint-Exupéry, copyright, 1932, by Harcourt, Brace and Company, Inc.

Harper & Brothers and Kenneth Tynan for excerpt from *Bull Fever* by Kenneth Tynan, copyright 1955 by Kenneth Peacock Tynan.

Holiday magazine for an article by Barnaby Conrad, copyright 1957.

Henry Holt & Co., Inc., and Whit Burnett for excerpt from *The Spirit of Adventure*, copyright 1956, Whit Burnett.

To Juan Belmonte
who knows more about the gates of fear
than anyone in the world.

Contents

Contents

Gates of Fear

Introduction

1. Introduction

THE BUYER OF THIS BOOK WILL SOON SEE, AFTER HE GETS HIS PURCHASE HOME and begins to browse through it, that he has been duped. This is not really a technical guide to the bullrings of the world, a bullfighting Baedecker, as he might have hoped. There are some spindly facts about the plazas here and there, but the reader will soon discern that the format is just a framework, an excuse, a sneaky device, an expediency for the author to tell his favorite stories about his favorite subject and to quote from other authors whose writing on the bulls he has admired over the years.

Mostly the chapters are about men, not plazas de toros: in other words, the Fear is more exciting to the author than the Gates. Most bullfight writing is about courage or lack of it. I find it an interesting theme, one of the most interesting in life. Just what is courage—a definition of it—would be interesting to explore. Isn't the clerk who, day after day, makes the drab haul to his accounting stool exhibiting a type of courage? It would take more guts for me to live out his life than to pursue the career of an arctic explorer. And isn't Schweitzer more courageous than all the bullfighters of all time?

But here we are concerned mostly with the obvious courage—physical. Saint-Exupéry didn't think too much of physical courage. In a letter to André Gide, quoted in Gide's foreword to *Night Flight*, he said:

> I have just pulled off a little exploit; spent two days and nights with eleven Moors and a mechanic salving a plane. Alarums and excursions,

3

The gate of fear.

varied and impressive. I heard bullets whizzing over my head for the first time. So now I know how I behave under such conditions; much more calmly than the Moors. But I also came to understand something which had always puzzled me—why Plato (Aristotle?) places courage in the last degree of virtues. It's a concoction of feelings that are not so very admirable. A touch of anger, a spice of vanity, a lot of obstinacy, and a tawdry "sporting" thrill. Above all, a stimulation of one's physical energies, which, however, is oddly out of place. One just folds one's arms, taking deep breaths across one's opened shirt. Rather a pleasant feeling. When it happens at night another feeling creeps into it—of having done something immensely silly. I shall never again admire a merely brave man.

Intellectually, well said and true. Yet emotionally, how the average person rejoices in feats of bravery—a Captain Carlsen riding it out alone on his ship, a man running across a busy street to catch a baby as it falls from a second story, a lone man sailing around the world, a bullet-ridden cop killing the thugs before he dies, a roustabout breaking the fall of an aerialist with his own body, Hillary and Tensing reaching the top, a woman diving off the sinking *Andrea Doria* to save her baby. "Bravery never goes out of fashion," wrote Thackeray.

But these feats we generally only read about. How often do we see bravery displayed before our eyes in peacetime? For some reason it is hard for me to attribute great courage to either football players or boxers, although I am sure I would change my mind if I were trying to get off a pass with four Neanderthaloid types bearing down on me or if I were looking across the ring at a Marciano working his feet in the resin and eagerly punching his gloves together. To drive a racing car seems to me a very brave thing, even though "immensely silly" in Saint-Exupéry's words, since no esthetic end is attempted or achieved. It seems to me infinitely more valid to risk your life gracefully trying to "throw a triple" on the flying bars than to go over Niagara Falls in a barrel. In our times, the circus and the bullring seem to be the only places where esthetic courage is localized, spotlighted, and exhibited on schedule.

Most stories about bullfighting are tales of adventure; and of the basic categories of narratives, adventure stories seem to have the most universal and lasting appeal. It seems to me that the more cowardly one believes himself to be, the more he delights in stories of brave deeds. As Whit Burnett writes in his book, *The Spirit of Adventure:*

> There is something in the breast of many of us bidding us to be up
> and away, lance in hand, mounted, riding off into the distance to meet

4

the dragon of our destiny. There is also in our bosoms something of the romantic Don's companion—the fat and reasonable peasant, Sancho Panza, soberly submitting all such dream stuff to the proverbs of common sense and seeing a sheep as mutton rather than enchantment. Yet even Sancho Panza was talked into the journey by the lively witted Don. Even realists appreciate the fact that a little jaunt, a change, will do a man no harm. The adventurer, deep within us, is sometimes sorely hedged about. And some of us are fashioned, as was Alphonse Daudet's Tartarin of Tarascon, with both the glorious Don and the dull peasant encased within the same body, and he who wants to slay a lion cannot kill a fly, he who'd roam the world must stay and pay the taxes—a pretty kettle of fish, as Daudet observed, when the Don Quixote in our bosom cries, "Cover yourself with glory," and the voice of Sancho Panza cries from the same throat, "Stay, and keep on your warm long underwear!"

We are all cowards—it's just that we are each afraid of different things. I vividly remember taking the fearless Sidney Franklin—fearless in a bullring, that is—for a fast ride on a midget motorcycle through the winding streets of Sevilla's barrio de Santa Cruz, and he was babbling with fright before it was over. Grantland Rice says, in *The Tumult and the Shouting:*

"Stribling . . . was the oddest fighter I ever knew. He was dead game—out of the ring. He was seldom game in the ring during a tough fight . . . yet he would drive a shaky aircraft in front of a hurricane, or a motorcycle through a heavy wall. I have seen him do it. He was killed on that motorcycle."

"Many would be Cowards, if they had Courage enough," wrote Thomas Fuller back in 1732.

Probably many toreros fight bulls simply because they lack the courage *not* to fight bulls. As I wrote in the introduction to Carlos Arruza's autobiography, much mystic claptrap has been ascribed to the reasons men fight bulls, from religion to homosexuality to thwarted matricide, and perhaps in rare instances it has some validity. But in Arruza's case, and I believe in the cases of the majority of men who get a supreme thrill from "making a bull pass by their legs," the basic underlying reasons are contained in this excerpt from the excellent paper entitled "The Counter-Phobic Attitude" by the late psychiatrist Otto Fenichel:

When the organism discovers that it is now able to overcome without fear a situation which would formerly have overwhelmed it with anxiety, it experiences a certain kind of pleasure. This pleasure has the character of "I need not feel anxiety any more. . . ."

The counter-phobic attitude may really be regarded as a never-end-

5

ing attempt at the belated conquest of an unmastered infantile anxiety. . . .

The most outstanding example is probably the entire field of sport, which may in general be designated as a counter-phobic phenomenon. No doubt there are erotic and aggressive gratifications in sports just as they are present in all the other functional pleasures of adults. Certainly not everyone who engages in sport is suffering from an unconscious insoluble fear of castration, nor does it follow that the particular sport for which he shows a later preference must once have been feared. But it will generally hold true that the essential joy in sport is that one actively brings about in play certain tensions which were formerly feared, so that one may enjoy the fact that now one can overcome them without fearing them.

I am convinced that the reasons for one's taking up bullfighting are usually neither more nor less neurotic or mystical than those that propel a man to take up high diving, mountaineering, or sports car racing.

The one thing that all bullfighters have in common is that they are true adventurers; they are pure, uncompromised Quixote inside, with no trace of Sancho in evidence. They are not modern American professional athletes with hearts that are basically commuter and bourgeois. Toreros generally start life by running away from home, and they usually remain restless and untamed and undomesticated until they die. And this is the way it should be. As William Bolitho writes in his classic, *Twelve Against the Gods*:

> A feat, a danger, a surprise, these are bonbons which adventure showers on those who follow her cult with a single mind. Their occurrence even repeated does not constitute a life of adventure.
>
> Here also we renounce utterly the comfort of Mr. Kipling, who believed commuting, and soldiering in the British Army, and buying English country houses, adventurous; and Mr. Chesterton, who was certain that a long walk on Sunday and a glass of beer set one spiritually in the company of Alexander, and Captain Kidd and Cagliostro. All this amiable misconception is as touching as the children's wish for a good pirate, for bloodshed in which no one gets hurt, and roulette with haricot beans. Tom Sawyer knew better. The adventurer is an outlaw. Adventure must start with running away from home.

So this is a book about adventurers and about the principal places where the adventures occur. Of course I have not included all the bullrings of the world in this book; in Spain alone there are over 400 plazas that hold

6

more than 5000 people. I am sure to get complaints from aficionados who do not find included their own special plaza de toros, the place where they saw *that* great corrida. Why not, some will wail, a chapter on the good ring at Cádiz, or the charming one at Aranjuez where you eat those marvelous strawberries between bulls, or Granada and Alicante and Logroño and Murcia, all good plazas; or Ronda, the oldest plaza in Spain; or Algeciras and La Línea across from Gibraltar; or Toledo, where Manolete, Arruza, and Parrita made history that day in 1945; or San Sebastián, where the chic summer crowd goes and the wind off the sea is terrible for the toreros' capes; or Bilbao—certainly Bilbao and Zaragoza, with their traditionally fine fighters and big bulls, should rate chapters.

And how about the many Latin American plazas that have been slighted? My only excuse is that space would not permit chapters on all the rings, so I chose those plazas that meant most to me or that had the best stories to tell. For example, Salamanca is a good enough plaza de toros; but Manolete and Joselito didn't get killed on its sand, Arruza didn't put up the greatest fight of his life there, the town hasn't produced a Belmonte, and García Lorca never wrote a poem about a happening there.

The plazas I did choose are, generally speaking, the most important in the world and the most colorful. Many have been around for a long time— like the almost two-hundred-year-old Maestranza—and they will be around for some years to come. Perhaps they will be changed into soccer stadiums, as so many writers have warned, but I doubt it. In an article written way back in 1930 in *Fortune* magazine, Hemingway gloomily warned of the threat of soccer to la fiesta, and for years there have been articles that "futbol" is weaning all the aficionados away, but the facts don't seem to bear this out. For example: in 1915 there were 241 corridas, whereas in 1945 there were 288.

The British critic John Marks says in his excellent book, *To the Bull-fight:*

> For some time past it seems also to have been supposed, outside Spain, that the pursuit of a ball was gradually ousting persecution of the bull from pride of place among the Spaniards. One read that they had only to take up sport in earnest, on a popular scale, and before long they would be sure to tire of such a shameful amusement as that of watching literally gilded youths tease a formidable brute for money and renown. Once the Spanish masses felt the fascination of professional football [i.e., soccer], the end of their own benighted preference for a debased gladiatorial show would ensue as inexorably as day follows darkness. The flaws in this wishful theory are obvious enough

on the most cursory inspection. The discovery of football was not exactly new in Spain during the first Great War, when bullfighting reached its peak in the golden age of Joselito and Belmonte—but anyhow it so happens that the respective seasons of the two contrasting entertainments scarcely overlap.

Back in the 1880's the bullfighting magazine *La Lidia* used to moan in its editorials, "You call these bulls—you call these men? La fiesta cannot survive one more decade."

Cossio lists the biographies of over ten thousand toreros since 1700 in his monumental work *Los Toros*. Whether the next 250 years will produce another ten thousand one cannot tell. But bullfighting, anachronistic as it is in this jet and atomic neon world of today, appears to be here to stay. The extraordinary interest manifested by Americans in the last ten years should insure steady customers by itself. Bullfighting clubs have sprung up all over America, and a San Diego periodical, appallingly named *The Bull Sheet*, keeps a small but intense group of what Tom Lea calls "aficionadillos" informed of what goes on in the pigtailed world.

Periodically there are attempts to hold corridas in the United States, but they are generally abortive attempts in Texas across the Mexican border or bloodless parodies in California. Far from encouraging this activity, I deplore it, and will do anything to discourage bringing bullfights to the United States. I am quite sure they would end up approximating this description of a fanciful corrida in Chicago dreamed up in a letter by the distinguished Peruvian architect and humorist, Hector Velarde:

QUERIDO AMIGO:

As you probably know, they now give bullfights in this wonderful country of America. They started them for Good Neighbor Policy Day. Of course they're not exactly like those back home in Peru, but I tell you the one I just saw here in Chicago was splendid. They signed up Spain's three greatest matadors, Chapalito, Carlete, and El Pita; for $2,000,000, $2,600,000 and $825,000, respectively. Six bulls crossed with buffalos from the pampas of Oklahoma. The arena—sensational—350,000 people!

What a commotion! Everybody was busy placing bets while the vendors shouted over loudspeakers: "Red-hot Spanish sandwiches, orange juice from the Alhambra, hot-bulldogs," etc. A few minutes before the fights, some youths pranced around the ring dressed like gypsies—"The Triana Boys"—and as they did front flips in front of the Mayor's box they shouted: "Rah, rah, rah—orehee, orehoo, orehaa, oreja, oreja, oreja!" Then they withdrew, and from the toril gate came a great quantity of vehicles and horsemen. In the open cars were several stacks of beautiful gringas dressed in mantillas, and on the horses were Argentine gauchos, wild west cowboys, Mexican charros, and Peruvian cholos. A Navy band was blaring furiously: "Spain, Spain, dear mother of mine. . . ."

Suddenly I heard a sound as though all Chicago's fire alarms had been set off; it was the signal for the parade of the toreros. There was no mounted constable. Instead a terrific-looking girl dressed like a Flit soldier led the parade out, her back arched gracefully and the baton a whirling blur in her hand. Behind her came Chapalito, Carlete, and El Pita, handsomely dressed, and then the banderilleros and helpers, Americans from the Boston School of Tauromachy. Then followed a small division of light tanks with picadors on top, a group of nurses with stretchers, monosabios protected by helmets and with ace bandages on their knees, a squad of policemen, a group of firemen wearing gypsy hats, and lastly, the mascot of the corrida, a baby elephant.

The ovation was deafening. I asked what the tanks were for and they informed me delightedly that the S.P.C.A. had eliminated the picadors' horses and introduced other slight modifications.

The sirens again, and the toril gate was opened. An animal charged out furiously. Half bull and half buffalo, he had a big sign painted on his side saying: "Drink Coca Cola." The card over the toril gate said his name was "Little Bill." Then I saw that his horns were yellow. "They paint them?" I asked. "No," a well-informed lady next to me told me, "they spray them with penicillin."

It was El Pita's bull. He did three majestic verónicas and I thought the world would come to an end; a group of Spanish experts gave the ovation signal and the applause machines went into operation along with 350,000 whistles, twelve bands of musicians each going its separate way, and a device that rattled out like a machine gun: "Olé, olé, olé, olé, olé, olé . . ." Once more the sirens and the tanks rumbled out. Here there is no question as to whether the bull wants to charge or not. A tank appears camouflaged like an appetizing bush, the bull steps forward to eat, and the picador lets him have it with a type of modified bazooka: ta, ta, ta, ta, ta—like a pneumatic hammer.

During this act, the crowd got up for snacks, and to make bets as to who would win, the matador or the bull.

The banderilla part was interesting. They were made of long thin springs covered with cellophane. The toreros from the Boston school

9

placed them. But something terrible happened. Johnny Maxwell, a good banderillero, tripped and fell as the bull charged. "He's going to get killed!" I cried, covering my eyes. When I looked again, Johnny had disappeared and everybody was calm. What had happened? Just that in this arena there are no burladeros, only trap doors, with a technician at a control board whose skillful finger is ever ready for the right button. Unfortunately, they tell me, the bull has gone down with two or three of the men . . .

El Pita dedicated the bull to the Mayor, throwing up his montera to him. His Honor was so pleased that he put on the hat and announced over the loudspeaker that he was presenting the torero with a Frigidaire.

El Pita was unlucky with the sword. But the bull did go down finally, and instantly between the man and the animal there appeared a fellow dressed in white who held a stop watch in one hand and began to toll off the seconds with the other: the referee. If the bull doesn't die by a knockout in 120 seconds, he wins. If he does die, he loses. This time the bull won. The nurses appeared with injections and took the bull out.

The second bull of the afternoon was for Carlete. It was big, brave, and had the face of a sea lion. But why go on? It was the same, *exactly* the same, as the fight before—you know how well organized they are here. Next season is going to be held in Detroit in the new Plaza Ford before 428,000 spectators. Maybe I'll write you about it. I don't know, though. Maybe I won't.

Best wishes,
HECTOR

Farfetched? Not so very, I'm afraid.

No—let us leave la fiesta to the Latins, for only they truly have the proper talent and history and breeding and decadence to savor the pagan spectacle, to know how to enjoy the death ritual. Let us leave Madison Square Garden out of this, for once. Let us continue to go to the source. Let the gates of fear continue to swing on their original hinges in their original sites, for when the bolt is thrown they creak open onto yellow sand that is steeped in centuries of blood and lore with layer upon layer of cowardice and bravery on top.

And this, then, is what the book is about . . . those gates of fear and the men who wait, pale and with pounding hearts, to see what is going to come out of the dark tunnel.

10

Talavera de la Reina

Talavera de la Reina

2. Talavera de la Reina

TALAVERA DE LA REINA IS AN UNIMPORTANT CITY WITH AN UNIMPORTANT bullring that seats only five thousand. Only five thousand people, therefore, witnessed the greatest tragedy in the history of bullfighting. Talavera is a mere hour or so out of Madrid, and one can get there by the conventional methods of train and bus. I did it the hard way: I stopped there on my way from Lisbon, Portugal, to Madrid, Spain—by taxi.

The year was 1952, and I had been bumped off the plane at Lisbon. It was impossible to get any form of transportation to Spain that week because, as my seatmate from New York, Cardinal Spellman, had informed me, it was the time of the Eucharistic Congress in Barcelona; thousands upon thousands of churchmen were heading for what the wonderfully irreverent Spaniards called "The Black Olympics." There was neither bus nor train nor plane space out of Lisbon for a week, and I had to be in Madrid the following day. So when I came out of the airport I looked over the line of ancient, high-topped, stubby-nosed taxis, found a driver who looked pleasant enough to spend fourteen hours with, and got in.

"Where to?" he asked in Portuguese.

"Madrid," I said casually, savoring the moment, for how often in one's life does one tell a cab driver to take him from the capital of one country to the capital of another?

"Si, senhor, Madrid," he repeated mechanically, and started off. We drove for half a block before his head swiveled around and he exclaimed, "Madrid!"

He thought he'd better stop home for his passport and tell his wife. After a few moments he came out with another man, a large, serious-looking fellow.

"My brother-in-law Manoel will take you—better driver than me."

Manoel got in the car, in a nimbus of garlic, and grasped the wheel determinedly. We set off with a gurgle and a chug and a series of spastic jerks, and I tried to make myself as comfortable as possible in back amongst my suitcases. I was rather looking forward to practicing my Portuguese and learning something about the countryside from Manoel.

"How old is the car?" I asked as we wheezed among the brightly colored little towns in this fugitive from the Smithsonian; I had picked one of the better ones, but it still must have been twenty-five years old. The man didn't answer or turn around. I repeated the question. And again, louder. Then I came to the horrible realization that he was stone deaf and virtually mute.

It was a ghastly trip. For lunch we stopped at a little café and ate together in complete silence, smiling wanly at each other from time to time. By dinnertime we were too exhausted to smile. At one o'clock in the morning we were only an hour from Madrid, and I never wanted to reach any place so badly in my life. Yet when I saw the sign reading "Talavera de la Reina," I had to stop, for I was at one of bullfighting's historic shrines, and I didn't know when I'd have another opportunity to see it. Manoel thought I was mad when I made him detour off the road to the plaza de toros, and he made little impatient animal noises when I got out.

It was a moonlight night, and the ring lay slumbering there in the black shadows of a clump of trees. I found a gate open and went into the patio de caballos. The whole saga seemed to unfold before me. It must have been here that he smoked his last cigarette. And over there in the chapel he'd asked his special Virgin for his last bit of luck. And there was the infirmary where he'd called out for his mother before he died. I walked out on the sand, pale green in the moonlight, and found the spot, across from the presidente's box, where perfection in the bullring died. I found myself foolishly looking down, looking for blood that had soaked into the sand thirty-two years before, on May 16, 1920. Actually, the story of the end, the tragedy of Talavera, had begun the day before that historic date. It had really started forty miles east, on the hot sands of the Madrid ring

It was May 15, 1920, the day before the man's last day on earth, and it was a bad day. The bull, the one that ran his total kills to 1566, swayed and crashed over dead, and the twenty-five-year-old matador down in the arena wiped his sweaty face, looked up at the Madrid crowd, and swore as they booed him.

14

This was José Miguel Isidro del Sagrado Corazón de Jesús Gómez y Ortega, known to Spain and the world as Joselito, or Joselito el Gallo, or Gallito, or simply—The Best. Although he was universally accepted by other bullfighters, experts, and historians as the most perfect bullfighter who ever lived, this afternoon the crowd was shouting insults and howling for his blood.

It's a recorded fact that as he walked away from the dead bull toward the fence, a woman stood up in the stands and screamed, "I hope a bull kills you tomorrow in Talavera!" A cushion struck Joselito on the arm, and as he looked up into the hate of the crowd, his melancholy eyes filled with tears. "This," he murmured to his sword boy, "this *must* end!"

The crowd had made the idol and, just as they were to do with Manolete twenty-seven years later, they were out to murder the idol they had created. The treacherous bull of the next afternoon, Bailador, wasn't really needed for the job. Joselito was already dead. He had been dead for some time.

He was an old-young man when he died. But he had always been old. Born near Sevilla on May 8, 1895, one of six children, little Joselito never seemed to be a child. Joselito was the son, nephew, and brother of gypsy bullfighters, and his kindergarten was in the unnatural shadow of the bull-rings. His father, a good matador, died when Joselito was two.

"How—," his father managed to rasp in his dying sentence, "how did Rafael fight today?"

Rafael "El Gallo," Joselito's brother, was a promising young bullfighter then. Now seventy-three years old, colorful and revered, he told me most of this story of Joselito.

Another brother was also a novillero, and his three sisters married toreros, so it was only natural that Joselito's first photograph at the age of two shows him practicing an estocada with a miniature sword. Joselito's mother, Gabriela, was also from a bullfighting family, and she used to sigh and say wearily, "The only ones who don't get gored by bulls are the priests safe in the cathedral."

Gabriela fought to keep her youngest and favorite out of the ring. "Let's save one," she pleaded. "Let's just save *one!*" But she knew it was going to be a useless fight when she saw "the child of her right eye" growing a pigtail at the age of six.

Then at eight he began skipping school. Usually she found him in the back yard of a painter named Cayetano who had a spaniel trained to charge like a bull. The first time she saw his already marvelously graceful body leaning into a sweeping verónica, she knew she had a genius on her hands.

His first public success came when he was nine. It was a festival at a little village called Coría del Rio outside of Sevilla. The arena was make-

15

shift, formed by an enclosure of heavy wagons, but the bullfighters—and the bulls—were professionals. Joselito, wearing his first pair of long pants and with a cap covering the pigtail pinned on top of his head, perched up on top of one of the carts like the other spectators, and his sad young eyes watched every move the toreros made down in the arena. Inside his jacket he had tucked a pair of cortas. These are banderillas that are cut down to a third normal size; hence the person placing them has to be much closer to the bull, thus making the maneuver much more dangerous.

It happened on the second bull. The veteran banderillero was having trouble making the difficult animal charge the way he wanted it to so he could place the banderillas. Holding the barbed sticks ready over his head, he made false runs at the animal twice, challenging it gutterally with his voice and rapping the two long banderillas together to try to provoke a clean charge. The animal just shook his big horns and pawed the sand.

Suddenly a boy's voice was heard by the crowd.

"Where you're standing, man, it's never going to charge! Come, place yourself over there!"

The crowd laughed, and the banderillero looked up at the nine-year-old author of this statement and worked his mouth disdainfully.

Suddenly Joselito leapt down into the arena, and the crowd gasped. "Toro, hah-hah!" he called in as manly a tone as a treble can be, placing himself close to one of the wagons completely opposite to the direction the banderillero had been trying to force the bull's charge. He had the stubby banderillas in his hands, and he leapt up into the air once to attract the bull's attention.

The animal, twenty feet away, stared curiously at this new target in a different area of the ring, and then it charged hard. The boy stood there like a post, his feet flat on the sand, his back arched gracefully as the big animal bore down on him. The crowd screamed in crescendo, for it looked as though the horns couldn't miss. But when the sharp points were six feet from him, Joselito jumped his right leg out to the side, leaning his body with it, but without moving his left foot. The bull, thinking the target was escaping, veered off its course to intercept it. In that split second, Joselito sucked back his leg, leapt up over the lowered horns, and jabbed the darts into the animal's withers. Using the sticks themselves to push himself away and out of the bull's course, he pivoted and trotted calmly toward the barrier as the bull bucked and wheeled past him.

For a moment the crowd was too stunned to realize what they had witnessed. Then they set up a roar. But did you see it? A nine-year-old child! A pair of cortas al quiebro—and Espartero himself could have placed them no better!

16

The young Joselito.

Joselito held up his hand as he'd seen the professionals do and gravely acknowledged the applause as he climbed back to his seat. It was the first applause of his life. He liked it.

Word spread fast throughout Sevilla of the astonishing happening at Coría del Río. "The youngest of the Gallos is a prodigy," was the verdict of the experts. How else could one explain that phenomenal pair of banderillas placed by a child who had never faced anything larger than a calf before?

That was a milestone for Joselito. The next came a year later at a tienta at the Miura ranch. Miura bulls are the most famous of all fighting bulls. A vicious, purebred strain raised exclusively for the ring for over a hundred years, they have killed more famous matadors than any other breed and were labeled "the bulls of death." Tientas at the Miura ranch were highly exclusive, serious affairs, and Joselito pleaded with his brothers to be allowed to go. They kept him in the background during the testing of the calves, afraid of what old man Miura sitting up on the porch over the little arena would think about a child's being around and getting in the way. After the stubby-horned calves were caped by Joselito's brothers and the other aspirant toreros of fourteen and fifteen, a large five-year-old heifer with sharp horns was let into the ring. The toreritos, who a short time before were so eager, brave, and jealous with the two-year-olds, suddenly retreated behind the burladero shields and very generously began "you-firsting" each other.

And then they saw a figure flash by them with a magenta cape that was larger than he was. Joselito was out in the ring before his brothers could stop him, and he was holding the cape behind his body in the dangerous De Frente por Detrás pass.

Old Miura, sitting up on the balcony, leaned forward, tugged at his gray mustache, and watched incredulously as he saw Joselito execute pass after pass with astonishing grace and control. He sent for Joselito to come up to the big house for tea. Before the afternoon was over he had given the boy a horse and, most important, invited him out to practice with the calves any time he wanted to. Joselito took the old man up on his invitation, going out to "Don Eduardo's" every chance he got. Miura became very attached to this serious, honest boy who lived, breathed, and dreamt bullfighting and only bullfighting. He had never seen such dedication in anyone of any age, and he liked him for it. Once Don Eduardo said affectionately, "It's as though another son were born to me."

With every tienta, with every bullfight he witnessed, Joselito was learning and perfecting. When he was eleven he said to his mother very solemnly, "Please let me become a professional, since soon I will be too old."

18

His mother, horrified, managed to keep him at school one more year. Then, when he was twelve, he fought in his first organized fight, wearing his first "suit of lights" in his first real plaza de toros. It was in Jerez, and he was to receive ten whole *reales* (two dollars and a half) for fighting a pair of small bulls along with two other young "fenómenos." Joselito tasted triumph and tragedy that day. On his first bull he was superb, graceful, and brave, and he had the crowd that had merely come to watch a novelty act cheering as though they were watching a top "sword" in action. He killed after two thrusts, and the crowd went wild, making him take several triumphant laps around the ring.

Then came his second animal. He couldn't kill it. "It's made of concrete," he gasped to his brothers between tries. Finally the warning trumpet blast sounded, and three minutes later the second, and then the last, and Joselito, with tears of rage and frustration, watched the animal being led out by the trained steers. Except for Bailador, it was the only bull he ever took on that didn't meet death at his hands.

Joselito was miserable, but the critics overlooked the ending of the corrida because of the astonishing performance that preceded it. An impresario signed Joselito for sixteen fights in Portugal. He was on his way. He performed well in those becerradas—calf-fights—and turned the pittance he earned over to Gabriela with a manly flourish, saying as his father had said to her so many times, "Here you go, Mama—have a good time."

The next season he fought more, and by the following season he was being talked about all over Spain. But 1910 was his first really big year. Here's what the critics said of this fifteen-year-old boy—and these reviews come verbatim from the newspaper files, not from the hazy memories of some old-timers bemoaning the passing of the "good old days when men were men and bulls were bulls."

Of his presentation in San Sebastián the critic Santo-Mano wrote in *Sol y Sombra,* the bullfighting bible of that era: "I never would have believed it possible! What this child did yesterday with a large and dangerous novillo!"

After his first fight in Valencia, the critic wrote: "Gallito III is nothing more nor less than a phenomenon. Why bother to detail the faenas he did yesterday? Let me just say that never in my life have I ever seen better fighting by anyone!"

The eminent Don Ventura described Joselito's fight in Bilbao in a curiously anachronistic term: "Positively *atomístico* [atomic]!"

The year 1911 was a repetition of success, with the addition of a feat unduplicated in the annals of tauromachy. On the fourteenth of May, just a week after his sixteenth birthday, this boy killed six novillos, instead of

19

Above: Joselito's superb grace shown in this *muletazo* pass.

Below: Joselito placing banderillas.

the usual two—all by himself! Before a crowd of ten thousand people he was awarded the ears off four of the animals; and this was back in the days when ears were very rarely awarded, no one yet having cut an ear in Madrid or Sevilla, for example.

The usually blasé *Sol y Sombra's* review of this fight of Joselito's in Cádiz starts out like something by a Hollywood press agent: *"Un éxito immenso, colosal, sublime . . ."*

People in the rest of Spain were impressed by the feat, but they didn't quite believe it. "Cádiz is a small town after all," they said. "How would he do in a big city?"

The next year, Joselito's brother Rafael decided that the boy was ready to show them, and he arranged for a fight in Madrid. Appearing in Madrid for a torero is like making his debut in Madison Square Garden for a boxer, and the whole city was buzzing about the prodigy from Sevilla. "It's the result of paid newspaper propaganda," many scoffed. "He's just a calf-fighter. You'll see on Sunday what happens when he comes up against real novillos."

Joselito started the proceedings off in a highly unorthodox manner. The day before the fight he went to see the bulls in the corrals behind the arena. They were large three-and-a-half-year-old novillos, bigger than anything he'd ever fought. Joselito studied the animals snorting in the enclosure for a moment and then announced firmly, "I won't fight them."

"But why?" the impresario protested. "Certainly they're big, but I think you can handle them."

"They're too small," said Joselito. "I won't fight."

The impresario blanched. He had sold twenty thousand tickets for the next afternoon, and now his attraction was walking out on him. "But what am I going to do?"

Then Joselito looked over into an adjoining corral where there were half a dozen huge five-year-old bulls. "I'll fight those."

"But that's madness! Those are full-grown bulls—for full matadors next Sunday, not for a novillero who's never fought anything but calves!"

Joselito was adamant and got his way. His presentation in Madrid as a novillero was not with novillos, but with toros de verdad—true bulls. The first animal that blasted out into the sun to try to kill him was named Escopeta—Shotgun—and it weighed over fourteen hundred pounds! (Nine hundred is the official required weight these days.)

The first thing the monster saw was the slight figure of a boy kneeling alone in the center of the golden sand. Joselito's father had invented the dangerous larga cambiada, and Joselito was out to show Madrid whose son he was. He shouted at the bull as soon as it came through the toril gate,

21

and it pounded toward the boy, its head lowered to kill. Thirty feet, twenty feet, ten feet, and the boy stayed there unmoving on his knees, holding the cape spread out on the sand in front of him with his right hand.

When the bull was two yards from him he swung the cape over his head. The cloth leapt into life, blossoming out around his shoulders, and the bull veered off its course to slash at the cape. The bull's right horn passed just a few inches from Joselito's head as its momentum carried it a full fifteen feet beyond him.

After that Joselito did things that, according to his biographer Gustavo del Barco, "converted that august plaza de toros into a cage of howling maniacs."

He gave them everything. He placed banderillas three different ways, and people swore they'd never seen sticks placed like that, so elegantly, so surely, so dangerously. On the last pair he let the bull come into him so close that the horn split open his right eyebrow and he had to withdraw to the infirmary before continuing. For his opening muleta work he called for a chair, placed it in the middle of the arena, and, sitting in it, made the animal pass back and forth five times without standing up. Then he scratched an X on the sand with his sword, and, planting his feet on it, he did eight frightening natural passes without moving off. The tricks over, he settled down to the damnedest lesson in classic bullfighting ever seen in Madrid, ending up with a perfect sword thrust that dropped the bull instantly.

The next day one critic wrote halfway down his column: "I have run out of adjectives to describe the glory of this boy. For the rest of this review I will leave blank spaces and the reader can fill them in as he wishes."

Madrid had a new idol. For weeks afterward people discussed that incredible performance, jumping up in cafés to demonstrate how Joselito had placed the banderillas or to show how slowly and elegantly he manipulated the muleta. Three months later they went through the same thing again when Joselito took "the alternative." Usually calf-fighters graduate to the status of novillero and stay there for several seasons before becoming skilled enough to receive a doctorate of tauromachy and become a full matador. If they make the grade, it's usually when they're over twenty-one. Rafael el Gallo figured his brother had nothing more to learn about the science, so Joselito eliminated a long apprenticeship as a novillero and became a full matador de toros, the youngest ever to wear the title. This would be tantamount to a seventeen-year-old boxer's jumping from the Golden Gloves to top heavyweight contention overnight, without the educational fooling around in preliminaries and tank town main events.

The next season Joselito fought eighty corridas, and found himself the

22

top sword in all the world. The only others who could be mentioned in the same breath with him were his unpredictable brother Rafael and Gaona, the Mexican.

What was this young man like, this eighteen-year-old who was well on his way to becoming a millionaire and who was already Spain's greatest hero? To most people he was an enigma. The most completely dedicated of men, he was dull, remote, and taciturn on any subject but his own. Nothing in the world interested him except bulls and the raising of them. Even in the years when he fought over one hundred corridas in a six-month season, if he found himself with a spare day when he wasn't either traveling to a fight or performing in one, his idea of a relaxing good time was to get out in the fields and cape heifers for a few hours.

He was superbly built, handsome with a thick-lipped brooding quality; women went mad for him. He had his women, plenty of them, and the best, but not for long. He liked to get away by himself out on the ranches, to ride on a fine horse through long fields of his beloved fighting bulls. He loved animals of all kinds, but especially the bulls. It's said that he inspired this dialogue in Hemingway's *The Sun Also Rises* between the matador and Lady Brett:

"No. Don't do that. The bulls are my best friends."
I translated to Brett.
"You kill your friends?" she asked.
"Always," he said in English, and laughed. "So they don't kill me."

Though he was often aloof and stern, men liked him. He was generous, fair, and *"un gran compañero."* "Here's a man!" wrote a member of his cuadrilla. "This is the essence of manliness we all hoped we'd grow to be when we were children."

He had thousand of admirers, but no one except his mother broke through that aura of greatness to be really close to him. He didn't ask for loves or intimate friendships from this life; he asked only to be The Best. And now he was, sooner than even he had thought he could be, and life was good.

On July 3, 1914, Joselito reached the pinnacle. Alone, with no other matador, he killed six giant bulls in the Madrid arena (not young novillos as he'd done in Cádiz). As an added bonus he called for the substitute, killed that, and was carried out of the ring in wild triumph. He made 25 *quites* that afternoon, placed 18 banderillas, made 242 passes with cape and muleta, and never rumpled his hair.

A newspaper said the next day: "Nobody could applaud at the end because their hands were too sore, nobody could shout, only croak like delirious bullfrogs. The taurine Vatican has been opened and we have a new pope. If only Cervantes were here to describe it all accurately!"

Another one said: "Beethoven is music—Joselito is bullfighting. Genius like this comes along only once every three hundred years."

It looked as though Joselito would simply coast along, unchallenged like this, into immortality. But then something happened. Fate saw fit to produce a comparable genius, not only in the same century but in the very same period.

Juan Belmonte didn't look much like a genius. He was little and ugly and he stammered. Three years older than Joselito, he got a late start in la fiesta brava. There were no bullfighters in his family, but somehow he drifted into it, and at seventeen, an age when Joselito was already a seasoned matador, Belmonte fought his first corrida. He attracted attention immediately. With little science, he got contracts on guts alone for the first years.

"He's crazy," everyone said.

Literally, he was tossed every afternoon that he fought.

"This Belmonte spends more time in the air than on the ground," said one critic. "He's no matador, he's an aviador."

They called him "the torero of four olés and an *ay!*" because that's about how many passes he'd get away with before getting tossed.

"If you haven't seen this madman Belmonte," they said significantly, "you'd better hurry!"

Some people realized from the first that Belmonte's style was revolutionary and that as it developed it was going to change all bullfighting. But most people wrote him off as *un suicida loco*—terribly exciting to watch, but not long for this mortal coil. How could anyone fight in "terrains" that no matador had ever thought of invading and expect to live? The old rule, first stated by the immortal Cúchares, had always been: "You place yourself *there*, and when the bull charges, you either move yourself in a hurry or it'll do the moving for you."

Joselito had modified that somewhat, but Belmonte, perhaps because of his deplorable physical equipment, didn't believe in dodging out of the way at all. He thought it made better sense to plant one's feet permanently and to move the bull out of the way with the cape rather than to move oneself. It didn't always come off, but when it did, and Belmonte wrapped the bull around his waist with no daylight between him and the animal, the crowds couldn't believe their eyes. But no one yet considered him any threat to the most technically perfect matador in the world, Joselito.

Then suddenly Belmonte arrived. On the sixteenth of October, 1913, he was given the alternative by the great Machaquito in Madrid. Whether or not it was because of the sensational performance Belmonte gave that day no one knows, but Machaquito returned to his hotel after the corrida and said, "I will never fight again in my life!" And he kept his word.

Overnight all Spain was arguing as to who was the better, Joselito or this new upstart. They fought together for the first time in March of 1914, in Barcelona. It was the most important fight held in decades, and special reporters were sent from all over Spain to cover the event.

When Belmonte had the crowd screaming on his first passes, Joselito's manager scoffed, "But just look at the bull the man's drawn."

Joselito whistled through his teeth admiringly and retorted: "Just look at the man that *bull's* drawn!"

As it turned out, they each cut ears, and were both carried out of the plaza de toros on the shoulders of the crowd in complete triumph.

This was a historic happening, the beginning of what is always referred to as the Golden Age of Bullfighting, the greatest rivalry ever known in the bullring. Side by side they were to compete with each other for the next six years. Bitter rivals in the arena, they became best friends out of it. Never was there a better, more complementary pair. Belmonte, flamboyant, creative, frighteningly brave, gave the impression that he didn't know quite what hair-raising thing he was going to do next. One had the feeling that he was going to be tossed at any moment, and he usually was.

Recently I visited Belmonte in Sevilla, and as we sat on the porch overlooking his private bullring, I asked don Juan exactly how many times he had been wounded. He shrugged. "Twenty?" I suggested, but this just brought a smile to his lips. "Thirty?" He shook his head. "Forty? Fifty?" Then Belmonte's big jaw came out even farther as he said in his attractive stammering way, "Fifty is a nice number. Yes, let's say fifty, because I like the number f-f-fifty." The only accurate way to find out would be to have a doctor count the white scars that form grim patterns over his entire body.

Competing against this daily attempt to commit suicide was the sure, unruffled calm of the master technician. Where Belmonte gave the impression that each pass might be his last, Joselito's every move, even when working a millimeter from the horns, seemed to assure the audience, "This is easy—anyone could do it."

Belmonte declared, "There is no cow alive who can drop the bull that could hurt Joselito."

And even Joselito's mother said, "Any bull that wants to hurt my José will have to catch him asleep in his hotel room."

This was not strictly true, since Joselito was gored five times during his career; but this was nothing when one considered the risks he took and the fact that once Belmonte received four almost fatal wounds in a four-month period!

And so these two completely opposite figures, the greatest pair in bull-fighting's long history, fought on together almost every day during the season, and after each corrida the word would flash around Spain: "Juan gave Joselito the bath today in Valencia," or "José cut three ears to Juan's one in Bilbao," and the joselistas and the belmontistas would rejoice or lament according to the performance of their idol. More extreme than Dodger-Yankee partisans in this country, the aficionados went as far as wearing pins in their lapel proclaiming their loyalty, carving great profiles of their matadors in the cliffs outside Madrid, and sporting silver likenesses of them for radiator ornaments on their cars.

A famous story showing how vehemently everyone felt about the controversy tells how after putting up an extraordinary performance and cutting the first ear ever conceded in Sevilla, Joselito was carried on the shoulders of the crowd to the church of Santa Ana. There the mob tried to commandeer the platform base from under the Virgin in order to parade Joselito around town on it. The Guardia Civil prevented them from doing it, and the shocked priest berated the crowd, exclaiming, "What sacrilege! Imagine wanting to carry Joselito on the very platform of the Virgin!" He hesitated. "Now—if it were for Belmonte . . ."

Once a newspaper critic apologized as he was being introduced to Joselito, "I must warn you that I am a belmontista."

Joselito smiled warmly as he shook his hand. "That's all right, so am I."

Actually the most ardent belmontistas had to admit that Joselito was the more perfect and versatile torero, but they were overwhelmed by the fiery excitement that Belmonte generated and his startling disregard for the rules. Joselito studied Belmonte's revolutionary techniques, the lowered hands, the elbows close to the body, and the contempt for heretofore forbidden terrains of the bull in relationship to the man.

Belmonte was never strong, and he was limited by his physical short-comings. ("My legs were in such a state," he once said, "that if one wanted to move it had to request permission from the other.") On the other hand Joselito was a superb athlete whose every movement in the arena was as smooth as an ocelot's. He quickly assimilated Belmonte's exciting new style and perfected it. And in a like manner Belmonte learned something from Joselito every afternoon that they performed together. He acquired more and more control; his faenas began to look more planned, rather than just a series of unrelated, foolhardy passes, and he began to be tossed less frequently. Belmonte even learned some of Joselito's seeming ability to read bulls' minds.

26

The stories of Joselito's extraordinary knowledge of the ways of a bull are infinite. A famous one is the episode of the white horse. He once drew a bull who refused to charge the picador. Nothing could induce it to attack. No matter how close the picador rode his nag up to the bull it refused to charge. Adjudged cowardly, the presidente ordered the animal withdrawn. Joselito requested a delay, had the picador's horse changed from white to black, and the bull charged the new mount immediately.

"I could tell the bull was not basically cowardly," said Joselito, "so I guessed that the man who had tested it with a lance when it was a calf was riding a white horse. Bulls have excellent memories."

The test of a great matador is whether or not he can perform with a difficult bull. Too many matadors can shine only when they draw a pera en dulce—a "sweet pear" of a bull that charges unswervingly as though on rails. Joselito's greatest ability was in making nearly every bull that charged out of the Gate of Fear into a "sweet pear."

Sidney Franklin told a good example of this in an *Esquire* article:

> Once in Málaga Joselito found himself with a particularly cowardly bull. The animal kept hugging the barrier and refused to be attracted to the center of the ring. It looked like a poor fight. A lesser matador would have performed his capework around the perimeter of the ring, working between the animal and the center. Not Joselito. In this case he got between the bull and the fence, the most dangerous place in the ring, and jiggled the cape. The bull charged and smashed into the fence with a sickening crash, missing the matador by less than inches. Again Joselito called him. Another splintering collision of bull and wood. This required cool, pure daring, but it taught the bull a lesson: stay away from the fence. Thereafter the bull went to the middle of the ring of his own accord and Gallito was able to proceed with the fight in style.

The period leading up to Joselito's death is merely the telling of statistics and recounting of repetitions of triumphs: how he would tie his ankles together and give twelve passes of death in one spot; how he would fight entire faenas with his left hand, his right behind his back as though strapped there; how he fought 22 incredible corridas as the only performer (compared to Belmonte's one); how in 1916 he fought 105 corridas, killing 251 bulls in 210 days, more than anyone else had ever done in a single season. He seemed to get better and braver with each year, though everyone said it was impossible.

"You don't know the meaning of the word fear," a reporter once said in an interview.

Joselito smiled. "Nobody knows what I feel in my guts between the time the trumpet blows and the time that terrible gate opens for the bull to come in. Of course I know fear, but I hide it from the crowd—and the bull."

And Belmonte added, "If we matadors had to sign the contracts one hour before the corrida was to start, there would be no bullfights."

And so season after season the success continued. But, as Fitzgerald says, nothing fails like success. In 1919, when Fortune's Favorite Child was twenty-four and just attaining the peak of his physical and mental prowess, everything went wrong. First of all his mother died, and this was a blow from which he never really recovered. "Without that loving force," he said disconsolately, "I feel lost, untied, purposeless, cast adrift."

Then in the same year, he fell in love, deeply and for the first time. She was the pretty daughter of Andaluz nobility, and although her father raised fighting bulls as a hobby, he would hear none of her marrying a common bullfighter, even if he was the best and richest torero in the world. This was the first time in his life that Joselito realized the disturbing fact that there might be something else in this world besides bullfighting.

He tried to forget her but couldn't. He grew moody and restless. He went to Peru for a change and fought brilliantly there. Then when he returned to Spain in 1920, he found awaiting him a more fearsome adversary than any bull he'd ever encountered: hostile crowds.

No one can say when and why the public turns against an idol, but once it starts little can stop it. Joselito was fighting better than ever in his life; perhaps that was the very trouble. One can forgive a man just about anything except perfection. Gustavo del Barco says in his book on Joselito: "In bullfighting, as in other arts, the sin of constant triumph is unforgivable."

They were tired of applauding Joselito day after day, year after year. It suddenly became more diverting, more chic, more sophisticated to go to the plaza to boo him, just as it was to happen in the last months of Manolete's life, twenty-seven years later. Belmonte came in for some of the crowd's hostility, but the attacks fell with the most savagery on the head of the one they had labeled The Invulnerable. Joselito was confused, hurt, uncomprehending, as any performer would be who daily tried to do his best for the people who paid to see him. Belmonte saw the reasons more clearly, and del Barco quotes him:

"The public began to tire of us, precisely because of the sensation

28

Belmonte—"the torero of four olés—"

"—and an ay!"

Joselito and Belmonte during the former's last year.

of security and domination and the elimination of risk which we managed to give. This was worse for Joselito than for me since he gave the impression much more than I that he was completely invulnerable, that he never could be hurt. Seeing that time after time we filled the plazas and that neither of us managed to get ourselves killed, try as we might, the public felt defrauded."

At the start of their last fight together on May 15, 1920, the Madrid crowds began to boo them before they'd even started the parade into the ring, and Joselito was unnerved. A group of threatening spectators advanced on the toreros. "Gyppers! Thieves!" they kept yelling.

"But what have we done?" Joselito exclaimed to Belmonte.

Later in the fight, after the cushions rained down and a woman had yelled that she hoped a bull would kill him the next day in Talavera, Joselito talked to Belmonte. "I'm going to get out of all this," he said bitterly. "It's time for me to retire. I don't know how to fight this."

The next day, eight days after Joselito's twenty-fifth birthday, was the corrida in Talavera de la Reina. Originally, Joselito had no intention of performing in this second-rate arena, but he accepted the fight at the last minute to help out a friend. He took the train there, booked a room in the hotel, and napped until three when his sword boy, Paco Botas, and his brother Fernando woke him up. They remembered later that, though he had been terribly depressed by the crowd's attitude the day before, now as he dressed in the gold and scarlet "suit of lights" he seemed almost gay. He joked with them about several things and kept singing a bit of *cante jondo* from the "Coplas del Espartero."

> Little Miura bulls fear nothing now,
> For El Espartero, who used to kill them so well,
> Is dead, olé, olé, olé!

When his superstitious brother chided him for singing such depressing songs Joselito laughed and pointed to his pigtail, saying, "Why worry? This is coming off very soon." (A matador ended his career when he cut off his pigtail.)

When he kept singing Fernando said, "The truth is I don't like that song."

"Well, Fatty," Joselito said good-naturedly, "I like it," and he continued to sing.

"What goes for you goes for us," said Fernando.

The fight started much like any other corrida in the provinces. They left the hotel at quarter past four and drove through the gaily decorated town. "There he is, there he is!" the crowds who lined the streets shouted. Joselito was the most exciting thing ever to happen to Talavera.

It had been cloudy, but the sun came out as the toreros paraded into the arena, and the band blared and the five thousand people cheered. They seemed so much less hostile than the Madrid audience that Joselito said to the other matador, his brother-in-law, Sánchez Mejías, "Let's really give them something today."

But Joselito's first bull from the Viuda de Ortega ranch was impossible to work with, and even he could do little with it. The second bull was a little better, and Joselito let his brother Fernando make some passes with it. Fernando was a wastrel, fat and completely inept, but Joselito felt sorry for him and took him around as part of his cuadrilla. (The famous *pasodoble* "Gallito" was actually written about Fernando, when he gave promise as a novillero, and not about Joselito, as is generally believed.)

Sánchez Mejías' second bull was the best and bravest of all, and he invited Joselito to put in a pair of banderillas. This Joselito did while standing on the stirrup board, his back up against the fence, and the crowd wildly cheered the magnificence of the maneuver. This was the last sweet ovation the man was to hear.

The fifth bull was named Bailador—Dancer.* It came into the ring fast and low, corral dust blowing off its black hide, a big O branded on its flank and the number 7 on its side. The moment Joselito saw it he sucked air in through his teeth, and his green gypsy eyes never left the animal for a second.

"Get behind the fence and don't come out," he ordered his brother. "Everyone look out with this animal. Get on those horns and you won't get off."

Bailador was comparatively small, 259 kilos dressed, which was about half the size of the bull of Joselito's presentation in Madrid. But Bailador had a killer's horns and a treacherous killer's charge, which Joselito spotted immediately. He also discerned that the animal didn't see well close up, but at a distance its vision was good; "burriciego," the toreros call it, and it's a dread thing since bullfighters depend upon the bull's seeing well, so that they can control it and make it charge the cape instead of the man.

In the act of the picadors, Bailador, small as he was, killed five horses in six vicious charges. After the banderillas, which were placed with great difficulty since the bull was completely unpredictable in its charge, the animal took a stand in its querencia. A bull's querencia is an arbitrarily

* Sometimes spelled without the "d" to approximate the Andaluz dialect.

chosen spot in the ring where the animal feels secure for some reason of its own, perhaps where it killed a horse or tossed a man. In its querencia it will fight a defensive, impossible, come-in-after-me type of fight instead of the long, hard charges that both the crowd and the matador want.

When Joselito was handed his sword and muleta by his sword boy, he dedicated the bull. "It goes for the memory of my father who fought the inaugural corrida in this plaza so many years ago," he said as he doffed his montera and tossed it elegantly onto the sand.

The banderillero had managed to lure Bailador out of its querencia by repeatedly trailing capes in front of it, and Joselito pointed with the sword to where he wanted the bull placed. Then he ordered the banderilleros to leave him completely alone with the dangerous animal. He draped the muleta over the sword in his right hand and advanced on the animal. "Toro, ah-hah," Joselito chanted as he walked. "We'll teach you how to charge, little bull."

Fifteen feet from the animal he stopped and shook the muleta. The bull, seeing well at this distance, lowered its head, attacked hard, and Joselito gave it a beautiful trincherazo pass. Three more passes, and the animal was charging straighter and easier on each one, being controlled and learning how to charge from the master teacher. But on the fifth charge it suddenly broke away from the man and trotted back along the boards toward its querencia. It had been attracted by one of the banderilleros who had disobeyed his master and hadn't left the ring.

"Hide yourself, Enrique," Joselito called exasperatedly, "he's with you and won't take the muleta!"

Joselito went after the bull, headed it off, and gave it two more passes, but the capricious animal had lost interest in the muleta now and was looking around distractedly for the banderillero. Joselito blew out a weary sigh and retreated fifteen feet from the animal and wiped the sweat from his forehead. He took the muleta in his left hand, and looking down at the cloth he shook out the folds and started to redrape it over the sword in his right hand.

Then it happened. Joselito, by withdrawing those five yards from the animal, had stepped into the area where the bull could see well. Suddenly, and without warning, it lunged forward, heading straight for the man's body. A banderillero cried out, and Joselito looked up. At that long range it would have been no trick for him, the greatest athlete the ring has known, to have dodged out of the path of this animal. But he left his feet planted on the sand as though they were nailed there, and standing straight and gracefully, he flared out the muleta to distract it off its course as he had done with so many hundreds of other bulls.

32

But with the surprise of the attack he had forgotten for a fatal moment that this animal had a visual defect. Though the bull had seen the man clearly at a distance, as it came closer the target became more and more blurred until it saw neither the man nor the flared-out muleta designed to make it swerve. Without even seeing its victim, the bull crashed into Joselito. Its left horn hooked into the man's right thigh, and he was slammed up into the air.

As Joselito spun on the horn, the bull chopped its head from side to side viciously, and the right horn ripped open the man's lower stomach. He hung doubled up on the bull's head for a second, managed to push himself off the horn, and then fell to the ground.

The other toreros lured the bull away and ran to Joselito's aid. He struggled to sit up on the sand and was clutching his stomach when the sword boy reached him. There was terror and disbelief in the matador's eyes.

"Ay, *madre mía*," he moaned, "my guts are coming out!"

"Don't talk like that, Matador!" said the sword boy as he started to pick him up. "It's not true!"

But as he said later, "The truth is, I could see in the mouth of the wound a green ball . . ."

As he was being carried, Joselito tried to hold his viscera in with his fingers. "Mascarell, Mascarell!" he cried as they rushed him out of the arena toward the infirmary. This was the name of the great horn wound specialist in Madrid.

Once in the infirmary, the two regular doctors and two Madrid surgeons who happened to be in the audience slashed off the matador's "suit of lights." He was breathing feebly, his eyes closed.

"Leave the wound alone," ordered Dr. Pastor. "Take care of him first!"

They injected blood serum, caffeine, and camphor oil into his arms and sides. But the man was slipping away. His cuadrilla was allowed into the operating room, and they wept when they saw the look of death coming on the man. At eight minutes past seven Joselito opened his eyes.

"*Madre, me ahogo!*" he said. "Mother, I'm smothering, I'm smothering!"

Then he died. The doctor explained later that the wound, in spite of its horrible aspect, wasn't necessarily fatal, but that Joselito had probably died of shock, that his heart had given out upon seeing himself so badly wounded. "He had begun to believe, as we all did, that he was invulnerable."

The sword handler, sobbing like a baby, ceremoniously cut off his dead master's pigtail. All night a steady stream of weeping people from all walks of life filed past the dead man to pay their respects. His brother Rafael arrived from Madrid, but, though he tried three times, he was too shaken to enter the room.

Joselito was taken through Spain to Sevilla with the largest funeral cortege the country could remember, and there he is buried in a tomb topped by a magnificent monument by Benlliure. It depicts nineteen life-sized figures in bronze, weeping gypsies, bull breeders, and toreros carrying the marble, godlike form of the dead matador.

Today, all these years after his death, Joselito el Gallo is far from forgotten. Every May 16 the newspapers in Spain devote pages to his memory, featuring odes by famous poets, paintings, photos, and editorials. And every May 16 you will see the toreros wearing black arm ribbons in the big annual fight in Talavera. It's impossible to pick up a bullfighting magazine in Spain or Mexico without finding new Joselito anecdotes or comparisons between him and the current crop of toreros. There have been hundreds of songs and volumes written on his life and art. To show what a truly living hero Joselito is after all these years, the top popular song in Spain two seasons ago was not about him, but about his mother! Called "La Gabriela," the verse starts out: "Fernando is fighting in Puerto, brother Rafael is fighting in Jerez, but what really chills poor Gabriela's heart is that little Joselito, all by himself, in Cádiz, is facing six Miuras."

Nearly every young boy in Spain dreams of being as great a torero as Joselito. And there are many Gabrielas today and there will be more to-morrow whose hearts will be chilled as they watch the "child of their right eye" swirling a cape in front of a trained dog and hear him sing "Coplas del Espartero," but changing the words to:

> Little Miura bulls fear nothing now,
> For Joselito, who used to kill them so well,
> Is dead, olé, olé, olé!

Joselito at the age of thirteen,
preparing to kill a large bull.

Madrid

3. Madrid

THE MADRID RING IS THE MOST IMPORTANT PLAZA DE TOROS IN THE WORLD. IT is Mecca for all toreros, whether Spanish or Latin American, and has been since the beginning of bullfighting, since 1617 when La Plaza Mayor, the first real bullring, was constructed for an immediate audience of three thousand (and forty thousand more from surrounding balconies and windows and improvised stands).

Madrid is the history of bullfighting. In the beginning, of course, it was purely a royal equestrian pastime. Then the common people began playing the bulls on foot with a cape, and though it was crude and unorganized, the science was burgeoning. Around 1725, Francisco Romero, from Ronda, stuck a stick in his cape to spread it wider and give him greater flexibility and safety as he killed bulls. This was the creation of the muleta. Romero also invented the act of killing "receiving," i.e., letting the bull impale himself while the matador waits out the charge and distracts it with the muleta while plunging in the sword. Then in 1767, Costillares presented to Madrid the new look, the volapié style of killing, literally "on flying feet," instead of standing still. Costillares also is credited with perfecting the verónica pass, modifying the torero's clothing, and in general with giving the bullfight the aspect it has today.

In 1775 the son of Francisco Romero, Pedro, took Madrid by storm, perfecting what he had learned from his father and Costillares. For twenty-three years he was considered the maestro, finally retiring healthy and intact at the age of forty-five after killing more than 5500 bulls.

Pepe-Illo was the first important casualty in the Madrid ring and the second matador ever to be killed. Author of the bullfighting bible, *Tauro-machy, or the Art of Bullfighting,* he was an exponent of the gay Sevillan school, and the distinction between that style and the more somber and conservative Ronda school was first made in his day. Brave, graceful, superstitious, Pepe-Illo was enormously popular, and when he was killed on May 11, 1801, by the bull Barbudo, Madrid was so shocked that they suspended all fights for twelve months, at which time they held another corrida during which a bull leapt up into the crowd and killed the mayor of Torrejón!

For some reason the month of May has always been the bloodiest one for toreros. Of the approximately 125 major matadors since 1700, 42 have been killed, and 11 of these died in the month of May, including some of the most famous of all time: Curro Guillén, Fabrilo, Antonio Romero, El Espartero, Granero, Joselito, and Gitanillo de Triana. There is no way of counting up the terrible number of almost fatal gorings in the month of May. Toreros say they think it is because the bulls are strong from the spring crops and that the toreros are still green from the winter's lay-off. Twelve matadors have been killed in Madrid, as opposed to two each in Granada, Valencia, and Mexico City (this refers to full matadors, not novilleros, picadors, or banderilleros). Four of the forty-one matadors were killed by Miuras and four by Veraguas. Only one was killed placing banderillas. Most were killed while working with the muleta, generally at the kill, the best chance the bull has "to collect the man," as Robert Ruark says.

This might be as good a place as any to list the principal matadors since formal bullfighting began. Asterisks indicate those killed by bulls.

Francisco Romero	1700–17??
Juan Romero	1722–1824
*José Cándido (Exposito)	1734–1771
*Francisco García (Perucho)	174?–1801
José Romero	1745–1826
Costillares	1748–1800
*Pepe-Illo	1754–1801
Pedro Romero	1754–1839
*Antonio Romero Martínez	1763–1802
Jerónimo José Cándido	1770–1839
*Curro Guillén	1783–1820
*Francisco González (Panchón)	1784–1843
Juan León (Leoncillo)	1788–1854
Antonio Ruiz (El Sombrerero)	1792–1860
*Manuel Parra Fernández	1797–1829

38

*Roque Miranda (Rigores)	1799–1843
Francisco Montes (Paquiro)	1805–1851
†José de los Santos	1806–1847
*Isidro Barragán	1811–1851
*Bernardo Gaviño	1812–1886
Manuel Domínguez	1816–1886
Francisco Arjona (Cúchares)	1818–1868
José Redondo (El Chiclanero)	1818–1853
Cayetano Sanz	1821–1891
*José Rodríguez (Pepete)	1824–1862
*José María Ponce	1830–1872
Antonio Sánchez (El Tato)	1831–1895
*Manuel Fuentes (Bocanegra)	1837–1889
Antonio Carmona (El Gordito)	1838–1920
Rafael Molina (Lagartijo)	1841–1900
Salvador Sánchez (Frascuelo)	1842–1898
Francisco Arjona (Currito)	1845–1907
José Sánchez del Campo (Cara Ancha)	1848–1925
Fernando Gómez (El Gallo)	1849–1897
*Joaquín Sanz (Punteret)	1853–1888
Luis Mazzantini	1856–1926
(M)Ponciano Díaz	1858–1899
*Juan Jiménez Ripoll (Ecijano)	1858–1899
Rafael Guerra (Guerrita)	1862–1941
*Julio Aparici (Fabrilo)	1865–1897
*Manuel García (El Espartero)	1866–1894
*José Rodríguez Davie (Pepete)	1867–1899
*Manuel Lara (Jerezano)	1867–1912
*Juan Gómez de Lesaca	1867–1896
Antonio Fuentes	1869–1938
Antonio Reverte	1870–1903
Emilio Torres (Bombita)	1874–1947
*Domingo del Campo (Dominguín)	1873–1900
José García (El Algabeño)	1875–1947
*Antonio Montes	1876–1907
Ricardo Torres (Bombita)	1879–1936
Vicente Pastor	1879–
Rafael Molina (Lagartijo Chico)	1880–1910
Rafael González (Machaquito)	1880–1955
Rafael Gómez (El Gallo)	1882–
*Fermín Muñoz (Corchaito)	1882–1914
Francisco Martín Vázquez	1882–1946
*José Gallego (Pepete III)	1883–1910
Manuel Rodríguez (Manolete)	1883–1923

*Hilario González Delgado (Serranito)		1883–1908
*Isidoro Marti (Flores)		1884–1921
Manuel Mejías (Bienvenida)		1885–
*Augustín García (Malla)		1886–1920
(M)Rodolfo Gaona		1888–
(M)Luis Freg		1890–1934
*Ignacio Sánchez Mejías		1891–1934
Juan Belmonte		1892–
*Enrique Cano (Gavira)		1893–1927
*Florentino Ballesteros		1893–1917
*Manuel Vare (Varelito)		1894–1922
*Mariano Montes		1894–1926
*José Gómez (Gallito) (Joselito)		1895–1920
Diego Mazquiarán (Fortuna)		1895–1940
(M)Juan Silveti		1895–1956
Manuel García (Maera)		1896–1924
‡Juan Anllo (Nacional II)		1897–1925
Victoriano Roger (Valencia II)		1898–1936
Antonio Márquez		1899–
Nicanor Villalta		1899–
Manuel Jiménez (Chicuelo)		1902–
*Manuel Granero		1902–1922
José García (Algabeño)		1902–1936
(M)José Ortiz		1902–
Marcial Lalanda		1903–
Joaquín Rodríguez (Cagancho)		1903–
Cayetano Ordóñez (Niño de la Palma)		1904–
*Francisco Vega de los Reyes (Gitanillo de Triana)		1904–1931
*Manuel Baez (Litri)		1905–1926
(M)Heriberto García		1906–
Domingo Ortega		1906–
(M)*José González (Carnicerito de Mexico)		1907–1947
Vicente Barrera		1908–1957
(M)Jesús Solórzano		1908–
(M)*Carmelo Pérez		1908–1931
(M)Lorenzo Garza		1909–
(M)*Alberto Balderas		1910–1940
Victoriano de La Serna		1910–
(M)Fermín Espinosa (Armillita Chico)		1911–
Luis Gómez (El Estudiante)		1911–
Manolo Bienvenida		1912–1938
(M)Luis Castro (El Soldado)		1912–
Pepe Bienvenida		1914–
*Pascual Márquez		1914–1941

40

Rafael Vega de los Reyes (Gitanillo de Triana III)	1915–	
(M)Silverio Pérez	1915–	
°Manuel Rodríguez (Manolete)	1917–1947	
(M)Fermín Rivera	1918–	
Juan Belmonte, Jr.	1918–	
Manuel Alvarez (Andaluz)	1919–	
(M)Carlos Arruza	1920–	
Pepe Luis Vázquez	1921–	
Antonio Bienvenida	1922–	
(M)Antonio Velázquez	1922–	
(M)Luis Procuna	1923–	
(P)Manolo Dos Santos	1925–	
Rafael Ortega	1925–	
Luis Miguel González (Dominguín)	1925–	
(M)Rafael Rodríguez	1925–	
(M)Manuel Capetillo	1926–	
Pepín Martín Vázquez	1927–	
Paquito Muñoz	1928–	
Manolo González	1929–	
(M)Jesús Córdoba	1929–	
José-María Martorell	1929–	
Miguel Baez (Litri)	1930–	
Julio Aparicio	1930–	
Antonio Ordóñez	1931–	
(M)Juanito Silveti	1931–	
(V)César Girón	1932–	
Manolo Vázquez	1934–	
Jumillano	1934–	
Pedrés	1934–	
Chicuelo II	1934–	

(Notice how often the great toreros have produced great sons: Manolete, Dominguín, Bienvenida, Ordóñez, Martín Vázquez, the Gallos, Algabeño, etc. Also, it's interesting to note that Bernardo Gaviño was killed at the age of 74, still practising his profession.)

Besides the fatalities indicated in the above list, there were many other minor, though legitimate, matadores de toros who were killed in the ring. In the ranks of official novilleros there have been 111 recorded deaths since 1786, but there must have been at least another 100 left unrecorded. There

° Killed by a bull.
† Killed by own sword while diving over fence to escape a bull.
‡ Killed in an arena, but by a bottle wielded by a fellow spectator.
(M) Mexican.
(P) Portuguese.
(V) Venezuelan.

have been 57 picadors and 118 banderilleros killed since the middle of the nineteenth century. Unrecorded are the hundreds of almost fatal gorings, the cripplings, the amputations, and the number of young aspirants killed while trying to learn their profession out in the fields of some bull ranch.

For comparison's sake, the number of boxing fatalities since 1900, as quoted by *Time* magazine, is set at 327. But of course more people box than fight bulls. And consider automobile racing in America. Forty-seven persons have been killed at Indianapolis since the track opened in 1909. Of the thirty-three men who started in the big race at Indianapolis in 1951, twelve were killed in crashes by 1955, leaving less than two thirds alive.

But back to Madrid and the history of bullfighting in that city.

After the death of Pepe-Illo, bullfighting went into a decline, partly because of royal disfavor and the French invasion. Interest wasn't aroused again until 1831 when the great Francisco Montes, "Paquiro," made his appearance in Madrid. He awakened such excitement with his style and bravery that a new ring holding ten thousand people was constructed. Then came the great Cúchares and Chiclanero and Pepete. Pepete's death in 1862 occurred in the Madrid Plaza.

If there were only one piece of advice I'd be allowed to give an aspirant torero, it would be simply this: Do not call yourself Pepete. All three who have chosen that nickname have been killed in the ring. In fact, I would just generally stay away from the name José (of which Pepete, Pepe, and Joselito are nicknames) since of the 41 matadors killed, nine have been so christened!

Toward the end of the nineteenth century Madrid saw the blossoming of the brilliant rivalry of Frascuelo and Lagartijo. And in 1894 it saw the death of one of the most popular matadors of all time, El Espartero. In May, of course—"*en el mes de mayo, cuando huelen más las flores.*"

It was a Miura that killed him, as it should have been. He had always had an obsession about the Miuras, even though this was some time before they earned their reputation as the "bulls of death"; they were famous and respected, but the mere mention of the name didn't send toreros into a cold sweat the way it did later.

"If a bull must kill me," El Espartero said, "let it be a Miura."

Even when he had just commenced his career there seemed to be an air of fatality about the handsome Sevillano. A popular song of the time went:

> Espartero, Esparterito,
> Don't go get yourself killed,
> Don't make half the girls in Sevilla
> Have to dress in mourning.

He was a highly successful full matador for nine years. Though not a creative artist in any sense of the word, he was fantastically brave, with a "stoic, crude valour." They tell how once one of his banderilleros was having a hard time executing a maneuver with a difficult bull, and Espartero impatiently explained to him how it should be done.

"But if I do it the way you say," the banderillero protested, "this bull will toss me for sure."

"And does that matter?" El Espartero asked simply.

He was the stuff heroes are made of, and Blasco Ibáñez made him the protagonist of his antibullfighting novel *Blood and Sand*. When he died on the horns of the caramel-colored, partridge-eyed Perdigón, a national wail went up and the poets and songwriters set to work with a will. The most popular song, the one that they still sing all over Spain is the Sevillana "Coplas del Espartero," which ends:

> Ay what a shame!
> The king of toreros is dead
> And all of Sevilla is in mourning,
> So that's why the cigarette girls
> Are wearing black scarves.

After El Espartero the great names that performed in Madrid and made taurine history come thick and fast. Guerrita, Mazzantini, Bombita, Machaquito, El Gallo, and the great Mexican Rodolfo Gaona. But Madrid and the bullfighting world had never seen anything like what was coming. "La revolución belmontina," it was called when Belmonte broke all the norms in his first appearance in Madrid in 1913. Nobody had ever seen such fighting. And then to have the genius of Joselito in the same era was too much to be believed.

After Joselito's death and Belmonte's retirement, occasional great afternoons in Madrid were supplied by Cagancho and Armillita and Marcial Lalanda and Chicuelo and Manolo Bienvenida and Domingo Ortega and Niño de la Palma and Gitanillo de Triana, but it was never as good again. The new arena, which was opened in 1934, had little use in the next years due to the Civil War.

Then came Manolete in 1939 to raise bullfighting out of its decadence, and the streets of Spain were once more jammed on Sundays as the crowds headed for the arena to see how Pepe Luis Vázquez or Carlos Arruza would do against the modern master. After Manolete's death in 1947 and Arruza's retirement in 1953, bullfighting again seems to have gone into a decadent decline, in spite of the capabilities of Antonio Bienvenida, Dominguín,

43

Litri, Aparicio, Antonio Ordóñez, and the Venezuelan César Girón, who have followed.

But Madrid is still the center of the bullfighting universe, and great afternoons can still be seen there, afternoons of prowess and courage that make even the old-timers sit up and take notice. The best of the current crop of matadors and novilleros can be seen in Madrid, and the largest and best bulls are usually fought there. May is the best month, since the ten San Isidro fights are held then. And when you go to the ring you feel the weight and presence of the thousands of afternoons before this one when men have gone out into the arena in the capital of their world to fight for fame and wealth.

But in spite of all the history of the plaza de toros, the most exciting fight that ever took place in Madrid was not in the bullring and it was not for fame or money. It took place when a bull got loose and ran wild through the city in 1928, and it's worth telling in detail.

The bull escaped at eight o'clock in the morning. By eleven o'clock it had left a trail of one dead woman and seven wounded men, had thrown downtown Madrid into a panic, and had set the scene for the strangest bullfight ever to take place.

It was January 23, and a herd of fighting bulls was being sent to the slaughterhouse at the edge of the city of Madrid in the Carabanchel Bajo district. Bulls that prove too big, too wide of horn, defective of vision, or otherwise unacceptable for the arena are generally sent to the abattoir, and this was a routine shipment of five animals. With only occasional jabs from the poles of the herdsmen up on the high stone walls, they filed docilely enough through the dusty maze of corrals leading to the death chute.

All of a sudden the last bull, the largest of the lot, stopped. Perhaps it smelled up ahead the blood of thousands of animals that had gone before it. It snorted, and the huge tossing muscle on its black neck swelled. It wheeled and crashed back the way it had come. The herdsmen shouted and tried to head it off with their poles, but it snapped them like bread sticks. A steer shied into the animal's way, and the bull ripped open its abdomen and charged on.

It found the gate where it had come in, barred now by two heavy slats. The bull didn't hesitate, and when its half-ton bulk smashed into the boards, they splintered. The animal was free, and it trotted arrogantly down the cobbled street, while the people in the few shacks along the road stared in disbelief, gathered up their children frantically, and bolted their doors. But the animal left the houses alone and kept heading down the road toward the city. It met its first victim on the Segovia Bridge.

44

Diego Fortuna caping the bull
in the streets of Madrid.

The man, a clerk, was calmly riding his bicycle to work across the bridge when his horrified eyes saw a mass of greenish black muscle with a pair of long, sharp horns coming toward him. The bull dropped its head, and its tail shot up as it charged hard. The man skidded his bicycle around and pedaled frantically in the other direction, but it was like a bad dream; fighting bulls are as fast as race horses for short distances, and it soon overtook him. One of the horns, as thick as a boxer's forearm, jabbed into the spokes of the rear wheel, and the man was spilled to the ground. The bull paused to hook once at its scrambling quarry, but luckily it was running too fast to hit the man. The bull wheeled and started to charge again, but a passing taxi attracted its attention. It swerved away from the cyclist to attack this larger and more inviting target. The amazed cabbie gunned his motor and careened up a side street, but not before the bull had clanged once into the side of the car, jarring the whole frame and actually puncturing the heavy metal in one of the doors. The animal stood watching the taxi retreat, trying to decide what to attack and where to go next. It could head back across the bridge to the open country—or it could turn left into the heart of the city.

In America, when a bull or steer escapes from the stockyards for a few hours, it makes pleasant reading in the newspaper; Mr. Commuter muses on how he'd behave if confronted with the escapee, and it's a field day for the caption writers when they publish photos of the cops making like cowboys. And it's fun, because one is always on the animal's side as he disrupts convention, the constabulary, and the aplomb of several citizens in his wild break.

When a fighting bull escapes, however, you are no more on its side than you'd be for a rhino charging down on you in an African field or for a tiger loose from the zoo and circling your children. There's nothing comical about the escape of a *toro bravo*. As Hemingway says in *Death in the Afternoon*:

> The fighting bull is to the domestic bull as the wolf is to the dog. A domestic bull may be evil-tempered and vicious as a dog may be mean and dangerous, but he will never have the speed, the quality of muscle and sinew and the particular build of the fighting bull any more than the dog will have the sinews of a wolf, his cunning and width of jaw.

They have been bred for centuries for one purpose and one purpose only: to kill men and horses . . . but in a regulation arena in a controlled, organized fight. A *toro bravo* loose and running amok in a city is a nightmare,

46

and now it had happened. For this bull, instead of heading back to the open country, chose to trot into the metropolis of Madrid.

As it entered crowded Leganitos Street the first thing it spotted was a young woman leaving the market with her shopping basket over her arm and a small dog on a leash.

"¡Cuidado!" People screamed from the safety of doorways and windows. "Look out!"

The woman turned as the hooves of the bull clattered on the cobblestones, and she screamed as she saw the unbelievableness of the animal charging down on her. She lunged for a lamppost, but the bull veered like a polo pony and hooked out at her. The horn pierced the wicker basket before it hit her in the abdomen, but she fell mortally wounded in the gutter.

The yapping of the dog over its dying mistress seemed to annoy the bull and keep it from charging her again. It shied off down a narrow side street, and after a few blocks it came upon a deaf fruit peddler who hadn't heard the cries of warning of the other people who fled the street. The bull attacked the man from the rear as he fussed over his cart, hoisted him screaming on the point of one horn, and slammed him to the street unconscious. The animal slashed into the cart and demolished it, ending up with one wheel hooked grotesquely on a horn.

A sixteen-year-old messenger boy had been locked out of the house when the door was barricaded, and he frantically pounded and cried for admittance as the bull bore down on him. Possibly because of the dangling wheel, the bull didn't get a horn into the youth, but it slammed him up against the door so hard that he received a concussion and his right shoulder and arm were broken. He was dragged inside before the animal could charge again.

The bull shook off the wheel finally and went on its murderous way, creating havoc wherever it went. No one knows where the police department or the Guardia Civil were during all this; probably busy doing whatever the police anywhere seem to be doing whenever you really need them. Incredible as it seems, the animal wandered unmolested for three hours after its escape, when all that was needed to stop the carnage was a high-powered rifle in the right hands.

By eleven o'clock the bull had worked its bloody way downtown to the Gran Via, Madrid's Broadway. When it suddenly appeared on bustling Conde de Peñalver Avenue, panic went through the thoroughfare. The bull seemed baffled by the screaming crowds. Then it focused its attention on one group of about twenty-five people who were caught cowering in a cul-de-sac made by two buildings coming together at right angles. The bull was intrigued by the target, but didn't quite know how to handle it. It stalked the whimpering people, coming within thirty feet of them, and then standing there pawing the cobbles and staring at them huddled together against the glass of a store front. The bull looked bewildered: where to charge this amorphous mass?

Among the crowd who watched the bull from a safe distance was Diego Fortuna, a thirty-three-year-old matador. When he heard the cries of "¡Se ha escapado un toro!" and saw the animal burst out into the big street, his first thought was to do something about it. But he was on a cane. In his last fight he had had the cartilage of his right knee badly injured, and his leg still wasn't right. Besides which, fighting this enormous bull in an arena would be one thing; on these rain-wet cobblestones it would be something else. And if he were to trip, there'd be no one to help him. Better to wait for the Guardia Civil to come with their rifles.

But no Guardia Civil appeared, and the bull was edging closer to the twenty-five trapped people. There were several women and children in the group which was staring horrified at the animal as it wagged its horns, already crusty with dried blood, and tried to make up its mind how to handle them.

Diego Fortuna turned to his wife.

"Go home and get the estoque!" he ordered, stripping off his heavy overcoat.

Fortuna started limping up the street toward the bull. The crowd saw the wiry little man, and word spread through the people huddled along the sidewalks, crouched behind the stalled streetcars and taxis, and hanging out of the windows. "It's Diego Fortuna!"

Some didn't recognize him, for he was fairly old for a matador, and his luck the last few years hadn't been so good. Back there a few seasons he'd been on top, cutting ears in almost every corrida and alongside of such greats as Joselito and Belmonte. His real name was Diego Mazquiarán Torróntegui, but he had early been called "Fortuna"—Lucky—by everyone. And then his luck seemed to run out. It was the old story. For some reason, even though he was just as good as always with the cape and sword, the crowds began to grow tired of him; he'd been around too long. The statistics in Cossio's taurine encyclopedia tell the story: In 1925, Diego Fortuna fought seventeen corridas, in 1926, only six, and in 1927, three. And in the last one in October he had his knee injured and hadn't signed a single contract for the forthcoming season.

But the crowd didn't think of him as a has-been as they watched him limp up the street behind the bull. They saw him as a savior.

"Don't move," Diego yelled at the cornered crowd as he came on steadily, "don't talk, don't move!"

48

Twenty feet from the bull he draped the coat over his cane to make a bigger target, the way a muleta is spread by the sword. The bull had spun around at the sound of the man's voice, and it looked at this insignificant challenger curiously. It started to charge Diego, but at that moment the pressure of the crowd against the store front caused the glass to shatter. The sound made the bull whirl. Before it could charge at the people Diego sailed his hat at the bull's head.

"Toro, ah hah!" Diego shouted, lunging forward and shaking the coat threateningly.

The flash of the hat and the immediacy of the lone man made the bull turn back and charge him. Diego used all his ring knowledge to make the

"En el mes de Mayo,
cuando huelen mas las flores . . ."

"In the month of May,
when flowers smell their sweetest . . ."

animal go at the coat instead of at his body, and the bloody left horn skimmed by him. Diego passed the bull four more times, backing up after each pass so as to lead the bull out into the street away from the people. But each pass was more dangerous because the animal was losing interest in the small lure and because Diego was restricted in his movements by a cement island in the middle of the street. It was a delaying action, a fight for time.

Diego's wife finally arrived and shoved her way through the crowd breathlessly. Diego withdrew from the bull quickly when he saw her, grabbed the special double-edged sword, and went back to the animal. Being a matador out in the sun with a good audience, he couldn't resist doing one graceful, dangerous pase por alto before he lined the bull up for the kill, and the crowd cheered. Then he held the coat in his left hand, focused the bull's attention on it, and as it charged at him, flung himself over the right horn cleanly and sunk the sword up to its red hilt in between the withers.

The bull coughed once, swayed, and then crashed over dead. The roaring crowd surged forward, cut off the ears of the animal, handed them to Diego, and paraded him around town on their shoulders for an hour.

Because of the resultant publicity, Diego was contracted for eighteen corridas that season, and on October 11, 1928, at an impressive ceremony he was awarded the highest civilian order of Spain, La Cruz de la Beneficencia. The following seasons were good ones, and he has gone down in bullfighting annals as a fine matador. But no matter how magnificently he fought in the arena, he was and always will be remembered as the man who risked his life to kill the bull on the Gran Via.

Manzanares

4. Manzanares

Long after the physical structure of the plaza of manzanares and its ten thousand seats have crumbled, it will be remembered as the place that inspired the culmination of the art of two men. One, a playwriting matador, achieved his climax by dying violently, and the other, a doomed poet, by writing about it.

It happened in this colorless brick and cement arena a hundred miles south of Madrid on August 11, 1934. The stands were jammed, not to see the comeback of an old man of forty-three but for the other two performers on the program. Yet it was this old man, who looked like a sweaty Caesar, one of the most unusual men ever to grow a pigtail, who was making them shout and applaud. And though he was balding and there was still fat around his middle that he hadn't been able to work off, his intelligent face looked radiant and almost handsome as he came over to the fence. He glanced up appreciatively to the clapping audience. Actually, he shouldn't have been there at all. He had come on a fluke, a last-minute substitution for another fighter, and he had been warned not to come. But now it was turning out fine, he'd drawn a good bull, and he felt good and young in the sun. He motioned to the mozo for the sword and muleta. "We'll take him sitting down," said Ignacio Sánchez Mejías confidently, "the way we used to."

Then he went out to keep his appointment, for Samarra was in the Manzanares arena this day.

Born of a well-to-do family in Sevilla in 1891, Ignacio Sánchez Mejías had studied medicine to follow in the steps of his physician father. But his wild nature led him suddenly to quit school when he was eighteen to stow away on a steamship to New York. He was held by the authorities in America until a brother living in Mexico bailed him out.

A friend once asked the colorful gypsy El Gallo, an active matador for forty years, what he would have been if bullfighting hadn't existed. "If bullfighting hadn't existed," he replied thoughtfully, "I would have invented it."

If there'd been no bullfighting around when Sánchez Mejías came on the scene he might not have invented it, but he would have found a substitute as colorful and dangerous. Here was a man who yearned for the dashing, perilous life the way some men thirst for knowledge. From the time he was a young man he seemed to be seeking a dramatic death as dedicatedly as Ahab sought his briny nemesis.

Ignacio began his bullfighting career in Mexico and returned to Spain to join El Gallo's cuadrilla as a banderillero. Later he transferred to Belmonte's and then Joselito's, and was considered one of the greatest banderilleros of all time. But it wasn't enough just to be a matador's helper. In 1918, at the age of twenty-seven, an age when many matadors think about retiring, he decided to become a matador. He shot to stardom overnight. It's very rare for a banderillero to come up out of the ranks and be a matador. It's generally the other way around—the flopped or aging matador resigning himself to the inferior position of a "peón." But Sánchez Mejías did everything differently.

In the ring, it looked as though he wanted to die very badly. Not particularly graceful, except with the banderillas, he was considered one of the bravest men in the annals of bullfighting; brave not with an impulsive, hot-blooded, little-boy daring, but rather with a cool, impassive, contemptuous absence of fear. The critic Don Ventura wrote in 1919: "When there should be no danger in the ring, this torero goes out there and sees to it that there is, inventing it if necessary."

He was athletic and rugged and good-looking in a romanesque way. Néstor Luján, in his *Historia del Toreo,* writes:

> His valor in the ring was simply frightening, awesome. The most suicidal maneuvers he executed with the simplicity of a man who carries inside his head the furious comet of madness which gave him a forehead that was broad and Roman and livid like a statue, a forehead with the classic whiteness of a man touched by death.

He was not artistic in the ring, but he had great personality, and he knew

56

Ignacío Sánchez Mejías.

Granadino,
the bull
that
fatally wounded
Sánchez Mejías.

the arts of tauromachy backward and forward. All except killing. Once after a corrida he complained about it unhappily to his idol Joselito and the critic José María Cossío. In *Los Toros: Tratado Técnico E Histórico*, Cossío reports the conversation this way:

"The bulls don't bother me at all," said Ignacio—"I think of them as poor harmless creatures. But the moment I profile myself and start to enter to kill I suddenly don't know what I'm doing. I lose my head and do it badly and ruin the whole performance." I remember Joselito said nothing, and I made some obvious comment about the dangers of that moment. Ignacio spoke up again. "I don't know what happens to me then. I know it isn't fear. I just don't know what it is I do. Do you know, José?" When confronted by a direct question Joselito answered: "Yes, I know. You try to kill with your arm held close in to your chest, and then you try to shove the sword in with your whole body. If you want to kill easily you've got to unglue that arm from your body, free it, pull it back as you lunge forward, and then have more freedom and force to get it in. That's the only way you're ever going to kill a bull right." Ignacio listened to this intently, respectfully, the way he listened to all Joselito's pronouncements on bullfighting. Then he exclaimed: "We're like brothers, you've been watching me make a fool of myself for fifty corridas now, and not until today do you tell me what I'm doing wrong!" Joselito answered dryly: "You never asked me till today."

58

Sánchez Mejías.

His life was always tied in with Joselito's. They'd been friends as children, he married Joselito's sister, and he was given the alternativa by Joselito. And it was he who slammed a sword into Bailador after it killed Joselito in 1920, doing it the way the young Maestro had showed him; Ignacio went on to fight ninety successful corridas that same year, a staggering amount.

By 1922 Sánchez Mejías apparently figured he had proved whatever he had tried to prove in the arena, and he retired a wealthy man. But after a year of inactivity he came back, greater than ever, and he fought until 1927, when he retired once more. He killed seven bulls all by himself on that last day and declared to the press that he would never fight again.

He was an educated man, and he had always had a literary bent, so now he flung himself into a new arena with the same fervor he'd displayed against the bulls. He had two plays produced with considerable success, and numerous poems were published. He began sponsoring singers and dancers, holding elegant soirees out at his estate "Pino Montano," near Se-

Federico García Lorca.

villa; he would telephone to Granada in the middle of the night so his young friend, the poet García Lorca, could hear the impassioned heel-clicking of La Malena or the hoarse voice of the flamenco singer Manuel Torres as he "clawed the air" with his *seguidillas*.

But it was all sublimation. "His peaceful literary triumphs weren't enough for his unquiet nature," Cossío writes: "He needed to struggle with a hard reality and to subdue it by violence." He stood retirement for seven years, but then he decided to come back. His son, José Ignacio, was thinking of becoming a matador, and Sánchez Mejías exclaimed, jealous of his death: "If a body has to be brought back destroyed to Pino Montano, let it be mine, and not the son of this woman."

He was forty-three, which would be old even for a matador who had never left the game. He started to work desperately to get himself back into shape. His friend Cossío again writes:

Lacking in agility and overweight, he submitted himself to such rigorous training that he collapsed and had to be kept in bed, consumed with impatience. Finally he got himself into condition to face the taurine battles, or so he believed, and on July 15, 1934, he made his reappearance in Cádiz, on an afternoon that was made more dangerous by the strong wind. The emotion of his style of fighting had not diminished a bit over the years; in fact, if anything, it was increased because of his obvious lack of physical faculties, which didn't stop him from doing those extremely dangerous feats of his. Then other fights followed, and his efforts to overcome his handicaps were miraculous and pathetic and inspiring; he was fighting with the same spark that he had back in the days with Joselito and Belmonte, especially as his timing and reflexes came back to him.

But there was an aura of tragedy about him that upset audiences. As Néstor Luján writes in his *Historia del Toreo:*

Hemingway tells us—and he must have got it from the mouths of the people as he made his rounds of Madrid sopping up Fundador cognac with that lime-dry North American thirst of his—that during the year before his death Ignacio couldn't enter the Villa Rosa cabaret in Madrid without the gypsies warning that he smelled of death: the way Joselito smelled on his day, according to his banderillero Blanquet, and also young Granero before dying on the spikes of a Veragua.

61

And so came August. This had been a terrible year for toreros, one of the worst, because twelve were killed and forty badly gored. The month started off badly for Sánchez Mejías; death seemed to be all around him. On the fifth of August he fought in La Coruña with Belmonte and Domingo Ortega, and as Belmonte was killing, the sword was flung up into the stands and killed a spectator. During the same fight Ortega was informed that his brother had just died, and he left hurriedly for Madrid. The car overturned; Ortega was injured and his cousin killed. On short notice Sánchez Mejías was asked to substitute for Ortega in Manzanares, which he agreed to do in spite of the advice of his friends.

The first bull was Granadino from the Ayala ranch, and Sánchez Mejías went out with it and executed four fine verónicas, ending with a close half-verónica. They earned genuine "olés" for their merit, not sympathetic applause for a pathetic old man. Encouraged, he grabbed the muleta and sword and decided to start the faena the flashy way that had been his trademark in the old days. With the sword and cloth in his right hand he stalked arrogantly into the ring. He went to the barrera and sat down on the white stirrup board that runs around the base of the fence. This is a highly dangerous maneuver because a man is trapped up against the boards if anything goes wrong. But nothing went wrong on that first cambiado pass, which Sánchez Mejías executed perfectly, the bull swooshing under the man's arm as it hurtled by. The crowd roared with pleasure and astonishment. The bull's charge didn't carry it as far through as it should have, so that when it wheeled it wasn't at the proper angle to be "cited" correctly for another pass. But instead of standing up and getting out of that compromising position, Sánchez Mejías slid three feet down the stirrup board and remained in a sitting position. The bull lunged forward. It looked as though it would go by. But halfway through the pass the animal veered into the man, smashing him up against the fence and then hurling him into the air, his thigh slashed open.

He died two days later, and was buried in the same tomb with his brother-in-law, Joselito, in Sevilla. Afterward, Sánchez Mejías' son became a matador, in quest of his own individuality, but he flopped miserably and has turned impresario. He still lives at the estate of Pino Montano, which has become sort of a musty shrine, very full of the ghosts of Joselito and Sánchez Mejías and his son's failure. I went to a party there in 1945 with Belmonte, Joselito's brother El Gallo, and Manolete. It wasn't very cheery.

In 1935, a year before his own violent death at the hands of the civil guard, García Lorca published the heartfelt portrait of his friend which has become probably his best-known work, "The Lament for Ignacio Sánchez Mejías":

I

LA COGIDA Y LA MUERTE

A las cinco de la tarde.
Eran las cinco en punto de la tarde.
Un niño trajo la blanca sábana
a las cinco de la tarde.
Una espuerta de cal ya prevenida
a las cinco de la tarde.
Lo demás era muerte y sólo muerte
a las cinco de la tarde.

El viento se llevó los algodones
a las cinco de la tarde.
Y el óxido sembró cristal y níquel
a las cinco de la tarde.
Ya luchan la paloma y el leopardo
a las cinco de la tarde.
Y un muslo con un asta desolada
a las cinco de la tarde.

Comenzaron los sones de bordón
a las cinco de la tarde.
Las campanas de arsénico y el
    humo
a las cinco de la tarde.
En las esquinas grupos de silencio
a las cinco de la tarde.
¡Y el toro solo corazón arriba!
a las cinco de la tarde.

Cuando el sudor de nieve fué lle-
    gando
a las cinco de la tarde,
cuando la plaza se cubrió de yodo
a las cinco de la tarde,
la muerte puso huevos en la herida
a las cinco de la tarde.
A las cinco de la tarde.
A las cinco en punto de la tarde.

I

THE TOSSING AND DEATH

At five in the afternoon.
At exactly five in the afternoon.
A little boy brought the white sheet
at five in the afternoon.
A basket of lime already prepared
at five in the afternoon.
The rest was death, only death
at five in the afternoon.

The wind bore off the bandages
at five in the afternoon.
And the glass and nickel rusted
at five in the afternoon.
Now fight the dove and leopard
at five in the afternoon.
And a thigh with a desolate horn
at five in the afternoon.

The deep threnodies began
at five in the afternoon.
The jars of arsenic and the vapors
at five in the afternoon.
On street corners groups of silence
at five in the afternoon.
And only the bull is happy!
at five in the afternoon.

When the icy sweat began to come
at five in the afternoon,
and the arena covered by iodine
at five in the afternoon,
then death laid eggs in the wound
at five in the afternoon.
At five in the afternoon.
At exactly five in the afternoon.

Un ataúd con ruedas es la cama
a las cinco de la tarde.
Huesos y flautas suenan en su oído
a las cinco de la tarde.
El toro ya mugía por su frente
a las cinco de la tarde.
El cuarto se irisaba de agonía
a las cinco de la tarde.
A lo lejos ya viene la gangrena
a las cinco de la tarde.
Trompa de lirio por las verdes ingles
a las cinco de la tarde.
Las heridas quemaban como soles
a las cinco de la tarde,
y el gentío rompía las ventanas
a las cinco de la tarde.
A las cinco de la tarde.
¡Ay, qué terribles cinco de la tarde!
¡Eran las cinco en todos los relojes!
¡Eran las cinco en sombra de la tarde!

A casket on wheels is his bed
at five in the afternoon.
Bones and flutes sound in his ears
at five in the afternoon.
The bull bellows by his forehead
at five in the afternoon,
the whole room writhing in agony
at five in the afternoon.
From afar comes the gangrene
at five in the afternoon.
Trumpets of lilies on the green groins
at five in the afternoon.
The wounds burning like suns
at five in the afternoon.
And the crowd was breaking the windows
at five in the afternoon.
At five in the afternoon.
Ay, what terrible five o'clocks in the afternoon!
All the clocks were striking five!
It was five in the shade of the afternoon!

II

LA SANGRE DERRAMADA

¡Que no quiero verla!

Dile a la luna que venga,
que no quiero ver la sangre
de Ignacio sobre la arena.

¡Que no quiero verla!

La luna de par en par.
Caballo de nubes quietas,
y la plaza gris del sueño
con sauces en las barreras.
¡Que no quiero verla!
Que mi recuerdo se quema.
¡Avisad a los jazmines
con su blancura pequeña!

¡Que no quiero verla!

La vaca del viejo mundo
pasaba su triste lengua
sobre un hocico de sangres
derramadas en la arena,
y los toros de Guisando,
casi muerte y casi piedra,
mugieron como dos siglos
hartos de pisar la tierra.
No.

¡Que no quiero verla!

Por las gradas sube Ignacio
con toda su muerte a cuestas.
Buscaba el amanecer,
y el amanecer no era.
Busca su perfil seguro,
y el sueño lo desorienta.

II

THE SPILLED BLOOD

No, I don't want to see it!

Tell the moon to come,
I really don't want to see the blood
of Ignacio on the sand.

No, I don't want to see it!

The moon completely full.
Horse of the quiet clouds,
and the arena gray with sleep
with willows round the stands.
No, I don't want to see it!
I tell you the memory burns.
Inform the jasmines
with their fragile whiteness!

No, I don't want to see it!

The cow of the old world
kept passing her sad tongue
over a muzzle of blood
all spilled on the sand of the ring,
and the bulls of Guisando,
half death and half stone,
were bellowing like two centuries
tired of treading the earth.
No.

No, I don't want to see it!

Up the steps came Ignacio
with all his death on his shoulders.
He was searching for the dawn,
and there was no dawn.
He is seeking his strong profile,
and sleep makes him lose it.

Buscaba su hermoso cuerpo
y encontró su sangre abierta.
¡No me digáis que la vea!
No quiero sentir el chorro
cada vez con menos fuerza;
ese chorro que ilumina
los tendidos y se vuelca
sobre la pana y el cuero
de muchedumbre sedienta.
¡Quién me grita que me asome!
¡No me digáis que la vea!

No se cerraron sus ojos
cuando vió los cuernos cerca,
pero las madres terribles
levantaron la cabeza.
Y a través de las ganaderías,
hubo un aire de voces secretas
que gritaban a toros celestes,
mayorales de pálida niebla.
No hubo príncipe en Sevilla
que comparársele pueda,
ni espada como su espada
ni corazón tan de veras.
Como un río de leones
su maravillosa fuerza,
y como un torso de mármol
su dibujada prudencia.
Aire de Roma andaluza
le doraba la cabeza
donde su risa era un nardo
de sal y de inteligencia.
¡Qué gran torero en la plaza!
¡Qué buen serrano en la sierra!
¡Qué blando con las espigas!
¡Qué duro con las espuelas!
¡Qué tierno con el rocío!
¡Qué deslumbrante en la feria!
¡Qué tremendo con las últimas
banderillas de tiniebla!

He sought his handsome body
and he found his flowing blood.
Don't ask me to see it!
I do not wish to feel
the flow each time less strong;
the stream that lights up
the seats in the gallery and spills
over the plush and leather
of the thirsting crowds.
Who demands that I look!
Don't ask me to see it!

He did not close his eyes
when he saw the horns near him,
but the fearful mothers,
lifted up their heads.
And across the bull ranches
there came a wind of secret voices,
crying out to the bulls of heaven,
the herdsmen of the pallid mist.
There was no prince in Seville
that can be compared to him,
nor sword like his sword,
nor a heart so true.
Like a river of lions,
his marvelous strength,
like a torso of marble
his wisdom was portrayed.
His head was gilded with the
air of Andalusian Rome,
where his laugh was a tuberose
of wit and understanding.
What a torero in the plaza!
What a climber of mountains!
How gentle with ears of corn!
How commanding with the spurs!
How tender with the dew!
How dashing at the fair!
How tremendous with the final
banderillas of darkness!

Pero ya duerme sin fin.
Ya los musgos y la hierba
abren con dedos seguros
la flor de su calavera.
Y su sangre ya viene cantando:
cantando por marismas y praderas,
resbalando por cuernos ateridos,
vacilando sin alma por la niebla,
tropezando con miles de pezuñas
como una larga, oscura, triste lengua,
para formar un charco de agonía
junto al Guadalquivir de las estrel-
  las.
¡Oh blanco muro de España!
¡Oh negro toro de pena!
¡Oh sangre dura de Ignacio!
¡Oh ruiseñor de sus venas!
No.

¡Que no quiero verla!
Que no hay cáliz que la contenga,
que no hay golondrinas que se la
  beban,
no hay escarcha de luz que la en-
  fríe,
no hay canto ni diluvio de azuce-
  nas,
no hay cristal que la cubra de plata.
No.
¡¡Yo no quiero verla!!

But now he sleeps without end.
Already the moss and weeds
open with skillful fingers
the flower of his skull.
And now his blood comes singing:
singing through marsh and field,
gliding by the cold horns,
winding soulless in the mist,
meeting a thousand hooved feet

like a long, dark, sad tongue,
and then forms a lake of agony
near the starry Guadalquivir.
Oh white wall of Spain!
Oh black bull of sorrow!
Oh hard blood of Ignacio!
Oh nightingale of his veins!
No.

No, I don't want to see it!
There is no chalice that can hold it,
no swallows that can drink it,
no white frost that can cool it,
no song nor deluge of lilies,
no glass that can coat it with silver.
No.
No, I don't want to see it!!

Valladolid

5. Valladolid

VALLADOLID IS ABOUT A THREE HOURS' DRIVE NORTHWEST FROM MADRID, AND the annual fair, September 18 to 21, is worth catching since they usually have top toreros and top bulls. The ring itself holds about twelve thousand people.

Whenever I think of Valladolid I think of Hemingway's fine chapter in *For Whom the Bell Tolls* where Pilar tells of her matador husband and his horror when he sees the mounted bull's head at the banquet in Valladolid honoring him.

People in Córdoba tell of the great Lagartijo and a mounted bull's head he had in his home. It was the largest bull he had ever fought—so large that during the fight it had casually scratched its chin on the top board of the fence—and it had given him a terrible time before he managed to kill it. They say he never got used to having the beast in his house, even dead and mounted, and for years when he wobbled home drunk, he would take his cane and beat it, cursing violently the while.

But read Hemingway's mounted head story in chapter fourteen of the novel. It begins: " 'Never have I known a man with so much fear,' Pilar said. 'He would not even have a bull's head in the house. One time at the feria of Valladolid he killed a bull of Pablo Romero very well——' "

Then it goes on to tell of the banquet given at the Café Colón in Valladolid where Finito, Pilar's tubercular and horn-pounded husband, is to be honored by being presented with the mounted head of the bull he has killed. All during the riotous meal he stares at the tablecloth, afraid to look

71

at the head on the wall veiled by a purple shroud. From time to time he coughs blood into his handkerchief, and by the end of the banquet he has gone through three handkerchiefs and his napkin. Finally comes the presentation:

"So the president of the Club reached the end of the speech and then, with everybody cheering him, he stood on a chair and reached up and untied the cord that bound the purple shroud over the head and slowly pulled it clear of the head and it stuck on one of the horns and he lifted it clear and pulled it off the sharp polished horns and there was that great yellow bull with black horns that swung way out and pointed forward, their white tips sharp as porcupine quills, and the head of the bull was as though he were alive; his forehead was curly as in life and his nostrils were open and his eyes were bright and he was there looking straight at Finito.

"Everyone shouted and applauded and Finito sunk further back in the chair and then everyone was quiet and looking at him and he said, 'No. No,' and looked at the bull and pulled further back and then he said 'No!' very loudly and a big blob of blood came out and he didn't even put up the napkin and it slid down his chin and he was still looking at the bull and he said, 'All season, yes. To make money, yes. To eat, yes. But I can't eat. Hear me? My stomach's bad. But now with the season finished! No! No! No!' He looked around at the table and then he looked at the bull's head and said, 'No,' once more and then he put his head down and he put his napkin up to his mouth and then he just sat there like that and said nothing and the banquet, which had started so well, and promised to mark an epoch in hilarity and good fellowship was not a success."

"Then how long after that did he die?" Primitivo asked.

"That winter," Pilar said. "He never recovered from that last blow with the flat of the horn in Zaragoza. They are worse than a goring, for the injury is internal and it does not heal. He received one almost every time he went in to kill and it was for this reason he was not more successful. It was difficult for him to get out from over the horn because of his short stature. Nearly always the side of the horn struck him. But of course many were only glancing blows."

"If he was so short he should not have tried to be a matador," Primitivo said.

Pilar looked at Robert Jordan and shook her head. Then she bent over the big iron pot, still shaking her head.

72

And then, unfortunately perhaps, I can't help thinking of another bit of writing.

Cornelia Otis Skinner also mentions Valladolid in her piece entitled "For Whom the Gong Sounds," from *Soap Behind the Ears*, but in a slightly different vein. Nothing is sacred to Miss Skinner when she sits at her typewriter: not la fiesta brava, not life, not even the ringing prose of Ernest Hemingway. Here is an irreverent sample:

> "Thou wast of the street car, camarada?"
>
> "Come now? Why not?" Robert Jordan thought of the last street car he had blown up. They had found arms and legs all over the roofs. One femur had gone as far as Valladolid . . .
>
> The mouth of the cave was camouflaged by a curtain of saddle-blankets, matadores' capes, and the soles of old espadrilles. Inside it smelt of man-sweat, acrid and brown . . . horse-sweat sweet and magenta. There was the leathery smell of leather and the coppery smell of copper and borne in on the clear night air came the distant smell of skunk.
>
> The wife of Pablo was stirring frijoles in a Catalonian wineskin. She wore rope-soled shoes and a belt of hand grenades. Over her magnificent buttocks swung a 16th Century cannon taken from the Escorial.
>
> "I obscenity in the obscenity of thy unprintable obscenity," said Pilar.
>
> "This is the Ingles of the street car. He of the boardwalk to come soon."
>
> "I obscenity in the unprintable of the milk of all street cars." The woman was stirring the steaming mess with the horns of a Miura bull. She stared at Robert Jordan then smiled. "Obscenity, obscenity, obscenity," she said, not unkindly.
>
> "Que va," said Robert Jordan. "Bueno. Good."
>
> "Menos mal," said El Sordo. "Not so good."
>
> "Go unprint thyself," said Pilar. The gypsy went outside and unprinted himself.
>
> The girl with the shaved head filled a tin pail full of petite marmite and handed it to him and she gave him a great swig from the wineskin and he chewed the succulent bits of horsemeat and they said nothing.

I would like to see Miss Skinner do a humorous piece on bullfighting itself. There is little commendable humor about la fiesta brava. Perhaps it is because, as Manolete solemnly answered when asked why he so rarely smiled, "This thing of the bulls is very serious."

There are attempts at humor. The bullfighting magazines often run anecdotes about the great matadors. ("How did it go today?" El Gallo was once asked, and he mumbled this answer: "There was a división de opiniones." His manager broke in sarcastically, "Yes—half the plaza called you a dirty coward and the other half a clumsy bum.") Usually the stories are technical and quite special and rarely funny.

There are cartoons often. I remember a better-than-average one of a funny sort of George Price type railroad-crossing guard making a pass with his signaling flag at the passing train, looking away from it disdainfully in Manolete's "mirando al publico" style, while his wife leans out of the window of their little hut and shouts admiringly, "Olé, Nicomedes, and even looking at the crowd!"

But usually the cartoons are bad, too—though not as bad as charlotadas, the worst form of humor in the world. Charlotadas are so-called comic bullfights, and if you ever hear of one being planned in the city you are in, leave town so that you don't, through some gross inadvertence, find yourself attending. My feeling about charlotadas is like Frank Lloyd Wright's about Pittsburgh. When someone in a radio interview asked him, "And what do you think of our little city?" he growled this succinct and final word on the matter: "Abandon it!"

Kenneth Tynan, in a book I admire enormously, entitled *Bull Fever*, has described a typical charlotada in Valencia wonderfully well:

The show begins at midnight beneath blinding arc lamps with a march of brass bands, led around the arena by a demonstrative conductor with a face like the Kitchener of the recruiting posters. The audience warms to the strains of its local anthem, "Valencia." The ring is then cleared; a trumpet sounds; and a starved little bull—a yearling becerro—is let in, to be fought by a youthful volunteer, aged about thirteen but arrayed in the full glory of the traje de luces. There are no horses, but the rest of the ritual is microscopically reproduced: capework, banderillas, and a travesty of a faena, with the boy getting tossed again and again to shrieks of laughter from the crowd and tearful complaints from a few pop-eyed middle-aged women. He tries hard to kill according to the rules, while terror counsels him to run for his life, and the result is a sort of hit-or-miss brawl.

At length the bull dies, and the matador, burying his blushes in a nosegay, makes a hesitant circuit of the ring. Meanwhile, at lightning speed, a platform stage has been erected in mid-arena, upon which, already, a vast woman with hair like tarred rope is singing profuse flamenco into a microphone, stamping and swaying as she shouts her protestations of undying love for every rock of her native province.

Unexpectedly, there are now fireworks and a selection from *Oklahoma!* by the band, whose encore consists of excerpts from the score of *Radio Follies of 1926*, played at half speed with ponderous syncopation.

The stage is then whipped away. What next? One hoped for a lady bullfighter, like the remarkable Martina García, who fought her last novillo in Madrid in 1880 at the age of seventy-six; the nineteenth century saw many señoritas toreras, but their vogue aroused so much controversy that in 1908 the appearance of women on foot in the bullrings of Spain was officially banned. Mexico, however, still permits it, and many a lusty Texas heiress has tried her luck in the smaller plazas close to the American border. Valencia has to make do with charlotadas. The band lines up by the barrera, idly playing "A Pretty Girl is Like a Melody," and a second becerro trots into the ring. This time the clowns are the gladiators, wearing crushed toppers, baggy trousers, sequins, spurs, chaps, kilts, and pom-poms. One of them, in night shirt and night cap, feigns sleep on an iron bedstead. He snores loudly, then twitches, whereupon the little bull charges him; it is like a persecution nightmare come true. The clown jumps out of bed and, using the sheet as a cape, executes a few parody chicuelinas, and dives back again under the covers, holding his breath. The bull sniffs at him, and, wheeling suddenly, charges the musicians, who leap headlong over the barrera, leaving a sousaphone behind, which the bull gores and dents with its stubby horns.

The fight itself is a black fantasy, an absurd satanic inversion of bullfighting, as if *Everyman* were to be played by the cast of *Hellzapoppin*. Two of the comics join hands in a broadly effeminate tango, withdrawing to arm's length while the bull charges between them, and then coming amorously together again. The principal grotesque or "top banana" takes a pair of banderillas and, as he puts them in, somersaults over the horns; his partner inserts another pair and dives under the hoofs, all in one movement. One clown, in an outsize overcoat, climbs onto another's shoulders and begins the faena from a height of around nine feet. Everything, short of dressing it up in a tutu, is done to make the bull look foolish.

The kill, which cannot be faked or burlesqued, comes as a sickening shock; you cannot believe it is really going to happen. But the Spanish mind moves as readily as Hamlet's did from clowns to graves, and the maladroitness of the matador, who needed six thrusts to kill, was all that the crowd objected to. A mule hauls the body out and the band marches over the blood, swinging into a free arrangement of "Alice Blue Gown."

Much of comic bullfighting is brilliant and hilarious; even allowing for the smallness of the bull, there is more inventiveness in it than in nine out of ten formal corridas. But with the kill a new dimension is added; as if, in an old pantomime, Clown were to belabor Pantaloon not with a slapstick but with a crowbar. A fellow comedian is casually murdered before your eyes; the farcical tale is brutally followed through until it ends, as all tales sooner or later must end, in death.

How very well Tynan writes, about charlotadas or anything. I shall always be grateful to him for his line about Girón's executing a chest pass that was "as flamboyant as a starlet's autograph." I shall be grateful to him also for his parody on the overwriting that abounds in bullfight literature. Bullfighting often hits writers so hard when they are first exposed to it that they get carried away when it comes time to sit down in front of the Smith-Corona.

Here are Tynan's verbal banderillas de fuego, from *Bull Fever*, directed at those miscreants:

One of the bullfight's greatest enemies is the intense romantic. It is in many ways a pity that most of the books which have brought bullfighting to the English language (I except Hemingway's, still the soundest and best) have been written in a state of literary kif: "A dark, swelling knot tightened within José's gut. This was it, then, this was what men called fear and looked away. Mother of God, he needed another anís, how bad he needed it. His gut was a flapping, empty wineskin, like a man should not have if he is killing bulls. And he was out there alone with it, alone with the horned fury. Little Saint Penelope of the lollipops, but that Number 28 was an ayuntamiento with sabres, a bitch of a bull. I got to tie the bastard down, crooned José within himself, I got to make a beauty of the bastard. He went towards the horns, walking on fire and sick to his stomach. 'Thou art my toro, thou son of a tart,' he whispered in Spanish, 'this is my afternoon and thou art my art. O thou noble bull of Andalucía, be good to me and be not a pigeon-dropping.' After his first series of seventy-eight linked naturals with the left, the true and honest hand, he felt better. The dark knot was cut, a great passion came in upon him, and his blood flowed in mystic surges. The hilt was burning him, the hilt of the sacrificial spear. 'Kill now,' said the soul of José el Rubio, 'kill now, and let it be beautiful, that the old men may talk about it over their manzanillas in time to come.' Uhh-hah, Señor Toro, I am ready for

76

you, you chicken-pellet, said José el Rubio, and he straightened his old man's shoulders and he took the black bulk of the most noble bull of all the Conde's pastures full on the point of his singing sword. 'Was it well done?' he shouted to his peasant of confidence, 'Was it well done, Fepe?' And Pepe showed him his young man's thumb and said that yes, it was well done, it was well done indeed . . ."

This kind of thing deforms the bullfight, presenting it as the dream of a neurotic solipsist, substituting a phoney ecstasy for the stronger, sterner excitement of the reality. It makes the aesthetic error of identifying the torero with his job, just as bad dramatic critics will identify an actress with her parts: "And then, her wits awry with sorrow at the death of her father, Miss Bartlett appeared decked in flowers, poor woodland tokens of homage, and sang the sad, ribald, remembered songs of her infancy . . ." To sentimentalise the bullfight is to commit a crime against it. For its finest moments bullfighting depends on restraint and Olympian detachment, never on what Landor calls "the hot, uncontrollable harlotry of a flaunting dishevelled invention."

Puerto de Santa Maria

6. Puerto de Santa Maria

ONE USUALLY GOES TO THE PLAZA AT PUERTO DE SANTA MARIA AFTER A NICE
leisurely luncheon at Los Cisnes hotel in Jerez. Jerez is a wonderful,
friendly, white town in the province of Cádiz, about fifty miles due south
from Sevilla. In olden days it was called Xeres (pronounced shey-ress)
hence the generic name sherry, which is given to wines similar to the ones
found in Jerez. Nowhere else in the world can produce sherry comparable
to the jerez of Jerez. California red and white wines may bear comparison
with some European wines; but sherry produced anywhere else does not
even approximate the sherry that flows from this little district of ninety
thousand people.

Jerez is a very bull-conscious town, and it has a small ring of its own.
But when there's a good fight in Puerto de Santa Maria you'll see half of
Jerez' aficionados there, since it's only an easy half an hour away. The town
itself is attractive enough, and the bullring is impressive, holding fifteen
thousand when jammed, say, by a crowd come to see Arruza and Manolete.
Puerto has had an active bullring since 1768, and the great matador José
Cándido was killed there in 1771. But the most memorable event to occur
in Puerto's history happened in 1857, and the most memorable man to stalk
out on the sand of Puerto's bullring was Manuel Domínguez.

They called him Desperdicios afterward. It means "Cast-off-scrap-of-
meat"—a very strange nickname for a man, but gruesomely appropriate
when one knows the story of his brave and appalling act. Was his a hor-
rifying, senseless gesture to prove brute male courage? Not if one under-

81

stands what bullfighting and guts mean to Spanish audiences—and more important, what they mean to the bullfighters themselves.

Born in Andalucía in 1816, Domínguez became a professional bullfighter at the age when most boys are occupied in trying to find the square of the hypotenuse. He soon became known as the bravest matador in Spain. The crowds called him "the wild boar from Sevilla."

He went to South America at the height of his career and was so popular that he stayed there for sixteen years. He made a lot of money, but became involved in a revolution, lost it all, and was forced to leave the country. He returned to Spain without a centavo but confident that he could resume his career and regain his fortune.

A rude surprise awaited him. He found he could get no contracts, for people had forgotten him. Curro Cúchares was the new sensation, and was such a tremendous drawing card that he could control all the plazas de toros in Spain. Domínguez sought out the idol, finding him one morning in a Sevilla café.

"*Buenos días*, Señor Cúchares," said Domínguez. "I would like to discuss the possibility of some corridas."

Cúchares sullenly studied the older man's graying hair, the strong jaw, the eyes that looked as though they'd never seen defeat—and never would. Cúchares grunted, but he didn't reply. Again Domínguez asked to fight.

"There's no room for you," Cúchares told him arrogantly. Cúchares remembered Domínguez' suicidal style too well.

Domínguez was desperate. He had to get a fight! He jumped up on his chair, shouted that Curro Cúchares was a coward, and dared him to meet him in a mano-a-mano—a hand-to-hand corrida between just the two of them. "We will prove who is the braver man," shouted Manuel, "if this *cobarde* is man enough to enter the contest!"

The trick worked, for it was a challenge no Spaniard could let go by with honor—especially a torero.

"I am not used to competing with has-beens," said Cúchares, rising angrily from his chair, "but I accept your insulting challenge. And after I give you a lesson in tauromachy, you will have to slink back to South America!"

The fight was scheduled for June 1, 1857, and Domínguez insisted that the bulls be Concha y Sierra animals, the largest and most dangerous available in that epoch. It was to be the most memorable bullfight of the century.

Manuel was forty-one years of age, an old man in the bull game. His side chops were graying, but they framed a rugged, supremely confident face, and he had a powerful, heavy-set body to go with it. A modern bullfighter would never look like that, but this was back in the last century when

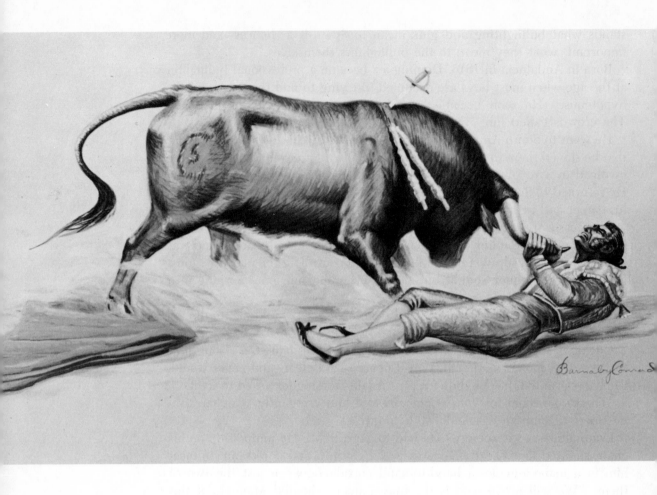

The goring of Desperdicios
in Puerto de Santa María.

bullfighting wasn't the refined, pretty-boy ballet it is today. Domínguez' style and silhouette no more resembled Manolete's, for example, than John L. Sullivan's would resemble those of Floyd Patterson.

Manuel was the last of the great classic style of fighters. He was an ardent disciple of Pedro Romero's School of Tauromachy of Sevilla, whose famous precepts were:

1. A coward is not a man, and bullfighting demands men.
2. Fear causes more wounds than the bulls themselves.
3. With a sword and muleta in his hands, a matador's code should forbid him from ever running from a bull.
4. A matador should never vault the fence; this is shameful.
5. Await the charge calmly, work in close, and always play the man.
6. A matador should not depend upon his feet but upon his wrists, and once in front of the bull he should either kill or be killed before giving down to the animal.
7. More can be done in the plaza with a pound of valor and an ounce of intelligence than the other way around.*

Those were the days when bulls were so big they were called "cathedrals" by the toreros. They were stronger and equipped with larger horns—a matter of grave concern to the individual fighter. They were harder to kill because the matador had farther and higher to reach so he could plant his sword. They were just more dangerous in every way. For instance, the bull with which Domínguez made his debut in Madrid weighed more than twice as much as the one that killed the famous Joselito in 1920. And the bulls for the Domínguez-Cúchares contest were the four largest to be found on the Iberian Peninsula.

The corrida was held in Puerto de Santa Maria, a town in Andalucía famous for its knowledge of "la fiesta brava," and people came from all over Spain to witness it. The two men didn't speak to each other as they arrogantly strode into the arena amidst the cheers of the crowd, but Domínguez spat very ostentatiously. This was a favorite trick of his to show his absence of fear.

Cúchares was the first to fight. His bull was the smallest of the four, and he could unfurl all his fancy cape-twirling tricks that had the crowd roaring. He took only two sword thrusts to kill the animal, and the audience applauded.

Manuel's big jaw was set determinedly as the bull named Barrabás skidded out of the tunnel. It was a black giant with tremendous horns.

* I like Hemingway's comment, in *Death in the Afternoon*, on Diego Fortuna: "He is as brave as the bull himself and just a little less intelligent."

Domínguez knew that his old legs could not compete with the fancy cape-work and athletic tricks of Cúchares; he knew that if he were to win this competition it would have to be on guts alone. And he *had* to win this fight, the most important of his life!

He crossed himself. Then he vaulted into the ring and dropped to his knees. The crowd gasped, for it was the first time a man had ever tried to fight a bull while kneeling.

When he made the animal pass back and forth ten times, the crowd cheered and screamed. Each time the horns cut closer and closer to his body until it seemed that the man was trying to commit suicide.

From then on, the fight was his. When it came time to kill, Domínguez elected to do it the most dangerous way of all—"receiving." That is, he stood absolutely still in front of the bull and shook the cloth to make it charge. Manuel waited calmly for the animal as it thundered down on him, and then he reached over the horns and made a perfect thrust. But Barrabás wrenched its head to the right and slammed Domínguez to the ground. As he lay there helplessly, the bull lowered its head and charged.

Domínguez saw certain death pounding toward him, but just as the giant horns reached him he grabbed the right one and managed to hold the animal off, the tip of the horn against his jaw, the bull skidding the man over the sand in its efforts to spike the horn through his head.

Finally the banderilleros were able to distract the bull and pull him away, and Domínguez lurched to his feet. The crowd saw a terrible sight. While there was only a slight scratch on his jaw, somehow the horn had gouged out his eye, and it hung down on his cheek like a peeled grape. But Manuel wasn't going to let himself be carried off to the infirmary. An old man? He'd show Cúchares and the rest of them what guts an old man could have!

He reached up, took the eyeball in his fingers, and flicked it away—as casually as though he were wiping the sweat from his brow, as disdainfully as though it were a scrap of garbage! Women fainted and men retched.

And then Domínguez turned back to the bull, for he was a killer of bulls and the animal was still alive. Bleeding, unarmed, and completely exposed to the clumiest charge, he walked slowly toward the bull with one hand raised. The heaving animal watched its quarry come, about to lunge forward, the sword jutting out between the shoulders. Suddenly the black beast coughed, backed up, wobbled, and crashed over dead.

Domínguez shook off the people who tried to carry him, and unaided he stalked out of the arena to the infirmary—and immortality. From that day on he was known as Desperdicios (Cast-off-scrap-of-meat) and for the rest of his life, wherever he went, people turned to look and murmur:

"*Allí va un hombre*—there, by God, goes a man!"

Barcelona

7. Barcelona

THE PLAZA DE TOROS OF BARCELONA IS THE STEPCHILD OF SPAIN'S BULLRINGS.
It is the second largest arena in Spain, holding 19,582 people, the best
toreros perform in it, and yet if a bullfighter has a great day there the rest
of Spain sneers and says, "What do they know about bullfighting in Barcelona!"

Barcelona is considered very un-Spanish by the Spaniards. The Catalans
are industrious, un-flamenco, rather Anglo-Saxon in their approach to things,
and horribly dull to the rest of Spain. To the colorful Andaluces, steeped
in the traditions of the fiesta brava, it is a grotesque joke for a bullfight to be
held at all in commercially minded Barcelona—the way New Orleans folk
might react if told that Pittsburgh was going to inaugurate a mardi gras.

Nevertheless Barcelona is a big city, it has had bullfights since 1387, and
it must be considered one of the world's important rings. The ring is now
called "La Monumental," but when originally built in 1914 it was called
"El Sport," which gives you an idea of the un-Spanishness of Barcelona.

La Monumental has seen some great afternoons, but only those who witnessed them will believe it because the other Spaniards automatically dis-
count the reviews in the newspapers about any triumphs in Barcelona. It
is highly unfair to the toreros because the public will believe the bad reviews, considering a Catalán critic of being capable of judging what makes
a bad fight but not what makes a good one. Manolete, Arruza, and recently Chamaco have had some of their greatest corridas in Barcelona and
received some of their highest fees—but they went knowing they were per-

89

forming for that audience alone, whereas when a torero fights in Madrid or Sevilla or Valencia he knows that all Spain is interested in the outcome, and whether or not he cuts ears will affect his prestige in the entire country.

Barcelona has only produced two toreros worthy of mention. Gil Tovar, the better of the two, took the alternative in 1930. He was a great stylist and could have been a truly fine torero if he'd had more guts in front of the bulls. But he is a very pleasant fellow and is today one of the important elements in the small but intense group of aficionados in Barcelona. Whenever I see Gil he gives me his marvelous smile and says excitedly that he's leaving next month for Mexico to marry an heiress there and raise bulls. He's been telling people this for nine years, but the banns are no closer to being posted.

The other torero is Mario Cabré who, ten years after taking his alternative in 1941, achieved certain notoriety in this country for his rather foolish affair with a beautiful Hollywood actress. Mario was a sturdy, yeoman-type torero, looking to perfection the way one would imagine a Catalán matador to be. Though competent enough, he is not taken very seriously in the annals of tauromachy. Handsome and humorless, he has tried acting and poetry in addition to tauromachy, and has received more publicity than acclaim for his endeavors. John Steinbeck tells of a time when they were filming a motion picture in Barcelona and Cabré was supposed to fight the bull in a certain area of the ring. The bull charged unexpectedly, and Cabré in his retreat to the fence somehow nicked one of the banderilleros with his sword. The crusty old veteran looked down at the scratch and said balefully, "I have been in this business for thirty years and this is the first time I've ever been wounded by a poet!" The quantity of *desprecio*— the contempt—with which the man imbued that simple word *poet* was quite remarkable, Steinbeck says.

My own most vivid recollection of Barcelona had something to do with bullfighting but nothing to do with La Monumental. It happened in the fall of 1945, and it was like this:

I was sitting at my desk in the American Consulate in Barcelona, going through the routine tasks of a vice-consul, when I remembered the midget.

He was six hundred miles away in Sevilla, frantically reproducing those statues. I had forgotten to tell him to stop making them when I'd been transferred from Sevilla the week before, and every statue he finished would cost me one eighth of my monthly salary.

I put aside the passport case I was working on and hurried through the big outer room where the clerks worked, past the senior consuls' offices, and into the consul general's lair.

"Go right in, Mr. Conrad," his secretary said, "Mr. Nash has just come in."

90

Arruza.

He always arrived at four minutes to ten. Not three minutes or five minutes, but always four minutes to ten. I gave my tie a nervous tug before opening the door.

I was only twenty-three, the youngest and greenest vice-consul in the Foreign Service, and consuls general to me were like brigadier generals to a second lieutenant.

"Good morning," said Mr. Nash cheerily, leaning back in his swivel chair. He was the unstuffiest consul general I ever met, but he was still very much a consul general. "How are you finding Barcelona after a week? Isn't much like the gay gypsy life in Sevilla, is it?"

"No, sir, but it's very pleasant." I hesitated because I knew how fantastic this was going to sound. "Mr. Nash——"

"What can I do for you?"

"I was wondering if I could go back to Sevilla this week end."

The consul general frowned. "You've only been here a week." He paused and scratched his head. Then he looked up at me with narrowed eyes. "If this has anything to do with bullfighting—" he slapped the desk for emphasis. "No!"

"No, sir," I said, and launched in. "You see, last month I made a statue of my friend Arruza. I thought if I had it cast maybe I could sell the copies for some extra money. I found a man who casts religious statues and told him to start making some copies. I only wanted a few, until I found out whether they would sell. Then this transfer came through, and in the excitement of getting here I stupidly forgot to call him off. He'll be up into the hundreds unless I can stop him."

"Send him a wire!"

"I don't know his name, except Antonio. He's a very small man—a midget, in fact. He lives in Gelves, a village near Sevilla. There's no telephone. I only know how to get there, I don't know the address."

It sounded so phony I didn't blame him for not swallowing it. He smiled knowingly.

"You know, we've heard about your amateur bullfighting for the two years you've been in Spain." He chuckled and lit a cigarette. "I'm a great aficionado and I must say it all sounds very colorful. But"—he brought his fist down on the desk—"not while you are a member of my consulate."

"But, sir——"

"I have no intention of having the State Department land on top of me just because you've been injured in some fool bullring."

"Mr. Nash, can't you see——"

"There are some things, young man, which an officer in the Foreign Service cannot permit himself to see."

"But, sir, honestly—I am not going to Sevilla to fight bulls."

He looked at me skeptically. "It's just a coincidence that the big fights of San Miguel are on there this week end?"

"Mr. Nash, I give you my word of honor that I will not fight any bulls."

He swung away in his chair and tapped his teeth with a pencil for a few seconds. Then he turned back and said, "All right. A vice-consul's word of honor is good enough for me. But if you're not back here in this office early Monday morning you will no longer be a vice-consul."

"I'll be back," I said.

The next morning, Saturday, I caught the plane to Madrid. There I transferred to one of the archaic trimotored Junkers of the Iberia Line and arrived in Sevilla in the afternoon.

The fair was on in full swing, and the beautiful town looked like something out of a de luxe travel brochure. There were Chinese lanterns all over and fancy decorated carriages and girls in gay gypsy costumes riding on the saddles behind caballeros in broad-brimmed, glossy black hats. The place looked the way all Spanish towns ought to look. I wanted to call Mari Harcourt, a girl friend, but after leaving my suitcase at the hotel, I grabbed a taxi and headed for Gelves; my midget could probably turn out a statue or two in the time it would take to phone Mari.

I arrived in the adobe village of Gelves about five, after frequent stops for stoking the taxi; like many of the ancient vehicles in Spain, the car was propelled by a *gasógeno,* a stovelike contraption attached to the rear, that burned coal or wood instead of hard-to-get gasoline. I knocked on the door where the midget lived. A filthy little girl answered the door.

"*Papacito no 'tá, Señó Vice,*" she lisped in her Andaluz accent. "He's gone to the stove to cook a big load of statues."

My heart sank, for I could see beyond her into the house. Everywhere there were replicas of my bullfighter swinging his muleta against a charging bull. They were perched on the mantelpiece, the chairs, under the bed, on the stove, on the window, above the sink. There must have been seventy-five of them—and now the girl was telling me another load had gone to the kiln to be fired!

"Where is the stove?" I asked her. "I have to stop him." I didn't know how I was going to pay for these, much less another batch.

She shrugged. "Another town." But she didn't know which. Anyway, the statues were already made. It was too late.

"Papa will return tomorrow at five," she said.

"Not until tomorrow?" I exclaimed.

I took one of the statues and got back into the taxi. I was supposed to take the ten o'clock plane the next morning. Now I would have to catch

94

the evening train at six-thirty. It would be a tight squeeze, but I could probably get back out to Gelves, stop Antonio, discuss arrangements to pay him by the month for the statues, and make the train. I had to make it. It was the only one that could get me to Barcelona before ten Monday.

Back in Sevilla I called Mari and made a date to meet her at the Bodega Bar in the Hotel Cristina. She showed up looking very American and pretty with her saddle shoes and white sweater and brown hair. Half English and half Madrileña, she was an art student in Sevilla, and though she was a very bad artist, she was a wonderful person.

We had danced once and toasted each other with a sherry when Carlos Arruza came in with his manager.

"Hola!" he shouted when he saw me. "Just the uncle we're looking for!"

Arruza was twenty-five, good-looking, and already had made two million dollars by being the bravest and most skillful Mexican matador ever to invade Spanish arenas.

"Look, chico," he said as they sat down at our table. "Tomorrow we're having a big festival fight. It's for charity and it's supposed to be international. I'm fighting for Mexico, Montani is representing Peru, Alfredo Pickman for Spain, and now you'll represent America."

I would have given anything I owned to fight on the same program with the great Arruza. "Look, Carlos," I said. "I can't. I'd really like to—but my leg. It's acted up again."

It was true that my leg had been badly injured by a bull when I was attending the University of Mexico years before. I felt Mari looking at me, and I knew she was thinking that it hadn't hurt my dancing a few minutes ago.

"But these are going to be really small animals," Carlos protested. "And the Civil Governor is going to give a gold bull's ear to the uncle who puts up the best faena."

I shook my head. "I can't do it."

"What an uncle you turned out to be," said Carlos. "I thought you were the big Niño de California."

"Listen," I said, "I'd like to, believe me, but I can't. I—I promised some-one I wouldn't."

"Your mamacita?" Carlos' manager grinned.

"Or some little girl up there in Barcelona?" said Mari.

There was an awkward pause. Then Carlos said, "Speaking of mamacitas, would you mind bringing my mother out to the fight tomorrow?"

"Sure, I'll be glad to take her," I murmured.

We had dinner and I went to bed fairly late. I couldn't get to sleep. I kept fighting a mythical bull—a wonderful, brave, cooperative bull that I

95

could make do everything but sit up and moo. And up in the stands, applauding deliriously, was the consul general. I finally fell asleep at dawn and slept almost till noon.

After lunch Mari and I picked up Arruza's mother at her hotel. I warned her that I would probably have to leave early as I had to take care of my statue problem and catch the six-thirty train. She said that was all right, she'd come home with Carlos.

She was hardly the pathetic little barefoot telling-her-beads type of bull-fighter's mother that one visualizes from literature. She was modern, attractive, and young. But she looked worried today.

"Carlitos has been fighting since he was thirteen years old," she said as we left the outskirts of Sevilla. "And I've never seen him in the ring. All the others, yes, as I am a great aficionada. But never Carlos. So finally I have said to myself, 'Look here, you are ridiculous, you just go watch today like any other spectator.'"

"You picked a good day," I said. "This is just a private ring and Carlos says the animals are very small."

"Small!" Señora Arruza snorted. "Remember, these are fighting bulls! The animal that killed Joselito the Invincible was no more than a calf." She bit her lip as though in anger for having voiced these thoughts. "I just hope he doesn't try to show off and do those *cositas* I read about—those little things."

Those "little things" that Arruza was famous for were acts like kneeling down with his back to the enraged bull or taking the horn between his teeth.

"Please ask him not to do *cositas*," his mother said unhappily, as we drove through the pillars of the entrance to the ranch. "No little things."

We saw herds of fighting bulls in the enclosed fields, and they raised their arrogant heads and snorted at the car, as if to say, "How dare you trespass!"

For scores of years this ranch had raised nothing but the toro de lidia, a strange, fierce breed of wild creature.

We drove past the white ranch house that hadn't been changed in two hundred years and down to the small bullring. We were late, and as we hurried up to the stands we heard a shout of "Olé" from the crowd.

Since it was a private festival fight, the audience was composed mainly of bull-wise people. There were professional bullfighters, bull breeders, promoters, and several duques and marqueses who dedicated themselves to amateur fighting. People squeezed over to make room for us on the stone seats when they saw it was Arruza's mother, and someone passed us a bottle of sherry and some crayfish.

Down in the ring the Peruvian, Montani, was putting up a good performance with a two-year-old bull. It would charge the muleta time after

96

time, and Montani gracefully managed to make the needle-sharp horns graze inches away from his legs.

The man next to Mari turned while applauding and said to us, "Too bad you came late—you missed a good performance by Alfredo Pickman. But this Peruvian is even better. He's certain to win the golden ear, unless Arruza decides to cut loose."

Señora Arruza looked very unhappy.

"I hope Arruza decides *not* to cut loose!" she said.

Montani's animal was wearing down, and he lined it up for the kill. This was just a festival, and the animals weren't to be injured, so he threw away the sword. Then, pretending he had the weapon in his hand, he lured the bull into a charge and flung himself over the right horn. He did it well and managed to slap the animal exactly between the withers—where the sword would have gone—as the bull hurtled by him. The audience cheered and clapped and stamped their feet, for the man had risked his life to execute the moment of truth perfectly.

A gate was opened and the uninjured animal trotted out to the corrals. Montani ran around the ring sailing back the hats and cigars and purses that the jubilant people threw into the arena.

We saw Arruza come into the ring and stand behind the fence, hugging his cape. He spotted us in the audience and waved and smiled. He was dressed in the broad-brimmed hat, bolero jacket, tight pants, and boots that matadors wear for festival fights.

Suddenly a bugle blew. Montani ducked out of the arena through a burladero opening in the fence, and the gate to the tunnel swung open. Out into the empty ring a greenish black shape exploded. It was a three-year-old heifer with long thin horns jutting from its head like rapiers.

Heifers are often more dangerous than bulls to fight. This is not because of the old myth that, unlike bulls, they don't close their eyes when they charge, since neither do. It's because of their nervous temperament and the fact that their conformation allows them to turn and swerve more quickly. Also, and most important, nearly all of them have been caped many times.

"Ai, ai, ai," Señora Arruza was moaning, twisting her handkerchief. Then as she saw her son getting his big magenta cape ready in his hands and preparing to fight, she couldn't keep from crying out, "No hagas cositas— no little things, Carlitos!"

Arruza went out into the ring chanting, "Ah-ha-ha-ha, vaca," to attract the animal's attention. On the first pass he knelt down gracefully.

As the heifer charged he swung the cape over his head, and the horns missed his head by five inches.

"Olé!" burst from the crowd, as though from a single throat.

I glanced over at Señora Arruza. She had her hands over her eyes. They remained there for the rest of the fight—and with good reason. Arruza did everything in his repertoire, including leaning his elbow on the animal's forehead at one crucial point; a shake of its head would have spiked a horn through his chest, if the man hadn't had the heifer so completely under control.

After Arruza had simulated the kill magnificently, and the heifer was removed from the ring, I persuaded Señora Arruza to remove her hands. She sat back limply.

"You still haven't seen your son fight," I chided. Then I looked at my watch. "I'll have to leave pretty soon, because I have to . . ."

I heard a voice saying my name from down in the arena. I looked down and saw Arruza in the center of the ring and heard him anouncing: ". . . and so the next contestant for the golden ear will be *El Vicecónsul de los Estados Unidos de América!*"

He pointed up to me, grinning. Everyone in the audience turned to look at me, and they applauded encouragingly.

I shook my head angrily. "No," I shouted, "no, I'm not going to fight!"

"Yes, yes!" cried the crowd.

"I have to catch a train," I said. "I can't!"

The tunnel door swung open and another heifer skidded out into the ring fast, shaking its head and looking for something to kill.

Suddenly it hooked into a burladero, the shield in front of an opening in the fence, and with a jerk of its head, it sent a heavy slat flying into the air. It did it so viciously that it broke off part of its right horn.

The crowd cheered the animal's strength and spirit and kept looking at me.

"Vámonos!" they shouted. "It's a brave animal—a good animal!"

"Come on, chico!" Arruza yelled, "Show them!"

"He has a bad leg," Mari protested to the people around me. "He can't fight!"

When the people saw that I wasn't going to accept the challenge, a sort of embarrassed silence came over the crowd. Spaniards put personal bravery above any other quality in a man. I heard murmurs of, "Well, let's not force him," and dry laughs following the words, "It *is* a rough animal for an amateur—and a Yanqui amateur at that."

One of the men, who was a known Germanophile, having been an officer in Spain's Blue Division which fought with the Nazis, announced, "You see, it was just propaganda that this American could fight bulls!" Several people booed his rudeness, and he shut up.

98

The author with the heifer of the story.

Montani went out in the ring with the heifer, and though he did some excellent passes with the cape, no one applauded. The people just watched sullenly. My failure to fight had put a damper on the whole festival.

Suddenly I knew that I had to do it. Hell, I said, if the consul general were here he'd insist that I fight! I rationalized thusly: This one action of mine, which a thousand Spaniards were witnessing, was ruining an inestimable amount of good will that the State Department so desperately wanted.

I stood up and pushed down through the rows. Word of honor or no word of honor, I was going to fight. The crowd cheered when they saw what I was going to do, and I'm sure the Nazi rubbed his hands with gleeful anticipation.

As I dropped down into the passageway the comforting thought struck me: I'd promised the consul general I wouldn't fight a bull—but nobody said anything about heifers.

"It's all yours, matador!" Montani called as he left the animal and vaulted the fence.

A sword boy handed me a muleta and sword, and without even taking off my hat or tie, I slid through the burladero opening into the ring.

"Ah-ha-ha-haaaa, vaca!" I called harshly, partly to bolster my courage.

The animal focused its attention on me, shook its one sharp horn, and prepared to charge. Down on its level it looked bigger and more vicious. But now that I'd picked up the gauntlet, I had to do something sensational to justify all the fuss. I'd try the "blind" pass that the immortal Manolete did.

I planted my feet, put them down as though unable to be moved even if the animal headed straight for my body. Then I turned my head away from where the heifer was standing and looked up at the crowd.

"Ahaaaaaa, vaquilla!" I shouted, still looking in the opposite direction from the heifer.

"No, no!" yelled someone in the crowd.

"Vaca!" I yelled once more, shaking the muleta and praying to God the animal would go for it and not at my legs.

I heard the heifer snort. I heard it start for me, heard its hoofs crunching into the sand, and my heart was in my mouth. I wanted to turn to see whether it was heading for me or the cloth, but I forced myself to keep looking the other way. Then I heard *swoosh* as the animal expelled air, and I felt the curly short hair of its shoulders brush against my trousers.

"Olé!" screamed the crowd. And again "Olé!" as I repeated the pass.

From then on I could do no wrong. The performance wasn't half so graceful or polished as Arruza's, of course, but it was every bit as suicidal.

100

In fact, it was more difficult because the animal's broken horn make it hook drastically to the right.

After a dozen passes, the closest and smoothest I'd ever done in my life, I lined the animal up for the mock kill. This was the most dangerous and important moment of all, and I wanted to do it right to round off the faena. Making the heifer focus its attention on the muleta in my left hand, and pretending to hold a sword in my right, I headed straight at the animal as it charged toward me.

But I tried to do it too well. I went in too straight. The heifer swerved to the right and the horn, instead of grazing by my knee, glanced off it. It was my weak knee, and the blow knocked it out of joint. I fell on top of the animal's head, and then I was tossed high up into the air as the crowd screamed. After I smashed to the ground, I saw the heifer wheel and drive at me, but I blacked out before it reached me.

When I came to I was stretched out on the grass outside the ring. Señora Arruza and Mari were bending over me placing wet handkerchiefs on my head. I blinked my eyes and propped myself on my elbows. I was covered with blood. I discovered later it came from the broken horn when the animal was trying to gore me on the ground.

My pants legs were torn and every pocket of my jacket ripped off. After a few minutes I attempted to get up. My knee was completely knocked out, and I couldn't stand. I looked at my watch, which somehow wasn't smashed. It was quarter of four.

They carried me up to the ranch house and cleaned me up a bit and gave me a glass of brandy. I rested until I felt a little better. When I finally checked my watch again, it still said quarter of four!

"What time is it?" I gasped. "I have to make that train at six-thirty!"

"Almost six," said Mari. "But there's a chance."

They carried me to Arruza's big station wagon and stretched me out in the back. Then with Carlos at the wheel, driving the way one would expect a bullfighter to drive, we streaked through the Andalusian country-side, plowing through herds of turkeys, careening around oxcarts, and honking our way through whitewashed villages.

We roared into Sevilla at six-fifteen.

"My suitcase," I cried, "at the hotel!"

"Never mind," said Mari. "I'm coming through Barcelona next week and I'll bring it to you!"

We sped straight for the station, already hearing the departing whistle and the clang of the bell. Mari ran to buy a ticket while Carlos and a porter carried me into a made-up berth just as the toy engine started to chuff and steam. They scrambled off the train, and I waved to them on the platform

101

weakly. I was close to fainting, and every bone and muscle in my body was bruised and aching. But I'd made the train.

And then as I lay back, and we pulled out, I thought of the midget. I hadn't turned him off—I hadn't even done what I'd come to Sevilla for in the first place!

The train arrived in Madrid at six the next morning. With porters carrying me to a taxi, I made it to the airport. Another set of porters carried me onto the plane, and at nine o'clock I was in Barcelona. I went straight to the consulate, and two of the clerks managed to hustle me into my office without any of the consuls seeing me.

There was a gabardine topcoat of mine on the coat tree. I hurriedly put it on to cover my bloodstained, shredded suit and sat shakily on the edge of my desk.

At four minutes to ten, the consul general opened my door.

"Just made it back," I managed to say cheerily. I shuffled through some letters and strove for the perfect picture of the eager young vice-consul unable to wait to take off his hat and coat before seeing what the day's tasks would be.

"Everything go all right?" said the consul general with an enigmatic smile. "Midgets and statues and all?"

"Fine," I said. I put my hand to my stomach. "I don't feel very well, though."

"You do look a little pale," he said, studying me. "Probably rancid olive oil. They all cook with it in Sevilla."

I waited for a few minutes after he'd gone, and then I had myself carried to a taxi and taken to the hospital. From there I phoned in word to the consulate that I was down with stomach trouble. It was true—my stomach was as black and blue as any other part of my anatomy.

After four days of massage and hydrotherapy, the doctors fixed me so that I could walk around with a slight limp. I went back into the consulate Friday morning thanking my lucky stars that my ruse had worked long enough to get me back on my feet.

Now my only problems were how to pay for a couple of hundred statues and how to stop Antonio from making more.

The consul general came in at his usual time and sent for me immediately. His hands were behind his head and he was staring out the window when I came into his office.

"Good morning," he said, and something about his tone made me uneasy. "Stomach all right?"

"Fine," I said.

Then I spotted the two objects on his desk. One was my figurine of Arruza. The other was a gold bull's ear mounted on a plaque. Underneath the ear was a little silver plate which said that it had been won by Carlos Arruza, giving the date and place. And under that plate was another which read: "Redonated by C. Arruza to *el vicecónsul Americano* for his brave performance of the same date."

My heart disappeared in the pit of my stomach.

"Your friend Mari Harcourt stopped here on her way to Mallorca yesterday. She left your suitcase, a note, and the statue. We—we had an interesting chat."

The way he said "interesting" left nothing to be said. He handed me the note.

It was crudely written in pencil, but the letterhead was very fancy. It proclaimed:

ANTONIO MORALES
Caster of Statues, Religious and Secular
By Appt. to his Excellency the American vicecónsul.

I skimmed through the note and learned that Antonio had bumped into Arruza's manager while looking for me, that the manager had ordered fifty of the statues and had introduced him to the head of the largest store in Sevilla, who wanted two hundred.

It was consoling to know that I would at least have a little money coming in now that I was out of a job. But it was a poor exchange for the coveted position of vice-consul in the Foreign Service of the United States of America.

I put the note in my pocket. "Mr. Nash, I must explain how it happened. You see, the crowd at the fight——"

"What fight?" growled the consul general, swiveling his chair around.

"Why—the bullfight," I said. "The gold ear——"

"What gold ear?" he said.

I made vague motions at the gold ear glittering on the plaque on his desk. "That gold ear, sir."

"I don't see any ear."

"Right there, sir," I said weakly.

He sighed with exaggerated patience. "As I remarked a few days ago, Mr. Conrad, there are some things which an officer in the Foreign Service cannot permit himself to see."

"Thank you, sir," I said.

"Young man," he said gruffly, "stop wasting time and get back to work."

I picked up my statue, my suitcase, and my invisible ear, and walked out of his office with almost no limp at all.

Malaga

8. Malaga

I USED TO HAVE A HOUSE NEAR THE SPOT WHERE THE PHOTO ON PAGE 109 WAS
taken; and sometimes, when there'd be a particularly bad novillada or a
comic charlotada that I wouldn't want to see close up, I'd walk up the hill
with my beautiful black-haired girl in the late afternoon. We'd look down
on the ring from way above on the cliffs and get quite a perspective of the
spectacle of la fiesta brava, with no distractions such as how close the man
was working or how small the bulls were or what vulgarity the charlot was
pulling off. And the lights would come on for the last bull, and out at sea
the fishermen would light those strong lamps they used to attract fish, and
the lighthouse at the end of the spit beyond the arena would come on and
stab out through the warm Mediterranean evening. It was a good time to
be alive and young and in Spain.

La Malagueta, as it's called, is a good ring and an important one, though
not as important as Sevilla or Valencia. It holds about fifteen thousand people. When I think of the Málaga plaza I think of when Litri fought there
for the first time in 1949 as a nineteen-year-old novillero. His brother, also
nicknamed Litri, was killed in this ring, and when it came time for the
kill we watched this boy lure the novillo across the ring with short choppy
passes to the exact spot where his brother had been gored. Then he squared
the bull up, "mounted" the sword, and flung himself between the horns to
sink it in up to the crossbar.

And then there was the time in 1952 when the bull managed to leap up
into the stands, and all the people who'd been yelling for the matador to

stand still and take the bull closer a few moments before now scattered in panic. Luckily the Domínguín brothers were in the audience, and they grabbed their overcoats and caped the bull down the aisles and back into the ring.

And the grim day in 1945 when Manolete was fighting and the bull slammed his picador up against the fence and snapped his back and the woman next to us had a heart attack upon seeing it and died before the picador did.

But when I think of the bullring in Málaga I think first of all of *that* fight of Arruza's, unquestionably the greatest corrida I've ever witnessed. It was that rare, almost unknown thing: the ideal bullfight.

In an essay on la fiesta brava in the *Journal of Aesthetics*, Patricia Hetter has written so very well:

> The ideal bullfight, as it has been described, exists only in the imagination. It is an ideal which the aficionado carries in his head and he will be fortunate if he sees the ideal approached more than a few times in his lifetime.
>
> Thus he attends every. Sunday afternoon in the season, drawn by the hope—not even an expectation—of seeing the theoretical corrida realized. Moreover, when the corrida falls very far short of theory, it is a brutal and degrading spectacle. Only a hair divides tragedy from travesty. Thus this particular aesthetic experience cannot be predicted. A concert-goer carefully calculates the quality of his pleasure beforehand. He has the program, the reputation of the conductor, and of the orchestra, perhaps past experience with both, to guide him. The aficionado may know the matador, but there are too many variables for him to know the serene expectancy of the concert-goer. No one can gauge the stature of a bull in advance of his actual trial, and the tragedy, once begun, must go on to the end, no matter how recalcitrant the bull or reluctant the matador. On such an occasion, beauty evaporates like a curtain of mist, exposing the pain and cruelty for which beauty is the only apologist.

Let me repeat the story of Arruza's fight from my account in his autobiography, *My Life as a Matador:*

> Since attending my first corrida when I was thirteen, I have seen hundreds and hundreds of bullfights, some of them excellent, many fair, most of them bad. But of all of them I have seen the ideal realized only these times:

108

Málaga.

Juan Belmonte with his one bull at Castillo de las Guardas, Spain, in September, 1945, when at the age of fifty-five he demonstrated how will can triumph over physical limitations and even age.

Manolete in Barcelona in the fall of the same year. After having been piqued by a spectator's bellowing "Better watch out—Arruza's coming!" Manolete glanced up and rumbled: "*Que venga*—let him come!" And then he went out with both his bulls to show us what a truly sublime, regal, cool, perfect machine he was.

Luis Procuna in Peru in 1946, when he was almost booed out of the ring for his cowardly and insulting performance on his first bull, a good one, and then came back with the last bull of the afternoon, a treacherous buffalo, to show Armillita, Manolete, and the rest of the onlookers the most startling and emotional faena Lima had ever seen.

Cañitas in Málaga, Spain, on August 26, 1945, when in the competition for the award for the best performance of the annual fair, he arose to artistic heights he didn't know were in him.

But best of all, without a doubt, was Arruza, in Málaga, on August 27, 1945. The man was twenty-five and the bull was five, just as the great Guerrita said it should be.

It's a good story and a true one, one that I've used as a basis for fictional tales. I might do well to tell in detail what can happen when all the elements that go into making la fiesta brava come off right. Maybe it will show how and why Arruza became such a hero to the Spaniards. Maybe it will help to convey what Hemingway calls "that emotional and spiritual intensity and pure, classic beauty that can be produced by a man and a bull and a piece of scarlet serge draped over a stick."

I had a fine big house in Málaga and I was known as a friend of Arruza's, so that's why the Town Council came to me. "*Mire*, Señor Vice-Consul," they said. "We are going to present a gorgeous diamond medallion to the torero who gives the best performance at the bullfights during our annual fair. It is an exquisite thing, made especially in Madrid, at a cost of 9000 pesetas, and we should enjoy the honor of presenting it to your friend Arruza in your house."

"The honor will be mine," I said. "And I shall plan a party for that date. But how can you be sure Arruza will put up the best show?"

"He cannot fail," they said. "First: he is fighting both Friday and Sunday; if he is out of form or the bulls are bad on Friday, he will have another chance on Sunday. And secondly, Manolete, Arruza's only real competition, has been wounded and will not be able to fight."

"And thirdly," spoke up the little treasurer uneasily, "he has to be the best, for we already have his name engraved on the medallion!"

On Friday Carlos arrived for the first fight and Málaga was agog, because he had become the most sensational thing in bullfighting. When I went to see him the afternoon of the fight his face was pale and drawn and I could see that the eighty fights he had already fought under this regime had aged him.

"*Chiquillo*," he said after we'd talked awhile and he wiggled into the gold-brocaded pants, "what's this about a medallion?"

I explained.

"*¡Caracoles!*" exclaimed Carlos. "They've put my name on it already! But anything can happen in a bullfight! How can they know if I feel like fighting? Or what about the wind? Or what about the bulls, eh? That slight detail must be considered—the bulls."

At four o'clock they paraded into the brilliant sun and the band blared forth with the *pasodoble*, "Carlos Arruza." Carlos grinned nervously and threw his dress cape up to me.

His first bull was a bad one, but he did pretty well, and the presidente let him take a lap around the ring to receive the crowd's applause. The second bull was the matador Estudiante's and he did a very good job, being conceded two ears from the dead animal as an evaluation of his bravery and skill. Morenito de Talavera felt the pressure of the two good fights that had gone before him, and surpassed by far his natural ability, cutting one ear and taking a lap around the ring.

Arruza, seemingly unconcerned by this competition as he waited for his second bull to come out, looked around, hugging his big red and yellow cape to him and smiling his little-boy smile at friends.

His bull skidded out of the toril and brought some boos from the crowd because it was so small. But the boos switched to *olé*'s when Arruza passed the bull closely three times, the lethal horns inches away from his knees. Few people objected when, after he had placed three beautifully executed pairs of banderillas, dedicated the bull to the glamorous gypsy singer Lola Flores, and dispatched the bull with one sword thrust, the presidente granted him both ears and the tail. Women threw down roses to him and men threw cigars, hats, even overcoats. A few people booed, though, saying he didn't deserve the tail, since the bull was so small.

However, the medal seemed cinched, especially after Estudiante and Morenito de Talavera were bad on the last two bulls, and I left the plaza jubilantly. The next day the program was Estudiante and Morenito again plus a little Mexican Indian named Cañitas. Nothing to fear, we thought, for the bulls were giants; we had seen what Estudiante and Morenito had to offer, and who ever heard of Cañitas? An ugly little Indian who had been around Mexico for years, he was a competent, brave craftsman, but hardly in the same league with Arruza.

None of the three fighters was anything but discreet on his first bull. But then the trumpet sounded for Cañitas' second. Out it came—a black and white monster weighing 750 kilos! *

Cañitas went pale when he saw the creature rip a section of the wooden barrier apart, but he set his Indian jaw and you could see him telling himself, "If I'm going to die I'll go out in a blaze of glory!" The bull ran around the empty ring twice looking for something to kill, and then Cañitas stepped out and dropped to his knees, letting it go by with a *whoosh*, as the great horns passed his head. A gasp of surprise went up from the crowd, who expected him to play the bull as safely as possible. Then when he passed the bull even closer, they set up a continuous roar. After numerous fancy passes with the cape, he placed three sets of banderillas with the arrogance of a gypsy, he accomplished a faena with the muleta that bullfighters dream about, and then drew back and dropped the bull with a sword thrust to the hilt. The crowd went wild and insisted upon his getting both ears, tail, and a hoof, the most you can possibly get. I left the plaza for the day, feeling a little sick.

The next day was Sunday, and the Town Council came to see me with long faces. "Now what do we do?" they asked reproachfully, as

* Almost 1700 pounds.

112

though it were my fault. "Order another medallion," was all I could suggest.

Arruza arrived at six in the morning, after having fought in Puerto de Santa María the afternoon before and driving all night to Málaga. I went to the hotel to awake him at three. The idol of Spain was a mess; he looked green, and staggered as he got up.

"I'm exhausted." The words tumbled out. "I've a fever of 102; I can't go on like this every day. I never want to fight again. I'm going to go to bed for ten years when the season is over. How was the fight yesterday?" Wearily he put on his frilled shirt. "I haven't seen the papers yet."

"Cañitas turned in the best fight of the season," I said.

Carlos stopped tying his tie. "Are you joking?"

It was no secret that he and Cañitas had thoroughly disliked each other for years.

"No," I said. "He got inspired—fought as he's never fought before—cut ears, tail—and a hoof!" I cleared my throat. "But—uh—you'll come up to the house for the ceremony anyway, won't you?"

Arruza regarded me quietly and said, "I'll be there, *chiquillo*."

I think for the first time I felt the tremendous will and iron determination of this man emanate from him. Under his pleasant, easy exterior he had a fierce, gnawing inability to allow himself to be second best to anybody in the world.

I made the error of taking two women to the last fight. Carlos was first on the program, and when he got to his knees and let the bull pass by him four times so close that it removed part of his embroidered jacket, the girl on my right passed out; the other girl was about to faint also, but she was too busy reviving her friend. Carlos did every pass in the book, plus two of his own invention, and the girls couldn't stand any more. They left just about the time he dropped the bull with one thrust. The crowd went wild, and the presidente signaled with his handkerchief for the banderillero to cut one ear, then the other. Next he signaled for the tail, and finally the hoof, and Arruza circled the ring, triumphantly, holding his prizes aloft.

It was a wonderful fight, a great fight, and we were limp from the emotion of it. But we all knew in our hearts that Cañitas had been just a bit more reckless, more daring, more suicidal the day before.

After Arruza came Parrita and Andaluz, both good bullfighters, but people were still groggy from the first fight and didn't pay any attention to them. When Arruza came out and stood there swaying, waiting for his second bull, people applauded wildly, but we really didn't ex-

113

Bull in the stands at Málaga

caped by the Dominguín brothers.

pect him to do anything more today. It is rare when a bullfighter is able to put up good performances on both bulls, much less great ones.

The trumpet blew, the torilero jerked the rope that clanged open the heavy Gate of Fear, and out blasted the bull. It was a monstrous creature from Villamarta. Arruza studied it as it charged viciously against a burladero and sent the top slats splintering into the air. Carlos was pale and looked as though he might throw up, but when one of his banderilleros started to go out to give it some testing passes, Arruza waved him back with a cut of his hand.

"Tápate!" he ordered. "Hide yourself!"

Carlos stepped out shakily into the ring and stood there swaying. He put his hand to his feverish head and pressed his hot temples. It looked as though he might faint. But then when the bull spotted him and lowered his head and started across the ring toward him, he collected himself. Taking the cape in one hand, he dropped to his knees.

"Toro," he called, swirling the cape out flat on the sand in front of him. And then I remember he called in a casual, invitational, mocking tone, "Eh, toro, why don't you try charging around this way?"

As the bull thundered down on him Arruza watched it come, his face resigned, as though saying: "Maybe you'll crash into my chest but I'm down here on my knees now and it's restful and I really don't feel well enough to get up and jump out of the way."

When the bull was four feet away, Arruza suddenly swung the cape over his head, flashing it from the left side over to the right. The bull veered off its course after the flare of cloth, and the animal's right horn grazed by Arruza's right eye.

A roar came from the crowd and then more roars as Arruza stayed there on his knees and did five liquid, fantastic faroles, so close that each time cape and man and bull made a beautiful blurry tangle of gold and black and magenta.

By the time the banderillas act came around the plaza was already a sea of white handkerchiefs demanding ears for the matador even if he did nothing else for the rest of the fight. Then Carlos placed the three greatest pairs of barbed sticks I've ever seen, running at an angle at the bull as it charged, and sticking them in the withers with his arms high, his chest only inches from the horns, and finally spinning to one side to let the bull hurtle by. He begged permission from the presidente to risk his life in still another pair. It was granted, and Carlos picked an impossible way to place them: with his back against the fence, he incited the bull, "Uh-huh, toro! Uh-huh-huh!" and stood there calmly watching it bear down on him. When the animal was

116

two feet away, Carlos raised his arms, dropped the banderillas in place, ducked to the side, the left horn grazing his waist as the bull crashed into the fence.

The trumpet blew for the death; with the scarlet rag and the curved sword in his hand, Carlos dedicated the bull, facing the crowd with exhausted, unseeing eyes. Then he went out for the last round.

His first pass with the muleta was the regal, dangerous Pass of Death. Carlos called the bull from twenty feet away, and as it *whooshed* by he remained absolutely motionless and straight, letting the bull choose whether he was going to crash into the cloth or into his legs. Still motionless, and without even looking at the animal, he let the bull wheel and charge again. And then again and again and still again, without moving an inch. Nine times he willed that bull into taking the cloth instead of his body, and nine times he should have been killed. By this time there were no *olé*'s from the audience, only wild gobblings and hoarse croaks and cries of "Oh God, oh God!"

Then he decided to show the crowd his invention—the arrucina. When he flipped the muleta around behind his back and offered the bull only the small corner of the cloth that protruded, and the audience realized what he was going to try to do, they began to chant, "No, no, no!"

But the bull was already charging. Carlos went up on his toes, his stomach sucked in, and as the horn knifed by, it caught on the inside of his jacket and ripped it open. But he wasn't hit. He immediately crowded the bull, the muleta still behind him, and cited the animal for another arrucina again. This time the bull got only halfway through the charge before lunging to the left.

The crowd screamed as Arruza went up into the air, not high but clutching onto the horns of the animal, clinging to its tossing head, and then spinning on the right horn. Somehow when his body slapped the ground, he was stretched out under the bull, the length of his body between the animal's front legs, and his head between the lowered horns. People hid their eyes, for there was no time for his helpers to get there and lure the bull off him.

Before the points could find the inert form, Carlos reached up and locked his arms around the bull's neck in a frantic grip. The bewildered bull spun around and around. Finally it gave its neck a great snap, and flung the man from him like a rag doll to the ground ten feet away. But before it could charge, Arruza's men were between them and attracted the bull's attention. Arruza lurched drunkenly to his feet and stood there swaying, bruised and dazed, his uniform jacket in rib-

117

bons, but miraculously not wounded. He picked up his sword and the rag.

"Fuera!" he yelled at his banderilleros. "Get out of the ring."

This is a customary theatrical gesture from matadors who have been tossed, but it is never taken seriously, and the men stayed in the ring, ready for any emergency. Arruza repeated it. "Fuera!"

The amazed men retreated several feet behind him.

Arruza whirled on them and snarled, "Fuera, I said! Leave me alone with him!"

When they had all left the ring, the matador turned to the bull, who was pawing the ground and studying him ten feet away. Carlos dropped to his knees. He stared into the bull's hot eyes. Then he began to inch forward toward the animal. Closer and closer he came. The bull shifted his feet and the crowd gasped, sure that it would charge. But it didn't; it was as though it were hypnotized and cowed by the enormous brute courage of this man-thing on its knees. Arruza kept coming, and coming, and coming, staring fixedly at the bull until he arrived in its very face.

Then, with the muzzle of the bull almost touching him, he leaned forward and rested his elbow on the bull's forehead! Then he rested his own forehead on the bull's right horn! Then he took the horn tip in his teeth! A sudden lunge, and the horn would have been spiked out through the back of the man's head.

He turned around and stared up at the crowd with the bull's nose against his back, a horn jutting out on either side of his head. We were afraid to scream for fear the noise would make the bull charge, but when he faced the bull again and, still on his knees, made it pass by four times, spinning in against the shoulder each time, a great roar burst from our throats. And then suddenly Carlos rose to his feet. He hurled himself between the horns, sank the sword in the shoulders to the hilt, and the bull only had time to cough once before it reeled and crashed over backward to the sand, dead.

Delirium took over the plaza. The presidente waved his handkerchief for one ear, again for two ears, again for the tail, again for a hoof—and still again for another hoof, for the first time in bullfighting's long history. But still the crowd kept chanting, "Más, y más, y más!"—more, more, more! Finally, as it kept up and kept up, the presidente just shrugged and said, "Hell, take the whole bull then."

So Arruza got the medal and we had the party, and what a party it was; but our honored guest left at midnight.

He had to hurry to Logroño for a fight the following day.

118

Arruza.

Huelva

9. Huelva

Tres cositas tiene Huelva
que le envidia el mundo entero:
la Rábida y Punta Umbría
y el Litri, de novillero,
la flor de la torería.

Huelva has three little things
that are envied by all the world;
La Rábida and Point Umbría
and Litri, as a novillero,
the flower of bullfighting.

—A *fandanguillo de Huelva*

LA RÁBIDA IS THE POINT OF LAND FROM WHICH COLUMBUS SET SAIL FOR THE New World.

Punta Umbría is an attractive spit of sand where wealthy Sevillans spend their summers, and where I remember there was a marvelous big dog trained to charge exactly like a bull and we would fight with him for hours on the white sands with a muleta. And when we would quit exhausted he would bark for more. I remember for some reason he loved the finishing-off pass, the pase de pecho, best of all, and he liked to go up into the air after the cloth.

And Litri? Well, Kenneth Tynan, in *Bull Fever,* writes wonderfully about Litri:

He lives in Huelva, a small mining port seventy miles from Seville, set about with ranches whose bulls, in ponderous silhouette, may be glimpsed from the road. The journey there springs for a few yards into fantasy, at the crossing of the Rio Tinto, which runs crimson and gold over rich surface deposits of copper. Huelva is fetid and tourist-scorned, though transient sailors prize it for its compact red-light district, where there is a bar whose proprietor, a defaulting poet, knows most of Ben Jonson by heart.

The town has four heroes, three of them dead. One is the nameless corpse, celebrated in Duff Cooper's *Operation Heartbreak,* which floated ashore at Huelva bearing forged information which embarrassingly misled the Germans about the Allied plans for invading southern Europe. Another is Columbus, who sailed westward from the estuary of the red river where his statue towers, staring quizzically at the sea. The third idol, a lean torero christened Manuel Baez and professionally nicknamed "Litri," was killed in 1926; and the fourth is my Litri, Manuel's half-brother, who outweighs, in local and national esteem, all the other attributes of Huelva put together. I have no doubt that when Columbus crumbles, the street-boys will still be chalking "VIVA EL LITRI" on the walls of the town-hall, and others after them will be adorning the inscription with forests of what the Spanish call admiration marks; for Litri is the marvellous boy who decided in 1952, the season of which I am writing, against perishing in his prime, and accordingly gave up fighting bulls. He announced his impending retirement two months after the Pamplona feria; he was then twenty-one and had put together in four sudorific years a fortune of twenty-five million pesetas, which is about $700,000. In Spain, where the return on capital is exceptionally high, that is very rich indeed. Week in, week out, few people on earth earn more than a popular matador; he can command up to $7500 for an afternoon's work; but Litri alone among the millionaire swordsmen can claim to have been a national hero at nineteen and a national enigma at twenty-two. When he retired, speculation about his future became something of a national pastime; one recalls similar curiosity about Garbo when her name vanished from the marquees. The cafés of Andalusia echoed with argument, as loud unshaven voices insisted that he would and would not

124

Litri.

Litri.

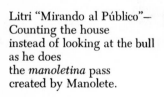

Litri "Mirando al Público"—
Counting the house
instead of looking at the bull
as he does
the *manoletina* pass
created by Manolete.

return to the ring, that he would surely marry an actress, that on the contrary he would become a monk. The rumours about him were and are luridly diverse, and the truth is strange enough.

I saw him first in 1950, and often in the two years that followed. He was without question a highly original performer, stormy and intense, though extremely limited in his repertoire: a true torero corto, or short bullfighter. With the cape he would be valiant one moment and grotesque the next; the excitement he communicated depended mostly on the muleta, and specifically on two idiosyncratic passes. For one of them he would skip thirty yards away from the horns and take the charge from that ridiculous distance. Holding the muleta behind him with both hands, as if drying his legs after a shower, he would stand stock-still until the bull was almost upon him and moving fast, when he would deflect the horns with a leisurely flourish of the left hand. This always bound a spell, and was as often accused of showiness as his second trick, which was quite simply to ignore the bull as it passed by his body; to stare away—not at the crowd (Manolete had done that) but up at the sky, as if inviting a thunderbolt. Litri knew how to perform most of the basic passes with the muleta, but it was his twin innovations that sold the tickets.

His father, Miguel Baez, was a stout fighter of the old school who appeared in the inaugural bullfight at the Huelva Plaza de Toros in 1902. Deficient in finesse, often and savagely punished by the bulls, he is remembered chiefly as a strong, clean killer. His first son Manuel followed him into the ring in 1923. This was the "brown-faced, bow-legged little boy with black hair" whom Hemingway describes in *Death in the Afternoon:* "A prodigy of valor and wonderful reflexes, but insensate in his bravery and very ignorant in his fighting." I never saw Manuel, but this is Miguel to the life: the old man somehow transmitted a crazy frailty to both his sons. In 1925 Manuel won the Golden Ear trophy at Madrid against stiff competition, and met a girl in Valencia whom he determined to marry. Publicly and privately he seemed to be thriving, when a galling complication intervened. He brought his sweetheart to Huelva, and his father, a recent widower, fell in love with her—immediately, violently and inconsolably. A bizarre triangle seemed imminent; but the solution arrived before the situation had time to develop. In February, 1926, a bull's horn found Manuel at Málaga and ripped through his right leg. The wound turned gangrenous as a result of faulty surgery, and amputation, the bullfighter's death-knell, had to be performed. It was as much from professional despair as from his injury that Manuel cried out and died.

127

After a decent period of mourning, the old man married his dead son's fiancée. Miguel, who was born in October, 1930, is the child of that haunted marriage and of his father's sixtieth year; fifteen months later his young mother was widowed. Shortly afterwards she gave birth to a daughter; thereby providing for Miguel an upbringing which could scarcely fail to produce abnormal results—he lived among women, with a mother twice bereaved, in a poor home where he was the only breadwinner. The qualities of over-mothered children, shyness, quick resentments, passionate cleanliness, guilt feelings, defiant independence, were early implanted in him; his childhood friends remember him as being always "absent" in his demeanour, moody and distrait. He left school at thirteen, disrelishing study, whereupon his mother began to indicate her hopes that he might, like her father, become a railway clerk; anything to preserve him from the bulls. He made no comment. When he was fifteen she was shocked to learn, from a friend who assumed she knew already, that Miguel was spending all his spare time practising. What kind of practising? With young cows, said the friend, on the ranches; practising bullfighting. Before long he was intervening in capeas, village scrambles with yearling heifers, and in June, 1947, three months before his seventeenth birthday, he killed his first bull at a country fight near Huelva. His mother tried to numb the sore part of her memory, and in the five ensuing years she never once saw him fight, never dared even to listen to the radio commentaries. In 1948 he fought a dozen times, with moderate success, as an obscure novillero. It is a safe bet that no one who saw him guessed that within a year he would ride in triumph across Spain and make bullfighting history.

In the ten months from February to November, 1949, Litri broke a record which had lasted thirty years. In 1919 Belmonte took part in 109 fights; Litri's tally for the 1949 season was 115.* Fighting three or four times a week, crossing and recrossing the country in dusty and fatiguing overnight journeys, he had the most successful year in all the chronicles of the corrida; his trophies totalled 225 ears, 68 tails and 31 hoofs. Huelva was systematically deafened by his admirers, who called him El Atómico and boasted explosively by letting off a fire-cracker for every ear he cut. He was usually partnered by a young madrileno named Julio Aparicio, the perfect foil for him, a "long" bullfighter (torero largo) with a spectacular all-round canniness far

* In defense of Belmonte's prestige, it should be remembered that his fights were corridas, whereas Litri's were novilladas.—K.T.

128

beyond his years; Aparicio was to Litri what Lagartijo had been to Frascuelo and Joselito to Belmonte. Their campaign as novilleros continued in 1950, astutely managed by José Flores Camará, a specialist in "phenomenons" who had handled Manolete's affairs and whose trade-mark was a pair of dark glasses bequeathed to him by the great Cordoban. Controversy crackled around the two boys, and Camará assiduously encouraged it, knowing quite well the truth of Unamuno's remark that Spain is divided into two groups, Anti-Exers who believe in Z, and Anti-Zedders who believe in X. The negative precedes the positive in that land of extremists, where a man cheers only that which diametrically opposes something he detests. Aparicio was applauded for not being Litri, and vice versa; theirs was the familiar rivalry of the demonstrative extravert and the stony introvert. Already it was apparent that Litri was more of an enigma than most bullfighters. At nineteen he was earning more than $20,000 a week, and it seemed to mean nothing to him; between fights he brooded at home, unsmilingly playing naïve card-games with his friends or, clad in outsize gabardine suits, staring with deep, accusing eyes at American comic books. Most prosperous toreros either invade society or woo film stars, forms of ostentation which Litri deplored. He was in the business of killing bulls for reasons other than those of social or sexual conquest; private reasons, at once incommunicable and immensely urgent.

He made his debut in the Las Ventas ring at Madrid on May 18th, 1950. His first bull came out of the toril at 5:45 P.M.; at five past six it was dead; but the intervening twenty minutes had passed into legend. After his first series of left-hand naturals, the crowd of 23,000 was on its feet in uproar, throwing hats and flowers into the arena in a display of enthusiasm unprecedented in the cathedral of tauromachy, as unheard-of as applauding after the first movement of a symphony. Litri did all the right, reputable things and all the extravagantly wrong ones; "he seemed," noted one reporter, "to be fighting in a hypnotic trance"; he brought off his two tricks to perfection, delighted both the experts and the tourists by the speed and valour of his kill, and was awarded both ears by unanimous petition. Madrid thinks the tail a coarse and repellent trophy, and hence never bestows it; but Litri's supporters in Huelva made up for the omission by giving him a miniature tail of spun gold when he returned home. At the end of the season he graduated to full matador status, which meant that he would henceforth be matched with the heavier four- and five-year-old animals. The critics shrugged and began to sketch out obituaries for the young suicide.

129

In 1951, to their confusion, he was earning more than ever, just as riskily, and was never dangerously gored. I saw him at the July fair in Valencia with bulls of Carlos Núñez, Antonia Urquijo, and Juan Pedro Domecq, three strains he especially favours, since they have provided for him more straight-charging "bulls on wheels" than any other breeders. To many toreros the bull is an instrument to be played on, and it was Belmonte who said that bullfighting was an art for which the Stradivarius and the stock cadenza already existed; but to Litri the bull was always the enemy, something terrible and infinitely to be hated. He was never much afraid. "When I feel the horn going in," he told me in a rare burst of consecutive speech, "I just switch off, like an electric light."

In October, 1952, three months after the Valencian Fair and a few days after his twenty-second birthday, he retired from the bulls, taking his farewell in a mano a mano with Pedrés, on whom he bestowed the alternativa. He made a few charity appearances in 1953, one of them at Madrid, where the warmth of the applause brought tears to his eyes; but he has not fought for money since. His first act in retirement was to buy a house, an old Andalusian mansion on the main residential street of Huelva. A firm of Madrid decorators was engaged to strip and refurbish it, which was done at a cost of $30,000; the place was transformed into a profusion of chandeliers, antique furniture and silver plate, with mounted bulls' heads and portraits of the young seigneur gazing down on marble floors. Here he ignored the press, which clamoured and clamours still to know why he gave up his métier. Why, having so recently proved that his powers had not diminished, did he abandon the ring after four short years? His mother, who manages the household and copes with her son's correspondence, piously believes that it was for her sake. An impassioned matriarch whose deep, crestfallen eyes Miguel has inherited, she has no doubts about his motives: "I have been father, mother, everything to him, and like a good child he has rewarded me. He leaves the bulls alone because he wants me to be at peace." Litri's sister, a lively hoyden, shares her mother's opinion.

There are other, less romantic views of the matter. Some say that Camará, who dominated Litri's professional life so completely that often he had no idea how much he was earning, advised him to retire at a peak rather than slide into decline. Others, pointing out that Litri was always shy of fighting Miuras, insist that he took fright when horn-shaving was outlawed, but the truth is that he announced his retirement months before Bienvenida's campaign began. I have also heard it said that he had a vocation for the priesthood, a theory scoffed at by his mother and sister. Yet he was undoubtedly among the most superstitious members of a superstitious profession. When fighting, he used to pack three images of the Virgin in his baggage, and the Virgin of the Sash, who guards Huelva, has a shrine in his bedroom, her vestment adorned with gold thread picked from one of his suits of lights. Even so, I agree with his family that he could never be a true contemplative. His mission, which is now accomplished, was to prove that one of his family could leave the ring famous and whole, not scarred like his father, or dead like Manuel.

Unless he returns to the game (and he probably will: matadors are like prima donnas),* a desert of ennui stretches ahead of him. He entertains seldom and hates it, smiling wanly and looking extremely uncomfortable. He sips whisky from time to time, without much enthusiasm, and is a moderate dancer. On occasion he has played inside-right for the local amateur football club. He once tried to persuade me that he read only history and biography, but the idea convulsed his sister: nothing, she said, but outdoor magazines and adventure stories. Like Manolete, he is a good shot. He rides well and has two horses; drives well and has two cars; sails well and has two boats. Above all, he has the torero's passion for cock-fighting. He owns twenty bantams, mostly English-bred, and the only time I have ever seen him carefree was at a cock-fight in Madrid, betting on his own birds. Frail, toothpick-thighed and markedly knock-kneed, he is always stirred by the smell of combat.

The ambassadorial opulence of his home does not impress him much. He bought it primarily for his mother and sister, and is usually out, sitting in silence at a corner bar, sipping a *manzanilla* and shrugging the corners of his mouth as his friends make jokes for him. Once he was summoned to Madrid to dine with the Caudillo. Loyalty demanded his presence, and he went: but by the first train he was back in Huelva, twiddling his thumbs and nursing his secret. His usual companion is Galápago, who was one of his peons. A peasant with the face of a flushed chimpanzee, Galápago had eyesight so poor that sooner or later a bull must have caught him. Aware of this, and aware, too, that he could not afford to retire, Litri brought him back to Huelva, where he was born, and gave him a pension for life. I found this out by chance, from a man in a café: no one I know has more pride in the ring and less out of it than Litri.

* He has.—B.C.

His mother's most ardent wish is that he should marry decently, "a good woman, not one of these clever modern wives," and then settle down to farming. If it is denied and he comes back to the ring, I have a feeling that it will be without much heart for the job. It was in his fourth season that Manuel was killed; Miguel, having seen four seasons through, may have decided that the family's luck has been tried far enough. I hope, for his sake, that he remains a recluse. His life has been governed by honour, pacts, and promises—to himself, to his mother, and to the Virgin. When he became a matador he promised the Virgin of Rocio, whose shrine is seventy kilometres from Huelva, that if he was preserved he would make a pilgrimage to her. In May, 1954, he made good the pledge, riding across open country for two days to the shrine, where he gave thanks for his life and luck. He also undertook to repeat the journey every year until he died. His contract with the bulls, for the moment, is over. His contract with the Virgin is for life.

Litri.

Valencia

10. Valencia

ALTHOUGH VALENCIA IS NOT ONE OF SPAIN'S MOST ATTRACTIVE CITIES, IT IS certainly one of the most ardent in taurine matters. The city's first recorded bullfight took place in August, 1373, and ever since then it has been one of the top bull centers of the world. Traditionally Valencia opens the bullfighting season at the end of March with the first corridas of the year. The present plaza was built in 1860 and holds 16,851 spectators . . . probably the most enthusiastic in the world.

Many toreros have had their first great successes develop in front of the ardent and knowing aficionados of Valencia: among them Joselito, Belmonte, Litri, and Manolete. Not as blasé and exacting as the Maestranza in Sevilla, Valencia still is almost as bull-wise, and the toreros like to perform there.

Carlos Arruza has had some of his greatest afternoons in Valencia—for example in the 1945 Feria he fought every day of the seven-day fair and cut nineteen ears, four tails, and two hooves off the fourteen bulls he killed. But as he writes in his autobiography, his most satisfying triumph came not in the ring but behind it, when he came to know Manolete.

Their first meeting in Portugal had been less than successful. Here's how he tells it in *My Life as a Matador:*

> With Manolete! Me—me with Manolete! I still couldn't quite understand how this had ever come about. But now it was all set, and in front of me I saw a big poster that roared "Manolete, Morenito de

135

Talavera, and Carlos Arruza"! The Portuguese bullfighting fans could talk of little else but Manolete, and they were delighted that a figure of such magnitude was fighting in their bullring.

My first desire was to meet him the moment he arrived in Lisbon. Dressing myself up to look as much like a real bullfighter as possible, I went to the hotel where he was staying.

"Is—is Manolete—could I meet him?" I asked the concierge.

"He can see no one," the man answered coldly.

A lot of people were milling around from the bullfighting world, but I didn't dare ask them about him. I went to the bar and had a drink (of soda water now) to see if he might not come down, and then I could snatch an opportunity to introduce myself. But he didn't show up. I left after a while but returned later in the afternoon, and still I couldn't get to see him. I knew him only from the photos and, like any aficionado, I knew what everyone knew, that he was ugly, that he was a phenomenon with a bull, that his was a new concept of bullfighting, and that he fought brilliantly with almost all the animals that he drew, no matter what their styles or conditions.

Throughout my career I have gone to the drawing of the bulls very few times, and almost never since I took the alternative. That day I went, just to see if Manolete might not go to the drawing and then I could get to meet him before the action started. But I was disappointed again, because they told me that he never went to see the bulls before they came out of the toril. At least the greatest bullfighter in the world and I had that much in common, and foolishly, I clung to that insignificant fact.

I wanted to go see him at the hotel after the drawing and introduce myself with some pretext or other, or simply to wish him luck, but I didn't dare. Instead, I went home to prepare myself for one of the most important happenings of my life.

That afternoon the plaza de toros was a terrifying monster, since it was jammed to the eaves with people who had paid large amounts to see the world's greatest torero fight two bulls; they would have filled the stands just to see him walk across the ring in the parade, so great was his attraction. As has always been my custom I was the first matador to arrive at the cuadrilla gate. Very nervous I was too. ("Nervous," I should tell you, is a highly technical taurine term meaning "scared to death.") A little while later Morenito de Talavera arrived, and I was introduced to him. A pretty big star in Spain, he seemed a modest person, and we chatted pleasantly for a while as we had a last smoke. Soon we heard a murmur, the murmur that one hears only on important occasions. Manolete was coming! The crowds gave way before him as though for a king.

I was struck immediately by his face. He wasn't ugly the way the photos made him appear. It was a good face, though scarred and sad. He was only twenty-seven, but he looked forty. Terribly serious, almost tragic-looking, he barely managed the hint of a smile in answer to the reverent greetings that the people gave him as he made his way through the crowd. I noticed that no one patted him on the back, the way they do with other toreros, any more than one would pat a bishop on the back as he made his way up the aisle to the altar. The moment I saw him I understood that this man had been born to be nothing more or less than a bullfighter. I saw that in just his regal mien and the way he carried himself and the way his uniform sat on his body. I believe he even smelled like a bullfighter.

I longed to be introduced to him, to shake his hand, to get to know him. But he moved away from where I was to the other side of the gate without so much as a glance at me. Then a friend said, "Like to meet him?"

"Would I!" I answered.

I eagerly followed him over to Manolete.

"Maestro," my friend said, "this is Arruza, the new Mexican matador."

Manolete turned his haughty face, and looked vacantly at me with those heavy-lidded eyes. All that the man muttered was *"Que tal—* how goes it?" so dryly, so stiffly, so aloofly that he sent a chill through me. Then he turned away.

I gave him some kind of stammering answer, somehow, and then I withdrew. Or rather I slunk away. Afterwards they took a photograph of us together, neither of us saying a word to the other. . . .

That is how I first knew the man who for me was the greatest bullfighter of this age. I didn't really know him then, of course, since I misinterpreted his manner, mistaking the reticence and seriousness with which he took bullfighting for dislike of me. I just didn't understand him; when dressed in uniform, and in or around a bullring, Manolete changed.

[Arruza then went on to discover a new style of fighting, fought an astounding fight in Madrid, and overnight found himself proclaimed a rival for Manolete. Their first meeting on Spanish soil was in the town of Cieza.]

I said to myself: "Now we'll see, Señor Knight of the Sad Countenance, if I can't make you notice me a little more this time."

137

The poor little town of Cieza was inundated by the people who poured in from all Spain for this event. Most of the people were ardent manoletistas and had come to see this Mexican upstart make a fool of himself. But I had many enthusiastic supporters too who would have given anything to see me "give the bath" to Manolete. I was almost as nervous as before the Madrid fight.

That afternoon Manolete was granted special permission to fight out of turn because he had to appear the next day at the other end of the country. So he just saw me on my first bull, where I did miserably. Of course he cut both ears off both his bulls, and justly so. My supporters were sunk, and those people who had never seen me before laughed at the crazy idea that this was the man who was supposed to be a threat to Manolete. I was booed on all sides as I went out for my last bull. But again this bull, while it looked terrible to everyone else, was the perfect type for my Lisbon style.

So when the bull was dragged out twenty minutes later, it went without its ears, tail, and, unbelievably, a hoof. The arrucistas were delirious, babbling with joy and vindication, and my enemies were silenced temporarily.

When I arrived jubilantly back at the hotel, Manolete was just leaving, dressed in ordinary clothes, with his ever-present dark glasses and followed by his banderilleros. We stalked by each other coldly, and as he got in the car his manager, Camará, grunted, "Well, how'd it go?"

Gago smiled sweetly. "Hubo patita," he said casually as though this were an everyday occurrence, "there was a hoof."

"A hoof!"

They all seemed to grow hard-faced. Manolete leaned forward as if to exclaim in disbelief, but then he sat back as though it were too much effort. He looked so bored and world-weary, so confident in his position of the Number One. They drove off, and as I watched the car go down the road I thought: I'm sorry you missed it today, Your Majesty, but we'll try to repeat for you. Your throne is not as secure as it once was. . . .

The next fight was Murcia, where I appeared with Manolete. The rivalry was again played up by the newspapers, and we were both out to give the other one "the bath." As it turned out it was a tie, with both of us cutting the same number of ears. The rival factions in the stands had to settle which one of their favorites had been better by fist fights after the performance. I still hadn't spoken to the Monster of Córdoba, nor he to me. If our glances crossed as we were waiting in the courtyard for the opening trumpet, it was more likely to be a

138

glare on my part. He looked as though he was too tired and bored even to work up a glare, so he generally just looked through me vacantly.

Even after the second fight at the Sevilla fair, when the bulls tossed both of us and we emerged with our uniforms in shreds, we still didn't speak. He was tossed in a frightening fashion and it was a shocking thing, because he looked so completely invulnerable and secure that I didn't quite believe any bull could do that to him. It seemed almost like sacrilege when the bull flung him ten feet in the air and then tried to get a horn into his skinny body as he lay on the sand. I was the first to get out there with my cape and lure the bull away from the fallen man, and, enemies or not, I remember how glad I felt inside when he lurched to his feet and I saw that he wasn't injured. I started to tell him I was pleased that he hadn't been hurt; at the same time, it seemed to me, he looked as though he might be about to say something, perhaps thanks to me for having made the *quite,* but at that moment the bull began to head toward us and there was no time. At the next fight's beginning we came together before the parade with the same aloofness and mutual dislike.

On the ninth of May in Valencia, Parrita, Manolete, and I had a historic fight. There were twelve ears, six tails, and three hoofs cut off those six bulls that afternoon by the three of us. We divided the trophies equally, and the next day the papers referred to the bullring as *un manicomio*—an insane asylum—because of the audience's reaction.

The next day I had a greater and more satisfying success. The impresario organized a party in the back part of the bullring, in the courtyard by the corrals, and the three matadors were invited as guests of honor. Deliberately, diabolically, they seated Manolete and me next to each other. I guess they just wanted to see the fireworks when the two enemies got together. At the beginning everything was serious, very cold, and completely silent. I nodded to him, however, and he nodded back. This, considering our past salutations, was practically the equivalent of an affectionate embrace.

Then something happened. I don't know even now how we started. It was something simple like "They call this food?"—but it broke the ice, and all of a sudden Manolete and I were talking.

"You missed a fine opportunity to let me get killed off there in Sevilla," he said laconically. "I've wanted to thank you for not doing it."

"What would I do for a rival then?" I joked back offhandedly. "I need the stimulus of the little competition you give me."

139

The beginning of the famous
"Paella" luncheon—
Manolete and Arruza
between their two managers.

Carlos Arruza.

Then I saw something I thought was impossible. His mouth widened and he gave a low rumbling noise. Manolete was laughing! Then we began, and we talked and laughed steadily all through the meal and stayed on afterward for another hour. We would have stayed all afternoon but we both had fights in other cities, and so after a warm handshake we said good-by until our next fight together.

That was how I began to know Manolete, the other Manolete, the charming, friendly, humorous one who existed only away from the plaza de toros. I had never met anyone whom I liked and admired so much as this man to whom bullfighting was a religion.

At first many people around us didn't like the idea of our being friends. They thought that our hate for one another was the motive for our going out there to work so close to the bull every day, and that once friends the rivalry would end. But that impression didn't last long, since our first ring duels after that friendly meeting were perhaps more intense than before.

Never have I seen a more noble companion than Manolo (as his intimates called him), nor anyone more fierce and jealous of his name and reputation. Yet many times after having cut ears and tail off his bull he would come over just before my bull came out and say in his deep, serious voice, "Come on now, Carlos, don't make me look like a complete villain—I'd like to see you with the ears of this bull in your hands."

"Anything to oblige, Manolo," I'd say to him, and if I managed to cut the ears, how pleased he would look.

We went along like this in perfect harmony, fighting together almost daily and appreciating each other more and more, but never letting anybody notice it inside the arena. Away from the ring we became like brothers, but inside the ring it was each man for himself. . . .

I liked the feeling of being in the arena with Manolo, because of the complete sense of mastery and security and even safety that he imparted to everyone. But one day in Alicante, while executing one of his perfect naturals, he worked in a centimeter too close to the horn. He was tossed very high and suffered a bad fracture of the clavicle when he hit the ground. I hurriedly finished off my last bull and went to see him in the infirmary. The doctors said he should be taken to Madrid immediately, so I sent the cuadrilla off in the station wagon and put Manolete in the back seat of my convertible. Then I set off with Pepe Bienvenida, the matador, to help spell me during the long drive. We had Manolete propped up with all kinds of cushions, but still the ride must have been agonizing. I glanced in the mirror from time to time and saw his sweaty pale face twisted in agony as we went over the rough roads, swerving to avoid herds of animals, but he never complained. Pepe passed him back a flask of brandy.

"If you're sure it's on you, I'll have one," Manolo said.

As I took a corner too fast and almost hit a tree, I heard Manolo suck in his breath in pain, but he merely gave a laugh and said between clenched teeth, "It's too bad this man can't work as close to the horns as he does to trees."

What a *man* he was!

Linares

11. Linares

ON AUGUST 28, 1947, A MULTIMILLIONAIRE AND A BULL KILLED EACH OTHER and plunged an entire nation into deep mourning. This took place in Linares, a small town about an hour and a half east of Córdoba in the province of Jaén, in a small plaza that holds exactly 8,268 people. Every year Linares fetes its patron saint, San Augustín, with a two-day fair, and this was the second day of feria fights. It was an important one since the great Manolete, aged thirty and past his prime, was going to compete against the brilliant twenty-one-year-old Dominguín. It was important to Manolete because Linares was near his home town of Córdoba, because of the pressure Dominguín and the press had been putting on him for the past months, and because of the Miura bulls—the famous Bulls of Death.

Actually, Manolete shouldn't have been there at all. He should have been home on his ranch raising bulls instead of fighting them. The year before he'd told me he was retiring. He came over to my studio in Peru, and after a few drinks he said, "I'm quitting as soon as this season is over." He said it vehemently, as though he expected someone to come back with "Oh yeah?"

I remember that he glanced over at his mistress and then walked over to the big picture window.

"Quitting." He stared out at the Peruvian sunset and nervously shook the ice in his empty glass as though it were dice.

"I'm going back to Spain and cut off the pigtail forever. I've made more money than five generations of my family put together, but I've never had

145

Manolete.

time to spend it. I'm young. Twenty-nine's not old. I've had my wounds, but I'm still in one piece, *gracias a Dios*."

A short scar notched the left side of his chin, and he put his fingers to it unconsciously. His face, ugly when analyzed feature by feature, was sad and drawn and old, yet at the same time it was compelling and majestic. If he were to walk into any café in any part of the world, people would immediately ask, "Who is this gaunt young-old man?"—for he had the look and aura of Number One. Hod-carrier, dancer, artist, banker, one might not know—only that he was the best in his field.

He ran long fingers over the black hair that had a wide path of gray down the center. "I've been able to spend about three months on my place in Córdoba in all the years I've owned it. I'm going back and enjoy it—never look at another bull except from up in the stands."

He went out to the pantry for another drink, and I turned to Antonia Bronchalo, for several years his "fiancée." She was pretty and seemed like a nice girl, but people said she was as hard as Toledo steel. She'd made a few Spanish movies under the name of Lupe Sino, but she was no star. Her fame would always rest in the fact that she was loved by important men— lots of them.

146

"What do you think?" I asked. "Will he quit?"

She smiled. "He's told me for several months now that he'll give it up the moment we get back to Spain and that we'll get married and raise bulls and half a dozen little Manoletes. He's starting to slip. He should get out quick, alive. But they'll never let him." She looked up at the portrait I had done of him. "That pretty gold uniform means excitement and money to too many people for them ever to let him take it off. They'll kill him first."

She was right. When Manolete arrived back in Spain in the spring of 1947, he received a tremendous reception. As the papers put it, no one since the conquistadores had so successfully carried the glories of Spain to the New World. Then, after he announced he was going to retire, they set about to kill him.

It's hard for Americans to understand why all this fuss about one bullfighter. But he wasn't just a bullfighter to the Spaniards. He was their only national and international hero. We have Eisenhower, Gable, Grable, DiMaggio, and hundreds of others, but they had just Manolete. And when he was killed, he died such a beautiful dramatic Spanish death that I swear, in spite of the great funeral, the week of national mourning, the odes, the dirges, the posthumous decorations by the government, that in his heart of hearts every Spaniard was glad that he had died.

He even looked Quixotic. Ugly in photos, cold and hard in the bull ring, he had tremendous magnetism, warmth, and gentle humor among his friends. Once in Peru I took a blasé American college girl to watch Manolete in the ceremony of preparing for a fight, though she protested she had no interest in a "joker who hurts little bulls."

"Excuse me, señorita, if I don't talk much," he said with his shy smile as they worried his thin frame into the skintight uniform, "but I am very scared."

After that he didn't say more than ten words to her. But she walked out of the room dazed. "That," she announced, "is the most attractive man in the world."

"To fight a bull when you are not scared is nothing," another bullfighter once said to me, "and to not fight a bull when you are scared is nothing. But to fight a bull when you are scared—that is something."

Manolete told me, "My knees start to quake when I first see my name on the posters and they don't stop until the end of the season."

But there was never any real end of the season for him. In 1945, for example, he fought ninety-three fights in Spain in six months, about one every other day. This meant body-wracking travel, for he would fight in Barcelona one day, Madrid the next, and then maybe Lisbon the day after. He would snatch some sleep in the train or car and sometimes had to board

147

Manuel Rodríguez "Manolete."

a plane with his ring outfit still on. Then followed Mexico's season and Peru's season, and when he got through with those it was March again and time for the first fights in Valencia.

What, then, made him run? What made him The Best?

Money was the obvious thing. In his eight years as a senior matador he made approximately four million American dollars.* In his last years he was getting as high as $25,000 per fight, about $400 for every minute he performed, and he could fight where, when, and often as he liked. His yearly income was abetted by such things as a liqueur called "Anís Mano-lete," dolls dressed in costume with his sad face on them, testimonials for cognac ads, songs about him, and a movie called *The Man Closest to Death*.†

Yet it wasn't the money; people seldom risk their necks just for money. It was that he needed desperately to be someone—something great.

He was born in Córdoba, in 1917, in the heart of the bullfighting country. His great-uncle, a minor-league bullfighter, was killed by a bull, one of the dreaded Miura breed that years later was to kill Manuel. His mother was the widow of a great matador when she married Manuel's father, also a bullfighter. He began to go blind, kept fighting as long as he could distinguish the shape of the bull, and finally died in the poorhouse when Manuel was five years old.

The family was always hungry-poor. Manuel was a frail child, having had pneumonia when a baby, and could contribute little to his mother's support. But he started carrying a hod as soon as he was big enough.

His two sisters stood the hunger as long as possible, and then they started making money in a profession even older than bullfighting. This was the secret of the driving force behind Manuel. He never got over it. He resolved to make enough money somehow so that his family would never have to worry again, and to become an important enough person so that his sisters' shame would be blurred. Bullfighting is the only way in Spain for a poor boy to become great. "Matadors and royalty are the only ones who live well," they say. Young Manuel decided to become the greatest bull-fighter who ever lived.

He was twelve and working as a plasterer's assistant on the Sotomayor ranch when he got his first chance. They raised fighting bulls, and little Manuel begged so persistently to be allowed to fight that finally the Soto-mayors put him in the corral with a cape and a yearling. Manuel, an awkward, skinny kid in short pants, was knocked down every time he went near the little animal. If the animal had had sharp horns instead of stubs, he

* As opposed to the one million Babe Ruth made in his lifetime.
† Never completed.

149

would have been killed twenty times; instead he was just a mass of bruises by the time he limped out of the ring. He decided to go back to plastering.

But he couldn't stay away from the bulls. In the next few years he got out with the calves every time he could, even after he had been badly wounded, at thirteen, by a young bull. There are always back-seat bull-fighters around a ranch, and they told him some of the mistakes he was making. He learned fairly fast, but he was no genius. He was awkward and tried to do the wrong kind of passes for his build. However, he was brave and took it so seriously that he finally persuaded someone to give him a fight with small bulls in Córdoba's big Plaza de Toros under the *nom de taureau* of Manolete.

In his debut he was clumsy, but so brave and obviously trying so hard that the home folks applauded the sad-faced gawk. It was the greatest day of his life. Flushed with success, he and two other boys scraped their money together, formed a team called the Córdoban Caliphs, and set out to make their fortune. They wangled some contracts fighting at night and in cheap fairs, and traveled around Spain for a year. Manolete was almost the comic relief of the outfit. The crowds would laugh at his skinny frame, made more awkward by the fancy passes he was trying. His serious, ugly face and his earnestness made it all the funnier.

"He looks as dreary as a third-class funeral on a rainy day," they'd say. But they couldn't laugh at the way he killed. He was so anxious to do well that when it came time to dispatch his enemy, Manolete would hurl himself straight over the lowered head, the horn missing his body by inches, to sink the sword up to the hilt between the shoulders.

"He's going to get killed that way some day," said the experts, prophetically.

His career, if you could call it that at this point, was interrupted by his being drafted into the army. After his discharge a year later, he resumed fighting without the other two Caliphs. Then came the turning point in his life, for Camará spotted him.

José Flores Camará, a bald, dapper little man of thirty-five with omnipresent dark glasses, might have become the greatest bullfighter of all time except for one thing: he was a coward. He displayed more grace and knowledge of bull psychology than anyone had ever seen before. He had the build, and he knew all about the different fighting habits of bulls and the rest of the complicated science of tauromachy. The only thing he couldn't do was keep his feet from dancing back out of the way when the bull charged.

When he happened to see Manolete gawking around a small-town ring, he knew that here was someone who could be everything that he had failed

150

to be. With his expert eye he saw what the crowd didn't, that the boy wasn't really awkward, but that he was trying the wrong passes for his build and personality. Camará figured that with his brains and Manolete's blood they could really go places. He signed up the astonished young man for a long, long contract.

Camará remade Manolete. He took him out to the ranches and showed him what he was doing wrong. He made him concentrate on just the austere classic passes, none of the spinning or cape-twirling ones. With the cape he showed him how to do beautiful slow verónicas, finishing with a half-verónica. It was the only pass, of the dozens that exist, that Manolete would ever do again with the cape. With the small muleta cape used with the sword, Camará let him do only four passes. He showed him how to hold himself regally, how to give the classic passes with a dignity never before seen in the ring.

When Camará thought he was ready, he launched his protégé. It took a little while for people to appreciate what they were witnessing, but soon they came to realize that here was a revolutionary, a great artist. His repertory was startlingly limited, but when he did the simple verónica the cape became a live thing in his hands, and the easy flow of the cloth, the casual way it brought the bull's horns within a fraction of an inch of his legs, was incredibly moving. Heightening the effect was the serious mien and the cold face, not unlike Basil Rathbone's, that gave a feeling of tragedy every time he went into the ring. No one laughed at him now. Camará had made a genius out of a clown. And always the nervous little man with his dark glasses was behind the fence while his protégé was out with the bull watching every move and saying, "Careful, Manolo, this one will hook to the left," or "Take him on the other side, he has a bad eye," or "Fight him in the center, he swerves when he's near the fence." And Manolete kept learning and learning.

If his first year was successful, his second was sensational. It seemed as though Spain had just been waiting for his kind of fighting. His honest and brave style seemed to show up the fakery that the cape-twirlers had been foisting upon the public. In 1939 he took "the alternative" and became a senior matador, fighting older and larger bulls. From then on his rise was dizzy, for every fight and every season seemed better than the last one.

By 1946 he was the king of matadors, and Mexico beckoned with astronomical contracts, the highest prices ever paid a bullfighter. Spectators thought they were lucky to get a seat for $100 for his first fight in Mexico City. It was the greatest responsibility a matador ever had, and he gave them their money's worth, although he was carried out badly wounded before the fight was half over. He came to before they got him to the ring infirmary, shook off the people who tried to stop him, and lurched back into the ring to finish the bull before collapsing.

After he recovered he went on to fight all over Mexico and South America. When I saw him in Lima he was exhausted. Most bullfighters can give a top performance one day and then get away with a few safe, easy ones. But not Manolete. To preserve his fabulous reputation he had to fight every fight as though it were his first time in the Madrid Plaza.

But the machine was wearing down. Though he was only twenty-nine, he looked forty. He was drinking a lot, and not mild Spanish wine but good old American whisky. His timing was beginning to go off. I remember once in Peru he took nine sword thrusts to kill a bull, and he left the ring with tears running down his cheeks.

Even Camará, who enjoyed having his wallet filled through risks taken by someone else, thought it was time to quit. But the public makes an idol, and then it tires of what it has made, and it destroys the idol. When Manolete returned to Spain and announced that he was going to retire, he found he had slipped from public grace. The people were saying that he had dared only to fight small bulls and that this new young Luis Miguel Dominguín was better and braver. Manolete had been on top too long. They wanted someone new. They amused themselves by changing the words of the once-popular eulogizing song "Manolete" to "Manolete, you couldn't handle a robust field mouse if confronted by one in the bathroom."

"Quit," Camará advised him.

"Quit," said Luis Miguel, who would then be cock of the roost.

"Quit," said the other bullfighters, who then wouldn't look so clumsy and cowardly.

Manolete had too much pride to quit under fire. He said he would have one last season, just a few short months, with the largest bulls in Spain, and fighting with any fighters the promoters wished to bill him with. He wanted to retire untied and undefeated.

His first fight was in Barcelona, and the critics said he had never been greater. Then Pamplona, and he was even better than at Barcelona. It looked as though everyone was wrong, as though Manolete was in his prime.

Then, on July 16, he was wounded in Madrid. The wound wasn't serious, but he left the hospital too soon to go on a vacation in the mountains with Antonia. He began fighting again long before he should have; it was as though he were afraid that if he missed any of these last contracts there would always be some people who would remained unconvinced that he was still The Best.

152

The next fights were not good. He just wasn't up to it physically, and he wasn't helping himself by the way he was drinking. He would stay up all night with a bottle of whisky, not go to bed, and try to fight the next afternoon. They say he drank because of Antonia, because he knew she was a girl "of a bad style" and a gold digger, but that he loved her and couldn't break off with her and hated himself for loving her. A friend of his said, "She dragged poor Manolo through the Street of Bitterness with her cheapness."

Also the crowds' new attitude toward him was intolerable, not because of egotism but because of his professional pride. Now they were always prone to applaud the other matadors more, no matter how close Manolete let death come.

"They keep demanding more and more of me in every fight," he complained to me. "And I have no more to give."

The Manolete myth had grown bigger than the real Manolete, and the people were angry at him instead of at themselves for having created it.

Then came August, and the fight in Linares. But Carlos Arruza tells it well in his autobiography, *My Life as a Matador:*

Now it was the summer of 1947 and I was forced to limit myself to Portuguese and French plazas, because the breaking of the bullfighting agreement again prevented us Mexicans from performing in Spain. I had two corridas signed for the twenty-seventh and twenty-eighth of August in the plaza of Dax in France, so we set out from Sevilla in the station wagon and on the way stopped at San Sebastián, where the fair was on in full swing. Manolete was fighting, and I went to see him in the morning.

To tell the truth, I was shocked by his physical state. He had been out on the town all night "de juerga," and I wondered how he could possibly fight that afternoon. The Spanish public had been brutal to him for over a year now, even though he had just returned from the most sensational season in Mexico and Latin America that any matador had ever enjoyed. He was fighting as well as he ever had, but after a while audiences become infuriated by perfection. They kept demanding more and more of him with every fight. Out of boredom they now wanted to destroy their once beloved idol. Manolete was too sincere an artist not to suffer under this treatment. I was worried, seeing his face even more tragic than ever and knowing of his present bitterness toward life because of personal and professional reasons. He was just thirty but he looked forty-five.

153

I decided to stay for the fight, and Manolo did me the honor of asking me to watch it from down in the passageway. Once out in the ring, he quickly dispelled any fears I had about what shape he was in by putting up a highly capable demonstration, if not one of his really great ones. But he did many wonderful things that day, things that only another torero could truly appreciate, that the crowd didn't even deign to applaud.

As he came over to the fence to change muletas I exclaimed, "Caraí, Manolo, what do they want!"

"I know very well what they want," he said enigmatically, "and one of these afternoons I just might give it to them to keep the bastards happy."

They took a photo of us in the cuadrilla gate, the last together. Then we said good-by warmly, but with what seemed to me a certain sadness and nostalgia for the great days we had shared that would never come again. As he climbed into his car, still dressed in his suit of lights, he turned and with that hint of tragic smile that could break your heart he said, "Make them applaud their hands off in France, compadre."

And then he set off, for he had engagements to fulfill. One special engagement was awaiting him, one terrible rendezvous in Linares, from which he wasn't to return, and he hurried off to keep it, almost eagerly, it seems to me now in retrospect.

After my first corrida in Dax I decided to take a spin in my car to relax. I flipped on the radio. With great alarm I heard: "The great torero Manolete has suffered a frightful goring in Linares and it might turn out to be fatal."

I didn't want to believe it. I had a great lump in my throat as I kept telling myself, This is just what they do, these people—exaggerate toreros' wounds to make the news more sensational. But I stayed glued to the radio, and my fears increased when I heard how the great horn wound specialist Jiménez Guinea had been rushed from Madrid because of the gravity of the situation. Then the next morning came the terrible blunt news: Manolete was dead.

I was stunned, empty, parched inside, my spirit shriveled. But he was invulnerable! How had it happened? No bull could kill Manolete!

Rather than my trying clumsily to reconstruct the events at Linares, here is a moving, detailed letter which gives the whole story. It's from Manolete's sword boy of so many years, El Chimo, written to Antonio de la Villa in Mexico five days after the tragedy.

154

My dear and respected Don Antonio:

I'm answering your kind cable, but I'm in a kind of trance, a trance so great that I'm not really sure of anything that's going on.

You'll have to forgive these badly written lines but in my condition and with my heart in shreds it is hard to see things as clearly as I would like.

My matador, may he rest in peace, went to fight in Linares with enthusiasm. It was the first corrida of the season for him in Andalucía and you know how much toreros want to please the aficionados there, especially those near Córdoba and Sevilla, which are the ones that have the power to bestow or remove fame.

For Manolete the Miura bulls were no worry at all since he'd had some of his best days with them. Balañá, who was the impresario of Linares, had bought two corridas, one from Samuel Brothers and the other from Miura. Manolo requested the Miuras.

And they try to say there's nothing to superstition! On the 21st of August Balañá arranged the fight, number 21 was the hotel room number in Linares, Manolete had fought 21 fights already this season, and 21 was the brand on Islero, the assassin of poor Manolo. These are forewarnings that never leave one.

I left Madrid with the cuadrilla in order to have everything ready in Linares. Manolo, with Guillermo, Camará and his friend Bellón, left Madrid at nightfall in his car (whose license plate began with "21.") He ate dinner in Manzanares with great relish—you know how he loved to eat—and afterward he sat around listening to some flamenco records and chatting with a friend of his from Manzanares who kept begging him to fight there. The friend began sucking up to Camará to get him to go for the idea, and to convince him, he took out his checkbook, saying to Manolo, "You put in the amount, any amount, and I'll sign it." But Manolete begged off, saying he had twenty fights in a row and he couldn't accept.

Manolete arrived at the Hotel Cervantes around 12:30 that night. There awaited him Domecq, Antonio Cañero, Bernardo, Carnicerito, and other friends. They stayed up talking and joking until nearly two in the morning. They didn't talk about bulls or anything unpleasant, only about things of the country, horses, and trips.

Manolo was a real sleepyhead. He was a real case. Whether he fought or not the next day, nobody could keep him from getting at least ten hours.

At 10 on Sunday morning I went into the bedroom to unpack the

155

capes and things and to arrange his suit of lights on the chair. "What suit are you fixing for me?" he asked. "The rose one," I answered. "See if you can't find me a pair of those stockings that we used to get in Barcelona," he said, "because those others wrinkle and with the balls of my feet so sore it bothers me."

He went back to sleep, and around 12 I served him lunch. When he sat up I saw a red blotch on his arm like a bite, and smiling I said, "You must have had some music in here last night."

"A Miura got to me sooner than I expected," answered the matador; Andalucía has lots of bedbugs and mosquitoes.

Then he ate a small steak, some grapes, and a cup of coffee.* He lit a cigarette and went to the bathroom to wash and shave. At one the parade of friends and the curious began; there was his friend the Count of Colombí and the newspaper critic K-Hito, an intimate of his, and the two of them began to joke. At one point, K-Hito, observing the darkness of Manolete's beard, asked, "Haven't you shaved yet?"

"Yes, I've shaved," said Manolete. "If my beard's getting darker it's fear that's making the whiskers come out."

Carnicerito arrived all dressed. "Why so soon?" Manolo chided. "Going to have your portrait painted?" And Manolo kidded him about his amorous weaknesses, which many times had kept him from doing his best with the bulls. Carnicerito had drawn the lots for the bulls that morning, and he said that the group of animals weren't too big and seemed manageable enough, judging by the way they let themselves be corraled.

Then came a newspaperman from the magazine *Life* from America with a photographer and an assistant, and Manolo, smiling, said to him, "We toreros are one person before the fight and another afterwards. If you're looking for a handsomer torero, take the photo after the corrida when the resemblance goes back into place. Fear puts a mask on us now."

Manolete was received in the Linares ring with a surprising ovation. Upon parading out the cry of "Manolo! Manolo!" was heard on all sides. There seemed to be less detractors today. Hat in hand,* like Gitanillo and Luis Miguel Dominguín, the matador stalked across the sand with that style and arrogance that only he had.

---

* Most matadors don't eat before a fight, to make things more convenient for the surgeons, but Manolete became too weak if he went without food.
* The montera hat is carried instead of worn when a matador is fighting his first corrida of the season in a certain plaza.

The truth is that on the first bull, which was Gitanillo's, there was nothing worth mentioning. Manolo only went out for one *quite* and then the cowardly Miura didn't charge.

Islero came out in fifth place and Manolo, as with his first bull, couldn't get any cooperation from the animal. Gabriel González and Cantimplas barely doubled the animal at all, and then with great difficulty, because Islero planted himself in the middle of the ring and just stood there wagging his horns wickedly, but with no desire to charge honestly. Manolo called out, "Quieto, quieto!" to Gabriel.

Then he opened up his cape and citing with gaiety, he gave it two verónicas with that inimitable style of his. But he soon saw that Islero was inclined to crowd to the right and hooked badly. Manolo tried again, but uselessly, since Islero just wouldn't respond. The animal kept putting on the brakes. Atienza really leaned on Islero in the first picking and again on the second.

The act was changed to the banderillas, and in the second pair Gabriel escaped by the skin of his teeth, and after leaping the fence to safety he said as he walked by Manolete, "He really hooks on that right side."

The worst kind Manolo could have drawn!

The matador took the muleta and went out and gave the bull a few cautious passes to feel it out. Then all of a sudden he gave the bull three tremendous right-hand passes, so beautiful and close to the horn that the emotion grabbed you by the throat. The audience held its breath until the pass that finished off and embellished the series, and then they burst out in a thunderous roar. They kept up this steady roaring as Manolete followed this with the rest of the brilliant and suicidally brave faena. And when Islero got its front feet together Manolo profiled himself for the kill just a very short distance from the Miura. He furled the muleta, cocked his left leg, and then, flinging himself on the bull, he sank the blade into the withers, centimeter by centimeter it seemed. It lasted too long. You could see him trying to do it absolutely perfectly, marking off the three classic positions of the ideal volapié.

The Mexican public must remember that superb and dangerous leisureliness with which Manolete used to perform the act of killing. Islero had time to wait, to let him come way in and then hook him, snagging him in the right thigh with the right horn. It lifted him up slightly from the ground, and Manolete, spinning on the horn, fell down head first. An ordinary tossing with no particular spectacularness to it, really. But the horn wound it left! A gaping hole, a hole big enough

157

to kill a horse, from which the blood spouted out like out of a faucet. You could see instantly that it was mortal.

I managed to get out there right away and grab him under his arms, Cantimplas and Carnicerito took his legs carefully, and two other helpers the middle of his body. Somebody made a mistake about the way to the infirmary, and two times we had to double back. Finally we got to the right door at the same time that Islero crashed over dead along the fence. The bull was black with some white hairs and a fine conformation and a good coat.

The infirmary was very bad, like most infirmaries in provincial plazas. And it became crowded with people. Thanks to Camará and Señor Domecq, with the assistance of two policemen, Dr. Garrido, the doctor of the plaza, was able to start to work on him. Manolo with his eyes very wide open as though they were going to pop out, tried to sit

Manolete.

up to take off his pants, but he fell back down on the table weakly. And turning his head to me he said, "This time they've really given it to me!"

Then the help arrived with the dress cape, which was white silk with embroidered red roses, and the Maestro said to me, "Chimo, this time the roses didn't bring luck." And all the time the blood wasn't oozing out, it just kept spurting in a steady stream.

Manolo was very pale, with that yellowness that frightens one. And the doctors began to work on him without chloroform, a fatal symptom for those of us who know. . . .

Kenneth Tynan continues the narrative in *Bull Fever:*

The cheers pursued Manolete to the infirmary, but he was already insensible, and did not hear the last ovation of his life. When the doctors were completing their examination, David burst into the room with the ears and tail of Islero, which had been won so purely. Swarms of well-meaning onlookers filled the air with cigar-smoke, and a jug of water had to be brought to moisten Manolete's lips. Blood was spurting from his leg in irregular gushes, and a transfusion was urgently required. The first volunteer was Juan Sánchez Calle, a police officer and close friend of the toreros. While the operation was taking place, wooden chairs were being arranged in the bullring for the film show which had been announced for later in the evening, and a silent crowd gathered around Manolete's great blue car, which stood empty in the courtyard outside. A medical report was posted outside the infirmary. It said baldly that Manolete had been injured in the groin, and that the wound had taken three trajectories—inwards, upwards and downwards: the result of the brief moment in which he had spun on the horn. The femoral artery was badly damaged, there was extensive haemorrhage and violent traumatic shock. "Outlook very grave." This was signed by Doctor Garrido and has been much commented on. Medical opinion now holds the view that Manolete was killed not by the wound itself but by the traumatic shock which it induced. Shock had unbalanced the vital triumvirate of brain, heart, and lungs by which we live; and his nervous system, already debilitated, could stand no further punishment. After a short conference, the doctors decided to summon the help of Jiménez Guinea, the Madrid bullring surgeon, who was spending the summer at El Escorial, more than two hundred miles to the north.

At eight o'clock Manolete regained consciousness. His peons were at his bedside, together with Camará, Gitanillo, and Luis Miguel. He murmured to Cantimplas:

"Ayee—but my groin hurts."

The peon mumbled a few words of comfort. Manolete turned towards Camará and asked:

"Is it in a bad place?"

It was in the worst place, but no one spoke. He then asked for water, and Luis Miguel poured a little through his arid lips. At eight-thirty a second transfusion was performed. His resistance was still very low, but he revived enough to grip the hands of those around him, saying:

"Move my leg a little. That's better. It was hurting me."

It was now agreed that he should be transferred to the municipal hospital in Linares. They carried him out of the infirmary on a stretcher. The crowd in the streets heard him utter two words. "Hurry!" he said: and again: "Hurry!" But the hospital of San José was a good distance off, and twenty minutes passed before he was on the operating table. Meantime one of his peons telephoned the diestro's mother in San Sebastián.

"What has happened?" she said.

"Listen," he said, "Manolo has been caught in the leg. Yes, it's a cornada, but nothing special, nothing of any interest."

"Go on," said his mother.

"Well, he cut the ears and the tail. Pay no attention to the papers and the radio—you know what they are. All that stuff about arteries and so on. It isn't important. Don't alarm yourself."

Just after ten-thirty, one of his mother's friends, the impresario Pablo Martínez Elizondo, spoke to Camará by telephone from San Sebastián and heard the worst. As casually as he could, he suggested to the señora that she might like to be at her son's side. "Not that it's very serious, but I think he would be pleased to see you." At eleven they left together for Linares. "Of course if it was really bad," she said, "they would have taken him to Madrid."

By this time word of the goring had spread across the whole country; in Madrid, Seville, and Barcelona no one talked of anything else. At midnight a third blood transfusion was performed and Manolete was removed from the operating theatre to a hospital bed. He asked for a cigarette, but could not smoke it: after three puffs it fell to the ground. He sighed, and said to Alvaro Domecq, the equestrian bullfighter, who had joined the group at the bedside:

"This is a bad feeling."

160

Professional pride revived for a moment, and he asked:

"Did I kill the bull with that estocada?"

They told him he had killed it.

"And—didn't they give me an ear?"

Camará replied that they had given him both ears and the tail. He smiled. A few minutes later, he shook his head and whispered:

"How my mother will suffer!"

At 4:00 A.M. he began to grow terribly pale. He was able to recognize Domingo Ortega when the latter arrived, but could do no more than make a feeble gesture of apology. Shortly afterwards Gitanillo, who had driven like a madman, drew up with Doctor Guinea in the blue car. Guinea examined the dying man and discussed the situation with Doctor Tamames, whom Luis Miguel had called in. They decided not to move him.

"Don Luis," said Manolete to Doctor Guinea, whom he knew well, "what can you do for me?"

Guinea told him to close his eyes and rest. To limit the circulation he then applied tighter bandages to both legs. Minutes passed and Manolete said faintly:

"I can't feel anything in my legs, doctor."

Guinea soothed him and again told him to rest. After a while he said:

"I can't see you, Don Luis."

His eyes were open. Guinea said:

"Close your eyes and don't worry. All is well."

There was no hope. A few minutes before five the hospital chaplain administered extreme unction. When this was done, Manolete called suddenly for his oldest peón.

"David . . ."

His lips went on moving, but the words were lost. At seven minutes past five, as the sky was clearing over the town, a brief convulsion took place, but with it no great agony. Then Manolete's head slumped to the right, so that it faced a picture of the Virgin of the Macarena which stood by his bed. Doctor Tamames, who was taking his pulse, announced that he had given up his soul. Antonia, his mistress, who had been kept away from the death-bed for fear of the effect her appearance might have on him, was now admitted, to weep over his body.

In the hospital chapel the first mass was celebrated in his memory. A little after ten o'clock his remains were taken in an ambulance to Córdoba, where they are now buried.

Pamplona

12. Pamplona

Uno de enero
Dos de febrero
Tres de marzo
Cuatro de abril
Cinco de mayo
Seis de junio
Siete de julio
 San Fermín!

—Pamplona drinking song

PAMPLONA IS THE ONLY CITY IN THE WORLD WHOSE ENTIRE MALE POPULACE IS made up of psychopaths, and in case there is any doubt about this fact they annually demonstrate it in the streets from July 7 to July 15 during the traditional fiesta of San Fermín.

Pamplona, which is about two hundred miles from Madrid, has always been a bull-conscious town. In fact the first document we have regarding professional bullfighting pertains to Pamplona. It is a royal order, dated August, 1385, by Carlos II, in which he says that fifty libra are to be paid "to two men, one Moorish and one Christian, that We have had come

165

from Zaragoza to kill two bulls in Our presence in Our city of Pamplona."
But although Pamplona, with its plaza holding 13,000 and its top programs
every year, is a major bullfighting town, its fame is clearly based on what
happens in its streets.

I saw the feria of San Fermín for the first time in 1945, when I flew up
from Madrid with Ambassador Armour in his plane. Along for the jaunt also
was the naval attaché, and a friend of mine, a mild, plump little lieutenant
(j.g.) from the naval Attaché's office who had been a history of art instructor at Yale before the war. That first night was a wild one in Pamplona, and
for what wild nights Pamplona can have I refer you to that splendid novel,
The Sun Also Rises. My friend Jim disappeared early in the evening with
some new-found Spanish friends, and when last seen he looked completely
out of character and was taking a bet that he couldn't empty a wineskin
held at arm's length from his mouth. The rest of us went to bed early,
got up at dawn, and were just starting out for the beginning of the race
through the streets when Jim appeared supported by two friends. He was
dressed now in the white trousers and red beret and scarf of the traditional Pamplonica runner, and from time to time he mumbled: "Riau, riau"
and waved a blown-up bladder on the end of a stick, which for some unac-
countable reason is what Pamplona people do during fair time.

"He's our little brother and he's going to run," said one of the Spaniards,
happily.

"Run where?" asked the naval attaché, frowning.

"In front of the bulls! He's told the whole town and everyone is waiting
to see the *yanqui* run in front of the bulls."

The captain frowned harder: "This true, Jim?"

"Well, maybe not *everyone*, sir," said Jim. He was pale and blinking
his eyes and trying to get sober. "Of course I can see how undignified the
whole idea is and if you order me not to I . . ."

The captain broke in angrily: "I'm not going to order you not to! I
think you've got yourself and America in a hell of a mess. If you've stupidly
told everyone that you're going to run, what are they going to think if you
back out now? We're about the only Americans they've seen here in ten
years, and what are they going to think if you chicken out? And just think
of how the newspapers and the Germans around here will play it up!"

When we got to the starting point, Jim was as sober as a man can get.
None of us had said a word in the car, and now we just shook hands with
him silently. Then he climbed over the heavy board fence that blocked off
the side streets, keeping the huge crowd safe from the bulls, and joined
the two hundred or so Pamplonicas waiting for the signal. The other runners were wandering around nervously, occasionally glancing back at the

166

end of the street where the bulls were to be released, but Jim got down in a sprinter's crouch and stared straight ahead, not daring to look at the bulls pawing and bellowing restlessly in the enclosure in back of him.

At seven-thirty on the dot a pistol was fired, the crowd roared, and the bulls were released. The veteran Pamplonicas around Jim were calm and unruffled because they knew the bulls were a good hundred yards behind, with dozens of other runners between. But not Jim; it was enough to him that seven wild bulls were loose anywhere in the county, and he shot off down the street ahead of everyone, running the way the old track coach had told him to, chin up and elbows close to his body. He was doing fine until he reached where Santo Domingo Street runs into Mercadores. Then he tripped on the string of one of his sandals. As he sprawled in the middle of the cobblestone street the other runners overtook him, running faster now that the bulls had picked up momentum. Wave after wave of them passed over Jim as he struggled and fought to get to his feet. He finally clawed his way up to find the lead bull a scant ten feet from him. When he began to run again it was like when the tiger chases one in dreams and one's legs won't work. But then he began to move, and throwing form to the wind he really strode out. The bull was gaining on him at one point, but it stopped to hook at a fallen runner and Jim pulled ahead. The street narrows down to the bullring gate, and it is here where the jam-ups occur. Already there was a struggling, amorphous tangle of people there, but Jim managed to scramble over the thrashing forms with the bulls right behind. When he finally made the arena and spilled over the fence to safety, he was very pale of face and wet of pants.

I recently sent Jim a present that must have brought the cold sweat to his forehead. It was a handsome picture book called *Fiesta in Pamplona*, which gives a terrifyingly graphic view of the goings-on at San Fermín time. The text by Dominique Aubier is especially good and is worth quoting. Herewith are some paragraphs from it:

"In the blind wound of the dawn," runs a song of the encierro, "they are waiting." Not one thousand or two thousand, numbers make no difference, this is humanity itself coming out of darkness. The great drive of the bulls to the bull-pen, the encierro, is the symbol of this birth, and within a few minutes it reaches the violent climax and so intensely that it is a true representation of man's first struggle to wrest himself free from animality. Some speak of this race, where men and animals charge through the narrow straits of the palisaded streets, as the Fall when man is driven out of earthly paradise. But whatever the image, and a thousand allegories may be inferred, the fact is the presence on the spot of the living, pulsing myth. And the essential

167

The running of the bulls, Pamplona.

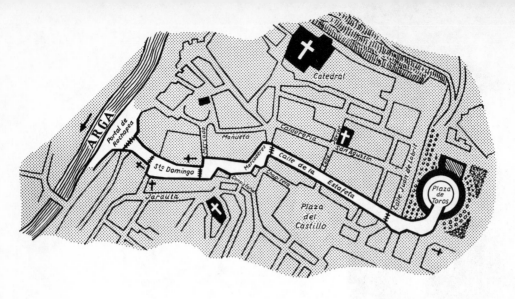

Pamplona.

point in the wrenching struggle is the accomplishment of the separation and the appearance of man. . . .

People say that the rocket explosion frightens the bulls and makes them jump faster into the street chased by the oxen and the herdsmen. You can see them burst out and head for the slope by the hospital. Since bulls have short forelegs, they are good climbers and can gather speed in the free space that is allowed them by the rules. But a few yards away the young men are waiting for them, some are ready to go, nervous runners afraid of missing the signal, others are provoking the animals by jota or banderillero gestures.

Near, or not quite so near the Plaza de Toros, there are the young men, spread out according to their courage and speed. Some go down farther than their fathers did, and from their tales you couldn't imagine where their bravery would drive them, if only the rules didn't forbid anyone's going farther than the end of the street of Santo Domingo! From one generation to the next performance must improve, which is good. The ideal is to go and face the animals at the gate, without taking any special advantage, and to get there first. Actually, all the official threats and genuine punishments were necessary to keep the most excited men, possessed by the strangeness and wildness of the moment, but who don't know what they are doing, from dashing toward the bulls just at the instant when even the policemen get out of the way and take shelter around a corner. This is not because fear has never hammered any nails into Pamplonese heads or hearts, it is simply that Spanish blood turns into carnations and invisible fields of flowers grow out of the encierro. Devotion offers them to San Fermín since this patron of the town is holding his cape with both hands, ready to throw it down from the heavenly heights under the bull's threatening eye with one of those wide sweeping "toreras" which are his secret. The ancient bishop understands the art of defense, and a bull's intentions have no mystery for him. He is guarding the destinies of the men of Pamplona. And he alone, for at this extraordinary instant of inauguration and competition no man may try to conquer death. Death and life are racing together, and the race is to whoever will run fast enough. Their action is one and the same: to run, to rush. Run and arrive. Run together in order to separate victoriously in the arena, there death's forces will be temporarily leashed until, for their final destruction, the community delegate a perfect representative, their hero, the matador.

Hero first, then sorcerer, his purity is protective, a sign that ordinary, preoccupied life has no existence for him, and his exceptional value

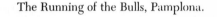

The Running of the Bulls, Pamplona.

makes him useless anywhere else. His particular courage is the intensification of all the forms of courage exacted very simply by life from day to day, his place is the center of the fiesta where he has the duty of accomplishing before a crowd what each man must do for himself. His act is the scope and the focus for every private action dying of exasperation in the margin. It is utterly inconceivable that such a man accomplish such a mission without skirting death, so the torero exposes his own life as proof of his merit, as the guarantee of his work, the wager of his human reality. "They think I am a prince," said Manolete after a fight when, though wounded, he continued until he fainted between the bull's horns. "Yet they must have blood in order to be sure. . . ."

As the procession advances the gates close; it is no longer possible to go back. What strange barriers they are, apparently there just for their usefulness as a safeguard, but they also have a completely different role. I have never watched one of these gates being slowly closed by a policeman, who has been granted some kind of superior authority, without thinking of how they stand for something utterly incomprehensible and terrifying. Mankind cannot turn back either, and these barriers are somehow like time's barriers. One minute is always pushing the next, and in this sense, we never reach the end of our own encierro!

. . . The public and the runners are told what they must respect and do or not do under pain of severe penalty, and the police like any police in the world tolerate only obedience; they have special authority on that day and doubly defend the chances for life. But their methods don't improve by it: I saw them beat up a man who did not at the exact second get out of the street which was to be cleared for the arrival of the runners. Seven o'clock had struck, and the rocket had proclaimed to the waiting crowd that the gates of the Rochapea corral were opening. This young man, who was plump and hesitant, brave enough to defy the rules, not brave enough to face the danger, had slipped through one of the palisades which continue the house walls at the cross-streets. He had squirmed underneath, and there was a moment when he stayed there, caught like an animal, with his chest between the feet of the people crowded against the boards and his legs in the street. The policeman was already trembling to have to guard this passage, which was on the point of being charged by the crowd of animals and men, and with his stick raised he ran for the young man and showered blows on him. There was just time for one to flee and for the other to flatten himself against the palisade, half in mortal fear and half in glory, when the violent torrent came pouring through.

172

The arena gates for the young men and the bulls are opened at two minutes to seven so that they can be used only by the runners who are coming just ahead of the animals; simultaneously the public gates are closed. In the circle which is still empty a few toreros, in civilian clothes but with their capes, are waiting, a little like doctors. When the mass bursts through the narrow gate the danger is enormous, in that strangling passage where men and animals are crushed, body to body in a cruel embrace.

Thus everything is regulated to the minute, so that the encierro may complete its plunging course to the Plaza de Toros. Nothing must hinder it and nothing must divert it from its goal and meaning. Shouting at an animal or isolating it and provoking it with a jacket or shirt could end the game, since it would defy the fundamental law and would take all the value out of the myth. Bullfighting is the symbol of willed and conquering action. It is the sign of man who wants for himself the place of the foremost earthly creature and who takes it and then proves that he deserved it. . . .

The encierro's symbol stands for mankind in a mass before they are split up into individuals, and it hardly matters if the Pamplonese realize this consciously or not, since they never make a mistake, or never for more than a minute, a tiny one. A mysterious cord attaches them to the heart of bullfighting, and the blood of the myth circulates in their veins. . . .

Castillo de las Guardas

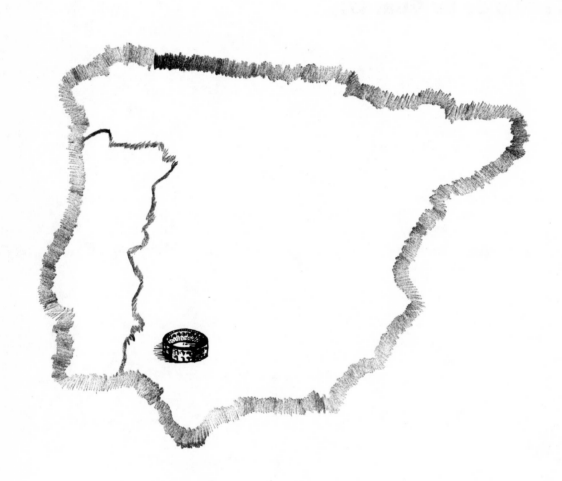

13. Castillo de las Guardas

To MOST PEOPLE CASTILLO DE LAS GUARDAS IS ONE OF THE MOST UNIMPORTANT plazas de toros in Spain. However, to me it is incontrovertibly the most important. For this is where, in September 1945, I appeared on the same program with the immortal Juan Belmonte, and every day since that date has been anticlimactic for me.

The arena itself is made of stone, holds about six thousand spectators, and is a 60-kilometer drive from Sevilla. The day before the fight, I arrived at Castillo at about seven o'clock with my two banderilleros and my sword handler. We looked over the Plaza de Toros first, to find out where the presidente's box and the entrances were and what they had in the way of burladeros. There were big posters all around advertising the fight. Below Belmonte's name I was billed as The California Kid—El Niño de California —which struck everyone, including me, as amusing. I guess it was Juan Belmonte's idea. Then we drove through the towered fairy-tale town up to the bull breeder's finca, a three-hundred-year-old ranch that probably didn't look much different, with its courtyard, carriages, and quaintly costumed farm hands, in the days when it was built. We arrived in time for dinner in the patio with the large family of the ganadero, and afterward a guitar was produced and we sang. Chico wailed out a gypsy song but stopped midway, saying he wasn't in voice; he was as nervous as though he were fighting the next day instead of just being my sword boy. Cascabel, a banderillero, did a stamping dance with Sona, the rancher's pretty sister, but we couldn't seem to clap in rhythm for him. I asked Manolo, my number one banderillero, to dance a bulería, but he said he wasn't in the mood. We were all jumpy and quarrelsome. We went to bed early.

I went right to sleep but tossed restlessly and fought a hundred bulls before waking up at dawn, sweaty and tired and with a sinking feeling. I made myself go back to sleep. When I awoke again, the sun was pouring in the window; there was the good hot scent of the fields in my room, and the swallows were wheeling and crying around the barn. What a fine day for everyone else, I thought; what a hell of a fine day! For the first time I asked myself if the glamour and excitement were really worth it.

Why was I, a twenty-three-year-old American vice-consul, signed to fight on the same program with Spanish professionals anyway? Well, mainly because I *was* American and *was* a vice-consul and they knew that my passion was bullfighting. Before graduating from Yale I had studied painting at the University of Mexico and become fascinated by the art and grace and color of the spectacle down there. After I imbibed a lot of tequila one day, some Mexican "friends" convinced me that I should jump into the bullring during a fight. I did, using my raincoat as a cape. I made a few half-hearted passes at the bull, made a fool of myself, and somehow got out alive. An amused professional, nineteen-year-old Felix Guzman, took an interest in me and began to teach me what an intricate science bullfighting is. I hadn't really grasped the first fundamentals before I was in a practice ring with animals too large for me to handle. One of the very first days, a large half-breed bull charged unexpectedly and smashed my right knee. I lay there on the ground for what seemed a century, waiting for a horn to go into my back. It didn't, because Felix jumped in the ring with no cape, struck the bull in the face, and when it left me to charge him, outsprinted it to the fence. I was carried out of the ring by the time the bull came back for me. Felix was later gored to death in the big bullring. I lost my enthusiasm for "la fiesta brava."

I was on a cane for a couple of years, and was still wearing a metal brace from ankle to hip, when the State Department sent me to Sevilla, Spain, as a vice-consul. However, after six months of swimming and Andalusian sun, my leg got better, so much so that I began to think about fighting again. One day I was taken by some friends sixty kilometers out of town to a bullfight party at Juan Belmonte's ranch. He is over fifty now and retired from formal fighting, but he fights about ten charity fights a year still, and when he does, he seems to have lost none of his skill; one can see why they used to call him "The Earthquake." He is little and twisted and ugly, but he is a tremendous personality, in and out of the ring.

That first day when I fought on his ranch with the cow calves they were testing for bravery, I made myself ridiculous. I had intimated to everyone

178

that I had been a pretty big bullfighter in Mexico—mainly to bolster my own courage—and I had half come to believe it. So when I got out in Belmonte's private ring and was shoved around by a knee-high calf, it was humiliating. I couldn't blame it on a weak knee, either, for it was just lack of knowledge that made me miscalculate the angles of a calf's charge and get knocked down by the stubby horns time after time. Belmonte was amused, however. He liked the idea that an American wanted to bullfight. I guess he liked the dumb, stubborn way I kept going back at the calf with the cape, making the same clumsy mistake, getting knocked sprawling each time, and then taking a terrible pounding on the ground from the vicious little animal. He finally persuaded me to stop this masochism and began to show me what I was doing wrong. It seems I was trying to make the calf pass between me and the fence. Fighting cattle have a tendency to hook away from the fence, so that halfway through a pass, the animal would swerve and hit my legs. I never made that mistake again.

When my bruised body would let me walk without groaning—about a week later—I went back for another lesson. This time I wasn't allowed in the ring, and I was just as glad. Belmonte had me practice for hours with just a cape and an imaginary bull. We started with the basic pass—the verónica—and he showed me how to hold the heavy scarlet cape, to keep my head down, my hands low, my footwork in rhythm with my arms. He would stand in back of me and work my arms like a golf pro until I learned to swing the cape smoothly. Then I graduated to a small boy hired to charge, holding a pair of sharp horns in front of him and simulating the action of a bull. He was not allowed to do anything that a fighting bull would not logically do, but if I made a mistake, such as holding the cape too far in front of my body or not fixing "the bull" properly after a series of passes, the boy would delightedly jab me in the legs. A bullfighter's performance is judged by his proximity to the horns, so now I had not only to think of manipulating the cape properly and gracefully but also to concentrate on working close to these sharp horns, yet making them miss me. Sidney Franklin, the American matador, lived in the same hotel with me, and he would help me with my homework. After the verónica was more or less mastered, I had to learn the half-verónica, and the chicuelina pass where you turn in toward the bull after the horns go by your knees, and the spinning "lighthouse" pass, and the butterfly, and the many others.

Then the muleta was produced. This is the small heart-shaped cape that is used for the last third of the fight and upon whose manipulation a bullfighter's ultimate success depends. It is essentially a one-handed cape, and I had to learn a whole new set of passes—the natural, the chest pass, the pass of death—with the added complication of always having the sword

180

Poster for the fight.

in the right hand. I seemed to have more aptitude for the muleta than the cape. For killing, I would practice with a mechanical bull made out of a bicycle and a pair of horns. One had to run head on to the contraption as a boy made it charge, go through the motion of keeping the bull's attention focused on the muleta held low to the right in the left hand across the body, while the right arm reached over the horns to get the sword into the five-inch wire mesh that represented the opening between a bull's shoulder blades. It was like rubbing your head and patting your stomach, only as Belmonte warned, if you did it wrong, the bull would pick up its head as your body went over the right horn and you would get spiked through the chest.

"Well, I think you're ready," said Belmonte casually one day after a long session with the cape and muleta. He said it with the deadly calm of a flying instructor climbing out of a plane and telling a student to take it up alone. He had calves brought in from the range to the ring, and I had to show how much I had learned. I got dumped several times, but I generally knew why now and set about to correct it. Belmonte would criticize from the porch or sometimes come down to show me how. It looked so easy when he did it.

The next time the calves were bigger. And then pretty soon they were no longer calves but half-grown animals with blunted horns. And pretty soon they were bigger. And all the time I was meeting and getting lessons from some of the greatest toreros in the business, Cagancho, El Gallo, Pepe Luis Vázquez, Arruza, and Manolete.

Then, after a year, I was signed by an impresario for a big charity fight on September 23, 1945, to kill my first bull. And on the same program with Belmonte! I wasn't sure I was ready. Killing the bicycle was easy enough, but I didn't know whether I could handle the bull.

For the month before the fight I'd thought of little else. When going over some consular invoices or passport applications, my hands would suddenly begin to tremble as I thought of the onrushing date. Or when I'd go to the movies and relax enough to laugh, right in the middle my brain would remind me, "You're fighting on the twenty-third!"—and the laugh would stick in my throat.

Belmonte.

And now here I was in Castillo, and today was the day, and there was no getting out of it. I think if there'd been an honorable way to get out of it, I would have. I was scared.

I got up and went down to the patio and practiced with the cape in the sun. Manolo came down and watched me. "You're crazy to practice on the day of the fight," he said. Manolo was a nice young Sevillan who had tried to be a matador but who gave up after one disastrously cowardly exhibition in Madrid. He was content to resign himself to the unspectacular and comparatively safe routine of a banderillero now.

I did some verónicas with an imaginary bull. "Don't do verónicas today, Bernabé," said Manolo.

"Why not?" I asked irritably.

"Because it's your weakest pass. They're no good and you get caught when you do them."

"Who the hell is the matador around here?" I snapped.

"You," said Manolo, going into the house. "You are, thank God."

I practiced until my arms got a little tired. Then I went back up to bed to rest. I could hear the others down below eating lunch in the patio while I had a coffee with milk. I heard some laughter. It seemed incredible to me that anyone could laugh today. I fell into a fitful sleep about two. I dreamed I was back in America—in San Francisco, riding on the cable car with a girl.

"Come on! To the fight!" Manolo had a rough hand on my shoulder and was shaking me. I had the idea that maybe if I kept my eyes closed and picked up my dream again, Manolo would vanish and there wouldn't be any fight. He shook me again and I got up quickly. It was five o'clock, and the fight was at six-thirty, since it stays light in Andalusia until about ten. My costume was laid out neatly on the chair, and after I'd shaved, Manolo helped me into it. I wore the big broad-brimmed hat and sash and white jacket used in fights without picadors. Manolo was serious and white and suddenly efficient.

"You look like a third-class funeral," I said, as we went down the stairs. I wanted to see if I was too scared to talk. "You'd think you were going to take the chances."

Belmonte.

"I'm not going to take any chances," he answered.

"I know," I said. "Then why are you scared?"

"I'm always scared," he said. "You know that."

"Why do you keep fighting then?"

"I can't help it," he said. "That's why."

We came down to the courtyard, and the rancher's family clapped and said, "Olé, matador!"

They took some photos of us when Chico and Cascabel came down. I looked at my watch. "It's almost six."

They all came up and shook hands seriously, wished me luck, and hoped I'd "get at least one ear." Except the foreman who shook his head and said pleasantly but positively, "He won't kill that animal. I raised that creature and I tell you he won't kill it with anything less than a hand grenade." My heart sank lower.

"Of course he'll kill it," said Sona. She was little and dark, with black Spanish eyes. "You'll see him come back with the bull's ear." She took a religious medal from around her neck and pinned it on the inside of my jacket. Then she kissed me on the cheek.

"Sure he'll kill it," said Manolo uncertainly.

We stood around awkwardly for a few moments.

"Let's get going," I said. It was six-ten. I gave Sona my watch to keep for me, and then we swung on the truck and rattled down the road. I could see Sona waving in the courtyard. She wasn't going to the fight because she said she couldn't stand it. We drove very fast, and on one of the curves, Manolo said, "This uncle's driving is scaring me to death!" It struck me funny he should be worried about anything but the bull that was waiting for us, and I remember trying to laugh. All the way in as we passed the big posters for the fight, I was constructing a wall of false courage, detaching myself from this person who was trying to be a Hemingway character, who was going to kill a bull with Juan Belmonte, but the sight of the gray and forbidding coliseum rising at the top of the hill brought me back into myself with a rush, and there was a sickening knot in my stomach.

It was six-twenty-five when we arrived at the foot of the plaza hill, and the cathedral bells were starting to ring. We started up the cobbled street, and the big crowd that was milling toward the plaza gave us a great ovation, shouting, "Suerte, suerte"—Luck, luck—and patting me on the back as we pushed ahead of them. I forgot the knot for a moment and smiled and waved. Then a great shout went up as Belmonte's Fiat pulled up and the Earthquake of Triana stepped out of his car in fighting costume and hurried after us.

"*Buenas tardes*," he said panting, smiling his great smile.

184

The author in the American Consulate,
Sevilla, 1945.

"*Muy buenas,*" we said.

"Who has seen the bulls?" he asked.

"I haven't," I said, "but I understand they're big."

"What do you mean, big, Bernabé?"

"I've heard that they are about a hundred and sixty, dressed."

"*Jesús, que miedo!*" he said, with his barracuda jaw jutting out. "Jesus, what fear. What a tragedy."

One never could tell what Don Juan was thinking. Had he expected them to be bigger or smaller?

We got to the ring, and it was already filled to overflowing. Belmonte's banderillero was holding his horse for him, a good-looking skittish chestnut. I saw a bronze plaque on the wall that read: "The novillero José Hernández 'Parraito' was killed in this plaza on February 27, 1885, may he rest in peace." It wasn't the sort of data I most wanted to be informed about at that moment.

As we lined up in the entrance to the ring, adjusting the capes over our shoulders, the third matador came up. He was a young novillero and looked nervous.

"Holá," he said, as he dragged rapidly on a cigarette.

"Holá."

"I'm Chavez," he said. "You must be El Niño de California."

"Yes," I said.

He smiled wanly. "You have a rare name."

"I thought El Andaluz was fighting third today?" That's what the posters had said.

"No," he swallowed dryly, "he's not. I am."

"What happened to the Andaluz?"

Chávez was working his feet in the sand like a boxer in a rosin box. I figured it looked pretty professional, so I did it too.

"El Estudiante got it bad in Logroño yesterday and the Andaluz had to substitute for him in Linares." He ground out the cigarette on the sand under his boots.

"So you're fighting third."

"Yes, I'm fighting third." He yawned, a sure sign that you're scared. I

Belmonte.

started one but swallowed it before it was out. "What a rare name," he said, frowning at its rareness.

"At least there's no wind," I said professionally. I'd heard Belmonte say it.

"No," he said, "at least there's no wind to blow the capes."

I remember thinking throughout the whole day that it seemed as though everyone had read Hemingway and was trying to talk and act like it.

Belmonte got on his chesty horse. We lined up in back of him on foot, Chávez and I in front and our cuadrillas—sword handler and banderilleros —in back of us. The crowd was getting impatient and stamping their feet. It was six-thirty.

Belmonte swung around in his saddle. I'll never forget the chillingly calm way he said, "I don't know any reason why we shouldn't start this thing."

I knew hundreds and would have been delighted to suggest a few, but his horse moved forward, and we all automatically started forward on the left foot. The band struck up with a clash of cymbals as we strode to the center of the ring, then wheeled and walked to the fence, bowing to the president as we did. We got behind the fence, and I looked over the crowd. It seemed that everyone was looking at me because I was American, and not at Belmonte, who was waiting for his bull in the center of the sunny ring. The look in their faces was a combination of amusement and commiseration and relief that it was I and not they down there. I saw Eduardo Miura and all my friends from Sevilla, and they waved and smiled. I nodded back to them and tried to look casual. They seemed so damnably safe up there.

There was a roll of ominous drums, and a trumpet split the warm air. Belmonte's bull ran in, black-and-white and bigger than we had been told. He fought it Portuguese style, on horseback, first, making the trained horse dodge the bull's charges skillfully while he placed banderillas, and then he got off to kill it on foot. He was magnificent. The president granted him the ears and tail of the animal, and the crowd gave him a tremendous ovation.

I saw all this through a haze, for drumming in my head was, "You're

The author
in front of the poster before the fight.

next, you're next, you're next!" But the crowd seemed in a receptive mood, and they weren't expecting much from an American. I made up my mind that I would either leave the ring with an ear or I wouldn't leave the ring. I had to be good—I couldn't let Belmonte down! These people had heard or read that I could fight, but they hadn't seen me and didn't quite believe that an American could fight at all.

Belmonte sent his horse outside the ring and climbed up into the stands. The trumpet blew for my bull, and the toril gate clanged open. Manolo and I stood behind a burladero, one of the shields in front of the fence, El Chico and Cascabel behind another as we waited silently for the bull to come out of the long, dark toril, or runway from the pens. I felt a little dizzy. It didn't come and it didn't come. Finally, Cascabel went over and cautiously flopped a cape in front of the passageway. Then he beat it for the fence as a black shape skidded out of the toril in a wave of dust. The bull hurtled around the ring jabbing and feinting with his horns and snorting, the dust from the corral blowing off its back.

"Line him up for me," I somehow said to Manolo. He took his cape and went out to run the bull up and down so that I could see which way he hooked; a bull has a right and a left like a boxer. After doubling him two or three times at a safe distance, Manolo got in trouble, the bull was almost on top of him, and he had to throw down the cape and duck inside the burladero.

"I can't see which horn he hooks with," I said.

"He hooks badly on both sides!" Manolo panted. "Don't go out there with the cape!"

When he saw me getting the magenta-and-yellow cape firm and right in my hands, he said, "All right, all right, but don't take him close and don't try verónicas! Face-fight him! For God's sake, no verónicas!"

Manolo didn't know that Belmonte had never really taught me "face-fighting," the only way to fight a bull that won't "pass." I'd always had good bulls and never had to learn.

Holding the cape for a verónica, I stepped out from behind the fence and called the bull:

"Huh-hah-ah-ah-ah, torito!" I called, and my voice sounded like someone else's. "Huh-hah!" It wheeled and charged for me, blowing out air as it did. It swooshed by, its horns much closer to my legs than I had intended, as I swung the capote just ahead of its nose. It came by again, this time even closer. It had obviously been fought before, and I couldn't control it because it went at my body instead of the big cape. It kept crowding me, making me back up. The third time it charged, it hooked to the right and slammed me up against the barrera with its shoulder.

189

I heard Manolo call, "Get the hell out of there!"

I was shaken up, but I changed the grip on the cape and called the bull again, stepping away from the fence. This time it came with its head high. The side of the left horn struck my chest a glancing blow and the right horn caught in the capote and yanked it out of my hands. I was disarmed. I wanted out! I fled for a burladero and ducked behind.

The crowd was laughing. They were holding their sides. This is what they expected of an Americano who was trying to invade a strictly Spanish art. They weren't laughing cruelly; they liked the fact that I had tried, and they were glad that I hadn't been killed—but then again they were glad that I had been knocked around. It was very funny to see me get knocked around, as long as I didn't get killed.

"Sabe latín," said Manolo, coming over, shaking his head. They say a bull that's been fought before is so smart that he knows Latin. Bulls are supposed to be simon-pure when they come from the range, but sometimes ambitious kids have sneaked out on moonlight nights to practice on them with capes.

The trumpet had blown for the banderillas, and Cascabel had to go out to try to put in the barbed sticks. He ran at an angle toward the bull, holding the banderillas high. The bull knew enough to lead Cascabel by several feet. The banderillero ran sideways frantically like a crab and managed to miss the horns, but he also missed putting in the banderillas and looked ridiculous.

"For God's sake," I yelled to Manolo, "go out there and show that tío how to put in a pair!"

Manolo went out. By sneaking up on the bull from behind, he managed to put in the banderillas with great difficulty, getting his pants ripped as he spun away. The crowd was still laughing as the trumpet sounded for the third and last part of the fight. Chico handed me the muleta and the wooden sword. A wooden sword is used to spread the small cape until time to kill because of the strain of holding the heavy steel estoque.

"Let the burros laugh," Manolo growled. "The animal was impossible with the cape and sticks, but with the muleta, I swear you can dominate him."

Belmonte.

"I don't know," I said.

I found Belmonte in the crowd; I went through the ceremony of extending my hand with the hat and dedicating the bull. "Thank you, Don Juan, for not having hidden," I started, and the crowd laughed—with me this time. "For you, master of the great masters, who has taught me what little I know, I am going to kill this bull, this difficult, cross-eyed bull." I flung my hat up and he leaned forward to catch it. He looked worried, and that made me even more worried.

The bull was against the wall in his querencia, that arbitrary, unpredictable part of the ring where he decides to stay because there he instinctively feels more secure. Under no circumstances did I want to take him on in there, as a bull fights a defensive and more dangerous battle in his querencia. I told Manolo to get him out and into another part of the ring. He went in as close as he dared and cautiously flopped the cape at him several times. "Get in closer!" I shouted.

"You get in closer, he's yours!" he answered without turning his head. But he got in closer and swirled the cape out on the dust in front of the bull again. The animal pawed the ground and shook his horns, but he wouldn't get out of the five-foot circle.

About this time I got mad, mad at the bull for being so rotten, mad at the crowd for not seeing that it was rotten, mad at the ganadero for raising such a rotten bull, mad at myself for being so rotten with the cape, and mad at Manolo for not being able to get the bull out.

"Hide yourself!" I shouted. When Manolo left the ring, I stepped out quickly from behind the fence in back of the bull. I took the sword and smacked him hard across the caboose with the flat of it. The bull whirled around, his tail went up, and he shot toward me. I waited with my back pressed up against the fence, offering him the heart-shaped rag, spreading it wide with the sword, shaking it, and praying to God that he take it and not my legs, for there was no way out for me if he didn't. Swoooosh, he went by, his head in the muleta. The crowd froze. The bull wheeled, came at me again, and setting my teeth, I made myself hold my ground as he hurtled by, the horns about five inches away from my legs.

"Olé!" screamed the crowd as I made two more closer passes without

moving, and now that I think of it, it was a very sweet sound, but then I was too busy with the bull and too scared to hear. I wanted to get away from the fence, so I worried the animal out across the ring, away from his querencia, with choppy, punishing passes. Once in the middle, I gave him every pass I could think of. I think I even made up one. On the most difficult, the afarolado, he tore my sleeve off and raked down my arm. It didn't hurt, but it made me mad, and on the next pass I took the wooden sword out of the muleta and broke it across his stern as he went by. This left me with just the limp rag and nothing to spread it with, so four times I had to pass him with the dangerous natural and pase de pecho passes. Finally, I walked away from the bull and Manolo ran out into the ring with the real sword.

"Kill him!" said Manolo.

I lined up the bull with its front legs together, so that the shoulder blades would open, as Belmonte had taught me to do. I sighted down the blade, shook the muleta to make him charge, and ran at him as he ran at me. But the bull had moved its leg position at the last moment and closed the small opening. The sword hit bone and flew out. I lined him up again. I had to do it this time. As the bull charged, I flung myself over the right horn on top of the animal, and the sword sank into him up to the hilt. The bull sagged, reeled, headed for the fence drunkenly, and then flopped over dead.

A roar went up from the crowd, and Manolo ran out and threw his arms around my shoulders jubilantly. I staggered over to the fence, and Belmonte tossed my hat down from the stands.

"Bastante bien," he said quietly. "Not bad, Bernabé."

The president signaled with his handkerchief that I was to be granted both ears. They dragged the bull out of the ring with the mules, and the crowd kept applauding and yelling for me to take a lap around the ring while they threw hats and cigars down to me. It was the happiest moment of my life. I started around shakily, the notched ears in my hands and Manolo in back of me throwing the hats back to the owners and keeping the cigars. But suddenly a trumpet blew, the toril opened, and we had to beat it for the fence as Chávez' bull skidded out into the pale sun, blinking its eyes and looking for something to kill.

Belmonte.

Sevilla

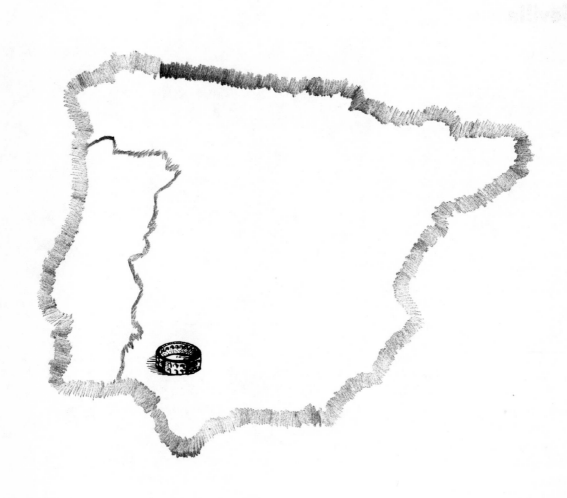

14. Sevilla

BULLFIGHTERS RATE THE TOP PLAZAS THIS WAY: MEXICO CITY THE BIGGEST from a standpoint of seating capacity, Madrid the most important for helping or ruining a career, and Sevilla the toughest. Not tough the way Zaragoza is tough. For some reason Zaragoza is considered by toreros to have the most demanding, most vociferous, and most unknowing bullfighting fans in the world. ("Sure, I'd go back," Arruza wrote after his one performance there in 1945, "for five million pesetas cash.")

Sevilla is tough because it is the most knowledgeable bullfighting audience in the world. Called the "cradle of bullfighting," it is in the heart of the bull ranch country, and it has been estimated that at least 80 per cent of the town's males have tried a cape pass on a charging bovine at some time in their lives; maybe just at a tienta at the neighboring ranches of Miura, Antonio Urquijo, or Concha y Sierra; or at a festival out at Joselito's old estate "Pino Montano"; or maybe at the annual Feria after a bottle or two of *manzanilla* at the caseta "Esta Es" where they have a miniature ring equipped with several heifers who have been caped so much they "know Latin." But at least the fans understand from first-hand experience the problem of luring a wild beast past one's body using only a hunk of cloth; and many even know the supreme thrill that comes from solving that problem with grace and dignity.

Physically and emotionally and historically, the town itself is a perfect setting for such "afición." This is picture-postcard Spain, the way one imagines all Spain to be before going to that country. *"El que no ha visto Sevilla, no ha visto maravilla":* He who hasn't seen Sevilla has missed a marvel.

195

Havelock Ellis has described the taurine atmosphere of Sevilla well in his *The Soul of Spain*. Though written in 1907, this lively description of Sevilla at fair time could be about the fair of April, 1957:

On the Saturday before Easter Sunday the ceremonies of Holy Week may be said to come to an end, not without a feeling of relief on the part of the visitor. At 10 o'clock on that morning the veil of the temple is rent in twain, in other words, the vast purple curtain which has been hanging in front of the high altar almost from the vaulting is swiftly drawn away; the signal is thus given for the bells all over the city to ring out joyously, while the people shout, guns are fired, and vehicular traffic, suspended during Holy Week, is resumed. On Sunday morning the women, who have all been dressed in black, with black mantillas, now appear in white lace mantillas and costumes predominantly white. In the afternoon a considerable section of the population, including some of its most characteristically Sevillan elements (also, it must be added, a large proportion of the British and American visitors, for it is only here their presence becomes obtrusive), are finding their way to the Plaza de Toros to witness the first bull-fight of the year. It may seem a long way from the cathedral to the bull-ring. In Seville one feels that it is not so. The Giralda, the cathedral tower, is the one outside object that we see towering above the walls into the cloudless sky as we sit in the ring, and it introduces no clash of discord. When the toreadors enter—grave, lithe, handsome men, in their varied and beautiful costume—and walk with hieratic grace and dignity of carriage to salute the president in his box, we feel at once that we are still in presence of the same spirit—in a slightly different form—which has dominated the proceedings of the whole week. One recognizes afresh that fundamental harmony in apparent opposites, which, though part of the Spanish temperament generally, may be said to reach its finest and deepest embodiment in the atmosphere of Seville. Gorgeous ceremony, elaborate ritual, solemnly accepted, we are just as much in the presence of here, as when we witnessed the Archbishop consecrating the holy oil or washing the feet of the thirteen old men. The whole process by which the death of the bull is compassed is nothing but an elaborate ritual, the detail of which the stranger is altogether unable to appreciate. In the church the ceremonies of every divine office gain their solemnity by association with the highest conceptions of the Christian faith; in the Plaza the sense of solemnity is gained by the possible imminence of death. But in both cases, ceremony, and a poignantly emotional background, furnish the deepest element of fas-

196

cination. The bull-fight is Spanish, and appeals to Spaniards, quite as much because it is a sacred ritual as because it is a sport.

As a sport many hard things have been said about it, and not without justice. In Spain itself only a section of the public cares for bull-fights; very many Spaniards of all classes do not go, and do not like it; the party of religion and the party of progress are equally opposed to it. Certainly it is the national sport of Spain, just as horse-racing and betting constitute the national sport of England; in both cases alike we must not identify the whole nation with the national sport. Apart from its repulsive elements—which are as objectionable to many Spaniards as to the stranger—the bull-fight is a fascinating exhibition of skill, and since the contest with the bull is very rapid, and the animal's death swift and certain, it must be said that if sport is to be defended at all, this kind of sport compares favourably with fox-hunting or pheasant-shooting. The element of risk also, the fact that the would-be slayer may himself be slain, adds an element of dignity which is wanting in nearly every other form of European sport. At the same time the bull-fight, reminiscent as it is of the feelings and habits of Roman times (though it is not actually a direct Roman survival),* is an anachronism under the conditions of modern civilisation. The continued vitality of such a spectacle, though rooted in the national temperament on more than one side, witnesses to the defects of the fine qualities of the Spanish character, to a certain hardness of fibre, a certain cruelty, if indifference to what is regarded as necessary pain, in oneself as well as in others, can properly be called cruelty.

In the middle of April the climax of the spring festival in Seville is reached during the Feria. Thousands arrive from Madrid and other parts of Spain to take part in or to witness this great picnic, and those who come late have to sleep where they can, on dining-tables or in corridors, for all rooms have been engaged. The Feria lasts three days, but for many weeks beforehand preparations have been going on in the Prado de San Sebastián, an open space just outside the city, close to its finest parks and promenades, and appropriately named after a tortured martyr, for this was once the Quemadero, where the Inquisition burnt heretics. Here are erected rows of wooden buildings, casetas or little houses, consisting mainly of one room—usually furnished chiefly with chairs, a piano, and flowers—entirely open to view on the

* The bull-fight was established in the eleventh or twelfth century, and has been traced to Moorish influence. "The bulls may have come from Africa," Ulick Burke observes, "the cavaliers may have had their origin in Damascus; but the savage solemnity, the orderly excitement, the whole form and feeling of the modern spectacle, are the heritage of Imperial Rome."

front side. Hither during the afternoon the people of Seville drive out in their carriages, each family proceeding to its own caseta. As evening comes on the sound of castanets and guitars begins to be heard in all directions, and ladies and children in nearly every caseta are seen dancing the gracious Sevillan *seguidilla,* while the paths are crowded with onlookers. This is the centre of the Feria, and hither the people flock; the broad avenues radiating in various directions—each softly lit up by its thousands of Chinese lanterns, a different scheme of colour prevailing in each avenue, and fragrant with the blossoming orange trees—are almost deserted, though delightful as a scene from the Arabian Nights.

Towards midnight the lights have begun to fail, and the Sevillians are quietly returning home. One hastens to walk away in the silence, under the wonderful southern sky, lest one should spoil the perfect sensation of this scene of gracious and sustained *alegría,* that quality which gives, sometimes a little proudly and self-consciously, so fine a distinction to the Sevillian. Yet as one recalls the impressions of Holy Week, of the whole of this spring festival, one feels that there has really been no break. The fair, like the bull-fight, has been no orgy in which the Sevillian seeks to drown and compensate the penances of Lent. "There is something traditional and sacred about these Sevillian holidays," a Spaniard casually remarks. "Something sacred"—even these domestic spring outings have not taken us beyond the region of ceremonial; even here we are in presence of an ostentatious though easy ritual; a holiday is here really a holy day. We are far away from those northern lands, whether Britain or Russia, where excesses of strenuous effort are followed by excesses of relaxing orgy. On Sundays and great moral occasions we people of northern race exhibit a tense and rigid virtue, like Sir Walter Scott's heroes, draw ourselves up to our full height, and then, in the blessed consciousness of that painful effort, we feel free to collapse in a heap. Here people neither hold themselves stiffly at full moral height nor awkwardly collapse. During Holy Week, in the Church ceremonies, one might note the vestmented dignitaries talking and smiling even beneath the Archbishop's eyes; and once, at a side altar, a kneeling young woman, whom I had supposed lost in devotion, slowly lifted and critically examined the lace border of the white altar-cloth; it was typical of the Spaniard's easy familiarity with divine things. But, on the other hand, at the Feria it was impossible to detect the faintest sign of drunkenness or the slightest impulse to rowdiness or indecorum; strenuous tension may be absent from the Sevillian temperament, but so also is any instinct or habit

198

of vulgarity. It would be fruitless to discuss which of these two methods of facing the problems of life is the more worthy of admiration. We may at least be thankful that, whatever men may elsewhere do or leave undone, this "something traditional and sacred" is still preserved in Seville.

Havelock Ellis does not talk about the Maestranza in his book, which is too bad since this is the most beautiful plaza de toros in the world. Built in 1761, it is second only to the plaza of Ronda from the standpoint of antiquity. It is stately and graceful; it has glistening yellow sand, like no other plaza in the world, which is made from crushed rock from the Huelva mining district; and it hasn't yet succumbed to "Tome Anís del Mono" or "Coca Cola—la pausa que refresca" advertisements around its perimeter.

The Maestranza has seen the greatest stars in history, for Sevilla has produced many more great toreros than any other region. Costillares, Pepe-Illo, Cúchares, El Espartero, Bombita, the Gallos, Chicuelo, Cagancho, Gitanillo de Triana, and Pepe Luis Vázquez, just to name a very few. But the greatest of all, as far as the evolution of modern bullfighting is concerned, was Juan Belmonte. Belmonte's story is bullfighting. Belmonte is Sevilla. Belmonte is more of a "maravilla" than Sevilla. As Leslie Charteris writes in his introduction to *Juan Belmonte, Killer of Bulls:* "If, without ever having heard of Belmonte, you were told that a man who was practically a cripple, who was certainly a physical wreck, could become the greatest bullfighter in the world, would you not say that if he did it he would be performing a miracle?"

The Maestranza saw him for the first time in 1910. He was a frail, ugly little youth of eighteen, but hidden beneath the cheap patched costume several sizes too large for him was a heart of amazing courage and the determination to become the world's greatest bullfighter.

The crowd laughed at his clownlike appearance, but their laughs soon turned to boos. Not only was he a ridiculous figure, but he was clumsy and could not handle the bulls. He took a dozen inept sword thrusts to hack down his first animal. He was utterly incapable of killing the second.

Pillows, bottles, and jeers rained down on the unhappy novillero. It seemed obvious to him that he would not only never appear again in the Sevilla ring, but that he probably would never be allowed to fight anywhere.

Tears flooded his eyes. He threw down his sword and cape and dropped on his knees before the animal.

"Kill me," he sobbed. "Kill me, bull, kill me!"

But the bull withheld even that honor and left the wretched boy to the howling mob.

199

The Face of Spain,
a portrait of Don Juan Belmonte.

Twenty-five years and 1650 bulls later, he entered the ring at Sevilla its most honored hero. The entire audience rose and cheered when he strode into the arena. As he marched around the ring the applause swelled, for this was to be his farewell appearance. In the intervening years he had revolutionized the technique of bullfighting and had brought the ancient art to its golden age. He had become the most famous living Spaniard, the idol of South America, Mexico, and the Iberian Peninsula. He was Don Juan Belmonte, "The Earthquake from Triana."

He was rich, famous, the owner of a huge estate, happily married, the father of three children. He had all he'd dreamed of and more. But according to a Spanish aphorism, God says, "Take what you want—if you pay for it." And Belmonte had paid for everything he had—paid with bull's blood and his own blood and with his best friend's life.

When I first knew him, he was a mass of scars, and there were still more to come. He had white scars up and down both legs, scars on his hips, and his chest looked as though someone had played ticktacktoe there with a soldering iron. The one on his neck, where a horn had torn through his jaw up to his nose, taking four teeth with it, caused a horrified British journalist to write an article entitled *The Corpse Which Fights!*

I asked him recently how many times he'd been gored. He didn't know, probably over fifty, including "three times where a man least appreciates it."

What makes a man take this kind of punishment? What makes a man take fifteen inches of horn into his body, spend two months in the hospital, and then limp out to take on another bull with the clammy feeling of the doctor's rubber gloves still on his flesh?

Belmonte isn't loquacious, but when he talks in his deep Andalusian accent with the occasional stutter it's worth listening to. He is intelligent, penetrating, and witty. During the years I studied under him a lot of the story came out.

He was born in 1892, the eldest of eleven children, and was brought up in the filth and hopelessness of Triana, the poorest slum section of Sevilla. His father was a drunken loafer, and Belmonte disliked him energetically. He went to school from the time he was four till he was eight, and that was the end of his formal education. He soon slipped into a gang that roamed the narrow streets, stealing, destroying, and generally getting into trouble.

"I was a thief," he answers pleasantly when anyone asks him what he did before he became a matador.

These hoodlums' heroes were bullfighters; they would constantly take their jackets and practice passes, caping each other, carriages, cyclists, and even dogs and cats. One day, when he was sixteen, Belmonte announced

The Maestranza, the most beautiful *plaza de toros* in the world.

that he was going to be a professional torero. He was hooted at, and with reason, for he was little and sickly and bandy-legged and ugly.

But inside the spindly frame, this little mushroom of a boy had a passion of *having* to be great, of *having* to get somewhere. It was not in spite of his physical shortcomings that he became the world's greatest bullfighter —it was because of them.

Though no one in his family had ever been a bullfighter and he'd never had enough money to see a bullfight, the fever of the bulls gradually came over him. It was mainly because he was so small and weak and because the gangs of tough kids held the toreros in such esteem. And also because it was the only way a poor boy could pull himself to the top in feudal Spain.

Soon Belmonte was going around telling people that he was already a matador. They laughed at him, but secretly he felt he truly was a torero because he had made up his mind to be one. He would swagger around town with his ragged jacket over his left shoulder like a dress cape. He was an avid reader and had a great imagination. It was not too hard for him to imagine that he was the pride of all Spain, with a fine house, wealth, women, and fame.

However, it was hard to reconcile these dreams with the fact that he had no talent for making money, could not keep a job, and had to go through the agony of watching his younger brothers and sisters taken off one by one to the poorhouse. He had decided to become a great bullfighter. But every other poor boy in Spain makes the same decision, and few come closer to realizing the ambition than a red-hot verónica executed with a gunny sack at a passing carriage.

Belmonte, though, was the best of the guttersnipes at the caping business. The others had to admit that this feeble *renacuajo* had an enviable style—different, certainly, and somehow very exciting.

One day a group of them were practicing in a sand lot. A well-dressed, dignified man stopped to watch. Belmonte did a series of verónicas against a companion charging fiercely with a pair of slaughterhouse horns held in front of him. As Belmonte finished, the man called "olé" and threw the youth five pesetas, predicting solemnly, "You'll be a great matador someday."

Belmonte says in the Charteris-Nogales book that he's often wished he knew the name of that unknown caballero who gave him his first bullfighting money and did so much for his ego.

Becoming a bullfighter is an extremely difficult business. It takes years of learning, and there were no schools available for the penniless Belmonte. It is much harder than getting a start as a boxer in this country. You can't just pick a fight, the way an incipient boxer might if he felt like a little

Above: Belmonte defying the bull to kill him.

Below: Belmonte in *traje corto*.

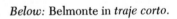

Above: The verónica
as performed
by Belmonte
in festival, or
traje corto, costume.

Below: Belmonte takes
a *vuelta.*

practice. For bullfighting you need bulls. Not just any bulls, but fighting bulls. A fighting bull costs around a thousand dollars, and that's a duke's ransom in Spain. A bull can't be borrowed to learn on, either, for it is against the law to send a bull that has fought before into the ring; bulls learn too much too quickly. They must enter the arena never having encountered a dismounted man, except once, briefly, at their trial for bravery as calves. So how was this wretched pollywog going to obtain the heights he'd set his sights on?

Fortunately, there was a roadside tavern near Sevilla that had a corral in the back, and in it a three-year-old fighting bull, discarded as unfit by some breeder. The innkeeper rented the animal to aspirant toreros at five pesetas a session. This was an astronomical figure to Belmonte and his gang, but as one pointed out with frightening logic, "If we are going to be bullfighters we should test ourselves out with bulls."

They scraped together the necessary amount, but when they arrived at the inn and actually saw the wicked-looking beast pawing the sand, they all backed out—except Belmonte. Here at last was a real bull to test his dreams against!

He leaped into the corral, ran out to the center, and knelt down, holding his jacket in front of him. He was starting with the dangerous, one-handed larga cambiada pass that has put so many professional matadors in the hospital. His heart was pounding in his chest, and he wanted to get off his knees and run as he saw the animal shake its head viciously and start toward him hard and fast. But he made himself stick it out.

When the bull was four feet away, Juan swung the cloth over his left shoulder. The bull veered after it, and the black mass rushed by his body, the horn a few inches from his head. Astounded and jubilant, he ran after the animal and gave it a verónica pass. Then another and another, while his companions cheered.

"It was an unforgettable revelation," he writes in his autobiography. "So one could really do with a bull the same things that one did with chairs and dogs and cyclists!"

Belmonte was fired with ambition now, confident that he could make his dreams come true if only he could get more practice. But he certainly could not pay five pesetas every day, and besides, this bull would soon "know Latin."

However his reputation had grown a bit because of what he had done in the corral, and he was admitted to a gang of older and more experienced aspirants who had a fine racket. On moonlight nights the six boys would swim the wide Guadalquivir River, or "borrow" a fisherman's boat, and make their way to the corrals on the ranches where the bulls for the regular big fights were kept. They would separate a small animal from the herd, corner it to start it charging, and then take turns "passing it." They took turns in order of experience and proficiency, and young Juan was the last in line for many expeditions.

But one night the largest bull in the herd suddenly separated itself from the others and attacked the group. All of them fled unashamedly to the safety of the corral walls. The giant animal stood triumphantly in the center of the enclosure shaking its horns and snorting defiantly at the boys.

Suddenly Juan grabbed the jacket out of one of the boys' hands, and ran in shouting belligerently, "Toro, ahaaaa, toro!" The bull's tail went up, and the head came down. It charged, hard. Belmonte held his ground, lured the animal into the folds of the jacket, and passed it perfectly. Again he made it charge. Back and forth, five times he received it. The barrel of the bull brushed against the boy each time. Then he gathered the folds up sharply on his right hip and by wrenching the animal around in less than its own length, he stopped it cold. He turned his back on the bull and strode away, his big jaw out triumphantly.

"The ovation I was giving myself almost deafened me," he says.

From that night on he never fought last again, but always right after Rivirito, the oldest and most experienced boy. One night Rivirito made a mistake and paid for it by getting knocked out and wounded. The other boys picked him up and started back toward the river, all naked as jays since they had left their clothes on the other bank. All of a sudden, in a patch of moonlight, they were confronted by a huge wild cow.* It let out a bellow and started to charge. Though their first thought was to drop their injured friend and run for it, they froze, knowing that a bull or cow won't charge at an object it believes to be inanimate.

"It was marvelous," Belmonte writes in his autobiography, *Juan Belmonte, Killer of Bulls*. "Everyone stood still, as if frozen into marble, in the position in which the warning had caught him. Naked, immobile, crushed together and holding up the inanimate body of our friend, we must have formed a most curious bit of sculpture. Fear gave us an amazing rigidity. One of us was caught with his arm raised, and thus he stayed, absolutely motionless as if he had been cast in bronze."

After an eternity the animal finally decided not to waste a charge on the curious object and went on its way.

The months were flying by; Belmonte's family was getting poorer and hungrier, and he was no closer to fame and fortune. Finally when he was

* In his "autobiography" it is referred to as a "big full-grown bull." Belmonte told me, "They changed her sex to make her more fierce—but they didn't need to, she was terrifying enough as she was."

eighteen a banderillero who knew his father arranged for him to substitute at the last minute for another bullfighter in a whistle-stop town in Portugal. He was to fight under the other bullfighter's name, buy his railway ticket, provide his own costume, pay his own banderilleros, and receive no money for his performance.

But Juan jumped at the chance. He rented a disreputable costume that was made for a man twice his size, which he had to mend and paint with ink where the silk was worn off.

He looked ridiculous in a hat three sizes too big for him, and the crowd received him skeptically when he entered the ring, but when they saw how close he worked to the bull's horns, how gracefully and slowly he swung the cape in front of the bull's nose, they hushed, and soon they were cheering.

However, his triumph in a small town under another name did nothing for his economic status, and hunger soon started him working as a day laborer dredging the river. But he pestered anyone and everyone connected with bullrings to give him a chance. Finally, more to get rid of him than anything, a promoter gave him a place on the program in a small bullring near Sevilla. He was to kill two young novillos.

That day the closeness of his capework thrilled the audience, though the unorthodox style bewildered them. Elbows close to the body, hands low, standing straight while working almost on top of the bull—here was the first inkling of the style that was soon to revolutionize a spectacle that was many centuries old. With the muleta, his passes were just as distinctive and his style more suicidal. It was a do-or-die performance. One pass took the bull so close that the right horn caught him in the forehead, leaving a long strip of bloody flesh hanging down over his eye. Swearing with rage, he lined up the bull, sighted down the sword blade through a screen of blood, and flung himself on top of the animal. When he wiped his eyes, he saw that the sword had gone into the correct spot between the withers and the bull was dead.

The crowd was roaring its approval of a fine performance and an honest kill, and it was the happiest moment of Belmonte's life. So it could be easy to kill a bull!

After he came back from the infirmary, he took on the second animal and did the same astounding capework. But when it came time to kill, he found that he'd had extraordinary luck the first time. Again and again he tried to kill the bull while the crowd booed. "Although it's true that there did come a time when it died," he says, "I believe it was more from boredom with me and my ineptness than from any lethal action of the sword."

But the day wasn't a complete fiasco by any means. Word of the boy's courage began to travel. He fought again in another little town, put on a great show, but was badly gored. When he'd half-recovered he was signed for a fight in the great Maestranza arena of Sevilla, the Madison Square Garden of bullfighting. After expenses, he would have four pesetas left—but to fight in the historic Maestranza! It was where every young bullfighter must prove himself, and here was his great chance.

He went into the ring ill and weak, from both hunger and the recent wound. He could do nothing with the huge and cowardly animals, and after a wretched exhibition with his first bull, he put up an even worse performance on the second. The exhausted boy was unable to kill, partly because the bull was so huge he couldn't see the place between the shoulders where the sword had to go. Every time he ran at the bull he was tossed. He would drag himself off the ground reluctantly ("How beautiful it was to lie there") and go back for another try and another toss. Over twenty times he was thrown into the air, until finally the third trumpet blew and the steers, with their bells clanking lugubriously, lumbered in to take the bull out. It was then that he gave up and begged the bull to kill him.

That one fight exiled him from all rings in and around Sevilla. He was in disgrace with his family and his friends and himself. He crawled back to day-laboring and tried to put bullfighting out of his mind. However, the next spring brought on the bull fever again. But where could he get a fight?

Then one day another last-minute substitute proposition came up, in the important ring at Valencia, when a matador refused to fight the bulls that had been selected.

They were monsters, so wicked looking that no one would rent Belmonte a costume for fear it would come back bloody and in shreds. He finally had to get one from a theatrical company. It was a frilly, tasseled mess, made originally for a hefty diva, and again the crowd had a laugh when Belmonte entered the arena. But he went in there resolved to make his name or die in the attempt.

He came very close to doing the latter, for the second bull gored him. He was carried unconscious to the infirmary, but not before he had showed the Valencians some of the damnedest bullfighting they'd ever seen.

Belmonte was in the hospital for a month. When he came out he found he was something of a hero. He secured several more fights and was as big a success. But he wanted to fight in Sevilla again. He begged his manager to get him a fight there so that he could redeem himself. But Sevilla wanted no more of this clown who had so thoroughly botched up his first attempt. The only way he managed to wangle it was by agreeing to fight free and as third matador with two young stars heading the bill to take the curse off the name of Belmonte.

Belmonte standing before his portrait
by Zuloaga.

The fight started off badly. On the first charge, the bull's sharp horns ripped the cape from Juan's hands. He hastily picked up the cloth and made another attempt, losing his cape again. The third time he was disarmed, the cape stayed hung on the horns until one of the other matadors very gracefully and calmly plucked it off and handed it to Belmonte with an insulting bow.

The crowd was laughing as Belmonte snatched the cape and went at the bull with tears of rage in his eyes. He planted his feet. He put them down on the sand as though they were screwed there. He was incapable of stepping back out of the horn's way. Then he gave the bull the five greatest verónicas he'd ever done in his life, ending with a half-verónica that was so close the horn ripped off one side of his jacket.

The crowd was too amazed to cheer on the first passes, but soon it began to stamp and scream, and it didn't stop for the rest of the time he was out there. Then and there began the revolution of bullfighting, for Belmonte was doing things that afternoon that even he had never dreamed could be done. He was even greater on his second bull. Drunk with emotion, caught up by the delirium of the crowd, shouting unconsciously with them at every magnificent pass he made, he was fighting for the sheer love of it, fighting the way he felt it, not knowingly thinking of style.

He kept working closer and closer to the animal until to get closer meant to be on the horns, and suddenly that's where he was—up in the air with five inches of horn spiked like an ice pick into his thigh, and then he was flung to the ground. He hauled himself to his feet, grabbed the sword, and lurched forward to sink it into the bull. It fell dead at his feet, and the crowd spilled down into the ring to hoist the groggy and bleeding matador to their shoulders and parade him out of the plaza and down the street, screaming in unison, "Viva Belmonte!"

This was a cry that was soon scrawled on Sevilla's walls and sidewalks, and then Barcelona's and Toledo's and Málaga's, for that fight was no fluke. He could do these amazing things every day and somehow manage not to be killed. His favorite climax was to crouch or kneel inches in front of the bull's nose, his great barracuda jaw out challengingly, his puny body insultingly exposed. Belmonte's sheer brute courage seemed to defeat the animals, but the experts said it was just a question of time.

After his debut in Madrid, the usually conservative critic Don Modesto wrote: "I swear by my honor as a Castilian *hidalgo* that there never has been a performance with the muleta as enormous, as formidable as yesterday. It was simply the greatest 'faena' since the beginning of bullfighting."

Another critic wrote: "His Majesty should erect a national monument to Belmonte."

With each new fight Belmonte seemed to do more extraordinary things, and the public was paying delightedly; for the last eight fights before becoming a full matador he received $9700, the largest sum that ever had been paid a novillero. He had suddenly become the hero of all Spain.

"Cervantes, Goya, Belmonte," declared Valdomar, the Peruvian philosopher. "You, Don Juan, stand for Spain in this age."

His face began to be reproduced everywhere.

"To each one of them I was part of himself," explains Belmonte in his autobiography. "Those who hoped to make a success of life looked at me as a mirror . . . of their own future success; those who were fighting a losing struggle for existence remembered that I had been even more handicapped and had overcome my handicaps, those who were conscious of being ugly and unshapely consoled themselves with the thought that I was ugly and unshapely too. They looked at me and saw me so weak, so insignificant, so different from what one would expect a conquering hero to be, that their own weaknesses seemed much less of an obstacle to triumph."

But while Belmonte's skill increased, he became physically weaker, paler, and more humped. The public gave him a nickname that they callously considered endearing: "Rigoletto." Yet this hunchbacked man would somehow manage to drag himself to the bullring, and once there he found some inner spiritual reserve that would enable him to perform his miracles. During the bull season he would force himself to fight several times a week, and in one period of 180 days he racked up the incredible record of 109 corridas. It still stands unbeaten, even though modern matadors have the benefits of planes and fast cars to take them from arena to arena.

Then there were the exhausting trips to Mexico and Peru, where he triumphed as no fighter ever had. On one of his trips to Lima he met Julia Cossío, the attractive daughter of a prominent family, and brought her back to Spain with him as his wife.

He had everything now. Belmonte, an intelligent, amusing person, had somehow managed to crowd a lot of self-education into his hectic life, and he had many cultured and talented friends. He had money, lots of it. He had a handsome wife, and soon two daughters. While still living, he knew he would be immortal.

"To die," a writer friend once remarked, "all you have left to do, Juanito, is to die gloriously in the bullring."

"I'll do my best, Don Ramón," Belmonte countered.

And that's what it looked as though he were trying to do, for instead of his ardor cooling under success and domesticity, it seemed he had never fought so suicidally. He couldn't last long at that rate, they said.

"A cool-headed scientist like Joselito can fight on forever," wrote a Madrid

212

critic. "But mark my words, Belmonte is doomed, if not this season, the next."

But, of course, it wasn't Belmonte who was killed; it was the invincible Joselito.

Belmonte was home resting after an injury. When they telephoned to tell him there was a rumor that his best friend had been killed, he laughed and said "Impossible" and hung up. Then he learned the truth. He writes in his book: "I was held speechless by terrible anguish. I looked around me, and I was afraid. Of what? I don't know. When my throat could no longer contain the flood of grief . . . I broke into sobs and wept as I had never wept before in my life. . . . I think I felt a little of my own death that day; and this egotistical reflection was what gave me the strength to pull myself together."

Two days later, in the Madrid ring, he put up the greatest show of daring in his entire career.

But not long afterward he quit the game. He said it was for good. His enthusiasm for la fiesta brava was gone.

Then one night in Sevilla, two years later, he felt the old passion return. He sneaked out to the ranches with some young hoodlums, and there in the moonlight he caped a big novillo to a standstill and felt the same thrill as when he was a kid. He returned to the ring the next week, and the critics said he'd never been greater.

He re-retired six years later, but the same thing happened. He couldn't stay away. When I first met him in 1944 he was retired again, theoretically content to raise bulls on his huge ranch for the new fenómenos to fight. He was in the best health of his life, not a gray hair on his head, and active. He had his daughters, his wife, his grandchildren, and Juanito, an illegitimate son whom he had recognized legally in 1935.

When I first walked inside the large and tastefully decorated ranch house, I wouldn't have known it was the residence of a bullfighter except for the big painting by Zuloaga on the wall showing Belmonte, standing out in the arena, jaw jutting out, his sword in his hand bloody, and a leg wound staining one stocking. There was a copy of *Ferdinand the Bull*, which Don Juan loves, on the table, but after that I saw no more bull motifs.

Then one of the many servants opened the living room doors onto a patio that overlooked a small bullring. Here was where the fighting bulls were tested, and here was where I was to learn most of what I know about the game from Juanito and his father.

Don Juan took an interest in my love of tauromachy. Every week end I'd be out there caping the heifers, and Belmonte would call down from the balcony, "No, you're not standing right," or "Keep your hands lower!" But he was unable to resist showing how it should be done, and in a minute he'd be down in the arena working the animal over himself.

Though supposedly retired, he still was fighting ten or fifteen "festival" fights a year for charity. In these affairs the animals were theoretically smaller, but since Belmonte himself generally furnished his own animals, he made sure they were dangerous enough to make for a little excitement.

In 1945, I fought on the same program with him near Sevilla, and the bull he fought was immense. The next day the headlines of the bull section of the newspaper shouted: "WE HAVE SEEN WHAT IT IS TO FIGHT A BULL!"

The article went on to say: "Incredible as it seems, at the age of fifty-four Belmonte is fighting better than his son, better than young Manolete, better than anyone in the ring today."

A few months later, Don Juan was doing a benefit show in Barcelona. He had put up a fine performance of Portuguese-style fighting—that is, a man mounted on a specially trained horse outmaneuvers the bull while placing banderillas. He was going to finish off the bull from horseback, but the crowd protested, demanding a display of the old magic.

214

Juan Belmonte y García,
the author, and Juan Belmonte y Campoy.

Actually the bull was too big and treacherous to be fought on foot, but Belmonte always felt a debt to the crowd that had made him. He climbed off the horse and threw his riding jacket up to me in the first row of the stands. With the red muleta cape draped over the sword, he went out toward the animal chanting softly, "Ahaaaaa, toro bonito"—charge, pretty bull, charge.

For some reason the sight of that incredibly courageous little man dressed in a gray riding outfit hobbling out there to take on a creature whose shoulders were on a level with the top of his head made me want to bawl.

In a few minutes I was up on my feet screaming "Olé!" with the rest of the crowd. What he did that afternoon with that unmanageable animal was unbelievable. But what he did with himself, with his body, the way he became young again, was more so.

When the crowd was hoarse from cheering, and Belmonte knew that the exact moment had come to kill, that the bull was learning too much, he "squared" it up for the "moment of truth." But the crowd set up a clamor, wanting more.

215

He knew very well that the bull did not have another pass in it, that now, and right now, and only now, was the time to kill. But for one of the few times in his life, he listened to the crowd and let them sway his judgment. He glanced up at me, shrugged with a grim smile as though to say, "You can never give them enough."

He turned back to do another pass. On the first charge the bull hooked into the man's chest, hard. As the crowd that had done it to him screamed, the bull carried him, dangling helplessly from a horn, out into the center of the ring and slammed him down to the sand bloody and unconscious. I remember how he lay there on his back, straight and stiff, his arms rigid in the air in a grotesque embrace, the fingers hooked as though ready to claw at something—maybe at death.

No longer a god, he was just an injured old man; and the crowd was shocked and stunned and guilty as we rushed his inert form out of the ring.

He came to in the infirmary, and he was frightened. He kept murmuring, "This is it, now this is it, I know this is it, to think that this is it now!" He sent me running for his favorite religious medallion he'd left in his riding jacket, so that he could die with it on his lips.

But that wasn't "it." A month later he was up and around, vowing he would never fight again. And four months later he was in his private ring working over the two-year-olds. And six months later he was again listening to the roar of the crowd from down in the arena of the big Sevilla ring, the plaza where he has fought so many "farewell" fights.

"The truth of the matter is," Belmonte has confessed, "that I shall probably never retire. When I can't handle bulls, I shall take on calves, and after that I shall probably swing my cape on goats, and then, perhaps, once again bicycles—but I am a torero, and fight I must!"

And what of the son of this colossus? What of the man with the unenviable name of Juan Belmonte, Junior?

Juanito became a bullfighter—what else?—and reluctantly—how else? He was a shy and gentle boy with much the same face as his father, better looking but without the power, and hence not as good-looking. He didn't look like a bullfighter, but strangely enough he had talent. However, he didn't have the heart nor the tigerlike fight of his father. This isn't to say he wasn't brave, because he was, extremely brave, but with an abridged, forced, I've-got-to-be-brave type of courage—not his father's kill-me-bull-kill-me type of guts. Everything in the beginning was too easy for him. He didn't have to swim any rivers and fight his bulls by moonlight; he could go down in his father's private ring any time he wanted and tell the vaqueros to bring in a good little animal for him to practice with. By the time he was

216

The son of Juan Belmonte
and the son of
Ignacio Sánchez Mejías in their first performance
together.

nineteen his technique was superb, but his craving to be great was not gnawing enough. True, he had the desire to establish his own identity instead of just going on being the son of Juan Belmonte, but apparently this isn't as powerful a goal as the craving to make oneself something out of nothing; by being born the son of Belmonte he was already something.

He took the alternative in Salamanca in 1938, and for the next five years he did well. If his name had been Juan Gómez he would have been considered a first-class matador, which he was. But the crowd could not forgive him for not being a genius. Spaniards add their mother's maiden names to their own—hence the father's full name was Juan Belmonte y García and the son's was Juan Belmonte y Campoy. Whenever Juanito would draw a bad bull or have an off day, there were always the wounding jeers of "Go home—you're not Belmonte, you're Campoy!"

Nevertheless he had his fine afternoons, and he held his own with great stars like Ortega, Manolete, and Pepe Luis Vázquez during the highly competitive years of 1941, 1942, and 1943. Aged twenty-nine in 1947, he retired to go into business, after killing some 750 bulls, most of them in a creditable and honorable fashion.

217

This business of the famous progenitor and the albatross it can hang around a neck has always interested and moved me. Even more than with Juanito Belmonte, I saw it crush Joselito's nephew. It happened with more dramatic focus than usually happens in life, and I wrote an account of it for *Holiday* titled "José and Joselito," a shorter version of which follows:

I first met the boy on the main street of Sevilla in 1945. He was with his uncle Rafael, "El Gallo," the famous old bald gypsy of whom Hemingway speaks so often in *Death in the Afternoon.* I had known El Gallo for a long time and he had always been the serene Elder Statesman, but today he seemed agitated as he took me by the arm.

"Bernabé, have you heard?" The little man was a trembling seventy, but he wore a rakish black sombrero tilted over one eye like a true flamenco. "The greatest—that's what he'll be!"

"Who?"

El Gallo jabbed his cigar at a young man standing a few feet away. "Joselito's namesake—José—my nephew. He's decided to fight! Finally!"

He led me over and introduced us.

"Honored," said the boy stiffly in a deep voice.

He was not good-looking like the photographs of his immortal uncle Joselito; in fact he was thick-lipped and almost ugly. But he had gentle gypsy eyes and an attractive shyness about him and a good toothy smile. He was only about seventeen, and I remember thinking that he had a perfect build for a matador and that perhaps his face could acquire the torero's disdainful steeliness in a few years. He had a big nose, and that seemed promising, since so many bullfighting greats have had powerful noses, like Belmonte and Manolete and Litri.

"I saw him in action yesterday, and I tell you, we're going to see a new era, a whole new era of bullfighting!"

"But I thought he hadn't fought yet," I said.

"Calves, man, practicing," said El Gallo. "I tell you, the grace, the control! He could"—he blew out a sigh at the enormity of what he was going to say—"he could be as good as my brother Joselito!"

I was impressed, for El Gallo was not given to rash statements.

"No!"

El Gallo closed his eyes and nodded twice. "As good!"

Young José shifted uneasily.

El Gallo opened his eyes and fixed them proudly on José. "Maybe even better," he said. He prodded his thumb into José's ribs. "Eh?" he said as he jabbed. "Eh? Maybe even better."

218

The boy drew one corner of his mouth up in the embarrassed, patronizing grimace that young men make around doting relatives.

"And when does this take place?" I asked, expecting him to say next year.

El Gallo automatically looked at his watch and then laughed at himself and said, "In thirty days. Next month we will see it. Everyone will see it."

They invited me to lunch, and we went to a little restaurant called Los Corales, on narrow Sierpes Street where the "pigtail folk" hang out. There's an old calendar painting of Joselito on the wall near the table at which we were put, and I remember that El Gallo made a charming little gesture when the waiter tried to seat him on the far side of the table.

"No," he said, moving over to the chair next to the wall, "here is where I belong—at the feet of my brother."

José drew a chair from another table and sat down next to him; every movement was like a dancer's—or a panther's.

Several men stopped by the table to say how wonderful it was that José was going to fight and how well they knew he would do. He took all this appreciatively but remained withdrawn and slightly uncomfortable. When they talked about bullfighting in general he listened politely, but I had the feeling he wasn't really very interested.

"I was studying the farming science," he told me hesitantly. "Crop rotations and . . ."

"Until he decided that bullfighting should be raised out of its decadence," El Gallo broke in.

"What made you decide?"

"Well . . ." José shrugged. He saw the café's cat and scooped it up.

"Love of it," said Rafael. "How could he have the same blood as Joselito and me and not love it?"

I remembered that Joselito had started fighting when he was a boy in knee pants.

"Why did you wait so long?"

José shrugged again and stroked the cat's white fur gently. "I guess some of us are automatically toreros and some are not."

"That's right!" Rafael declared enthusiastically, his arm around the boy. "And here is the most natural-born torero I have ever seen!"

I never did find out the motivation behind his decision. Maybe it was a girl he wanted to impress. Or maybe it was that all his life he had been referred to as "Joselito's nephew" and he was just bloody sick of it and wanted to become an entity himself. Or maybe he was goaded into it; after all, his family had always been connected with the bull-ring, and once, back in Joselito's time, thirteen members of his family fought in different rings on the same day.

I looked at José's taut face, and it was hard to guess what was going on behind those eyes that were fixed stonily on his uncle. He kept stroking that damned cat and I wished that he would put it down.

Someone proposed a toast and we drank to José, who lowered his head and scratched lines in the tablecloth with the tines of his fork.

Three weeks later I saw him practicing with calves at Juan Belmonte's ranch. I saw him only with one very small and easy heifer, but he looked magnificent. After a series of slow, sleek verónicas he did a media-verónica that I'll never forget, wrapping the cloth up on his right hip with an insouciance, grace, and old-fashioned elegance that I have never seen before or since. The heifer seemed hypnotized and only able to operate in slow motion as it twisted itself around his body after the folds of the cape.

Everyone looked impressed. Afterward, at the supper served in Belmonte's living room, there was an electric excitement at the thought of what we would witness next week in the big ring. Even the old maestro Belmonte said to me with his usual stammer and his great jaw stuck out, "There's t-t-talent here." Then he added casually, "But we shall see. The difference between a c-c-calf and a bull is a chasm."

People came from all over Spain for "el debut de Gallito." (Day-boot, they pronounce it.) They had already nicknamed him "Gallito," Little Rooster, which was one of Joselito's nicknames, and that's the way it read on the gaudy posters that screamed from every street corner: "Gallito Chico! La Nueva Sensación!"

Not that they needed posters to advertise the fight. Word of mouth and the newspapers had stimulated such interest that when I got to the Maestranza ring, two hours after the box office had opened, every ticket was gone and a huge crowd was mobbing the scalpers. But I was determined to see the fight after that tantalizing, exhilarating flash out at the ranch. I tracked El Gallo down in the Gallango café and touched him for a ticket. The little man looked very proud and very tense and younger than I had ever seen him. He said José was "calm and confident."

I didn't see José until the day of the fight. I was the American vice-consul in Sevilla, and the consular car was clearly the fanciest in Andalucía, so I offered it to José for the drive to the ring and back. I went to his house about two-thirty and already a crowd was there. All over town the people were taut with excitement.

220

It's hard to find anything in America comparable to the anticipation that was running through the city. Perhaps it would be somewhat the same if Jack Dempsey had a nephew named Jack Dempsey from Manassa who signed to meet the heavyweight champion in Madison Square Garden. But Joselito came much closer to deification to the Spaniards than Dempsey ever did to us.

I pushed through the crowd in front of the house and into the cool tiled interior and was silently ushered upstairs by one of the banderilleros. This was Joselito's house, and there were reminders of its former owner everywhere. A rather musty bull's head, with a plaque describing the details of its glorious encounter with the immortal matador, was mounted on the wall, and I remember being surprised by its smallness considering how enormous all the bulls he fought were said to have been. There were photographs of Joselito all the way up the stairs, pictures of him playing at bullfighting when he was three years old, others when he was a becerrista at the age of thirteen, when he took the alternativa and became a full matador at the age of seventeen, the youngest ever to receive the "doctorate." And there were action shots of his sensational style with the cape and banderillas and muleta. There was one of him currying his horse when he was thinking of retiring, and one of him standing chummily with Alfonso, king of Spain. And then there was one of his elaborate sculptured tomb in the Sevilla cemetery, with a dusty bow of black ribbon thumbtacked to the frame.

Over a dozen people, hushed and tense, were crowded in the blue-tiled room at the top of the stairs. I saw old El Gallo and Juan Belmonte and recognized the Marqués de Aracena and the Duque de Pinohermoso among the other prominent people gathered around José. He was standing in the middle of the room, wearing the gold-encrusted pants of a new "suit of lights," and he was slipping the red tie under the collar of the frilled shirt. He saw me come in the door and acknowledged my arrival with raised eyebrows and a polite dip of the head. Then his face went back to grimness, his thick lips drawn thin, his green gypsy eyes narrow with tension.

El Almendro, Joselito's favorite banderillero, who was with him at his death, waddled over to José with a folded red sash in his hand. "This was his, boy," he said huskily. "Wear it. Luck."

José reverently took the bit of cloth that had belonged to an uncle he had never known, and, as though it were a part of the True Cross, turned it over slowly in his hands. Then he held one end to his waist while El Gallo held the other. He spun twice, and the sash was wrapped tight around him, a talisman from the past to protect him.

There was a sighing sound, like "ai," from the corner of the room, and for the first time I noticed a woman who sat there, her giant frame oozing over the edges of the wicker chair, her fat neck shiny with perspiration. She kept snapping her fan open and fanning her face, breathing hard and whimpering a little from time to time. This was La Gabriela, Joselito's sister, the mother of José. She didn't look like a gypsy, except that the kind and unbelievably tired face had a hint of umber in it and the eyes were gypsy green. Granddaughter, daughter, and sister of bullfighters, now she was the mother of one. She looked as though she hated the whole mess but bowed to its inevitability. After all, what other profession was there for a man to follow? The farming José had talked about was always just a lovely, impossible dream.

Now José was helped into the stiff jacket of his glittering gold-and-white costume by Almendro and El Gallo, and he shrugged his shoulders against its newness several times. The costume was a beautiful thing. Manfredi's must have charged a fortune to make it. The whole family had chipped in to buy it, and it represented a sacrifice for them, for although Joselito had left a great deal of money, it couldn't last forever.

The room quieted as José struck a match and lit the candle in the little red glass before the Madonna on his bureau. He would pray again at the ring chapel, but this was his own particular Virgin. He clasped his hands together and stood before Her like a little boy.

"*Virgen mía, que no me pillen,*" he said softly. "Don't let them snag me, help me to be good."

He made a cross with his thumb and forefinger, crossed himself, and kissed his fingers. He turned around and took a deep breath. "A la lucha—to the battle." He said it quietly and undramatically, like a lieutenant telling his men they were going over the top.

The room was quiet except for the steady snap of his mother's fan. It was as though someone should say something. El Gallo shuffled forward and cleared his throat.

"Today . . ." he began. He cleared his throat again. "Today . . ." But he could get no further.

Another uncle, El Caracol, took over. He was a famous singer of *cante jondo*, the weird deep singing of the gypsies, and sword carrier for Joselito. He was a huge man, and he had a great goiter on one side of his face that hung down like a swollen turkey wattle.

"Today," said El Caracol, and for a moment he looked as though he

222

wouldn't get any further either, but then he said, "Today we will see the genius of yesterday return."

"Yes," said El Gallo.

"Yes," said El Almendro.

"Yes," echoed other people in the room. "Yes!"

I had the feeling that they were all counting on this boy not only to put up a great performance but somehow to eliminate the passage of a quarter of a century and make them all young again.

They handed José his kinky black montera, and he put it on his head, pressing it down almost to his eyebrows. He slung the dress cape over his arm and started for the door. Then he turned back and walked across the room to his mother. She heaved herself to her feet and took his hands and tried pathetically to make the corners of her mouth stay up in a smile.

"Well, José," she said, looking down at the floor, trying to control her quivering voice, trying to say it enthusiastically. "We're going to hear applause, José. It'll be so loud . . ." her voice broke before she could get it all out, "so loud we'll hear it from here!"

She sobbed and flung her fat arms around the boy. José and El Gallo helped her into her chair, where she sat with her hands over her face. José turned with tears in his eyes, strode from the room, and went downstairs. He was already walking like a jungle animal in the cocky, exaggerated paseo walk, his left arm slung in the cape and his right curved out from his side and swinging gracefully across his body with each step. Now, dressed in his suit of lights, he walked and looked more like a bullfighter than anyone I'd ever seen.

José's first bull was big and treacherous, with twisted horns and a peculiar charging style, so when he played it wide and safe, nobody in the audience complained. They blamed the bull breeder. They felt let down and uncomfortable, though. It was a bad bull, yes, a terrible bull. But Joselito would have made it into a good bull. Nobody yelled, however, and no cushions were thrown, and there were no insults. They were waiting.

There were two other novilleros fighting that afternoon, and they were inexperienced, but one, a buck-toothed Mexican of about nineteen, was superb with the banderillas on his second bull. He did well with the muleta, too, working in close, standing back-arched and graceful as the novillo's horns sliced only a few inches by his legs on every charge. He entered to kill straight and honestly, and left a half-thrust between the bulls' withers that killed it almost instantly. The boy was applauded soundly, and the presidente conceded him an ear for the performance. In any other plaza de toros it would have been both ears and tail, but not in the Maestranza.

As the boy took a jubilant lap around the ring, the man in back of me growled, "Not bad for a Mexican. But wait for Gallito; he'll show the Mexican what a Spaniard can do!"

As the kettledrum rolled and the trumpet bleated for the last bull, I saw José behind the fence down in front of me, his big magenta cape hugged to his chest, his eyes riveted on the toril gate. He was very pale, and there were little pearls of sweat on his upper lip. I saw him stifle a yawn, and hoped no one else noticed it, because this is a sure sign one is scared.

The bolt shot back, the toril gate clanged open, and out into the arena burst José's bull. A great sigh of expectation ran through the crowd, and there was spontaneous applause, and people cried, "Now!"

José motioned for his banderillero to "double" the animal to find out how it charged. The man behind me pounded his fist into his palm and rasped, "Now! Now we see it!"

For this black creature was just the right size, not too big, not too small, the horns uniform and turned in, and it charged honestly, bravely, and with no tricks. It was the kind of bull toreros dream of, and pray to the Macarena for, and get only once or twice in a lifetime.

José, behind the barrera, studied the animal as the banderillero clumsily flung the cape out in front of it with one hand, then dragged it along in front of the bull's hooking horns. The bull, trembling in its eagerness to kill, skidded on its back legs and almost slipped as the banderillero changed hands and lured it back the other way.

"Quieto, quieto!" José ordered in his deep voice, and the banderillero dropped his cape and vaulted the fence. José quickly slipped through the burladero opening and out into the arena, biting the collar of his cape while getting it right in his hands as he walked.

The bull was in the sunny portion of the ring, and José stalked across the shaded sand toward it, swagger in his slim body, command in the way his chin was down on his chest, disdain on his lips. When he strode out of the semicircle of shadow cast by the rim of the plaza de toros and the fiery late sun put a match to the dazzling gold of his costume, it was a reincarnation of Joselito the Perfect.

"Toro, ah-hah!" he chanted as he drew near the bull, arrogantly offering it the cape. "Toma, torito!"

Fifteen feet away José planted his feet flat on the sand, and waited, straight and graceful. The bull wagged its horns once. The great head

224

lowered, and nine hundred pounds of black bull started toward him.

It looked as though he were going to wait it out, as though he couldn't move. But then at the last moment, as the horns came near his body, he seemed to crumple. His knees gave a ludicrous dip, his arms suddenly flailed out, and his feet jittered him back yards away from the animal to safety.

The arena was so silent that one heard the *swo-oo-oo-osh* of the bull's breath on the first charge. Nothing can be as silent as a bullfight audience. And it stayed silent, chillingly, damningly silent all through the next six verónicas José made with that dream bull.

The terrible part was that he was obviously trying so hard. He was trying to swing the cape the way he had with the calves, he was trying to make himself stay in close. He knew what he was supposed to do. But he had absolutely no jurisdiction over his feet.

The crowd remained silent through the first two thirds of the fight. It waited until he went out with the muleta and sword for the last phase. He had given the animal only three bad, dancing, sloppy passes with the small red cape when the whole audience seemed to come down on him at once. The roar was deafening, the insults were personal and disgusting, not the usual amusing insults from the gallery. Everyone felt personally bilked and defrauded, affronted as Spaniards, cheated by someone they had trusted.

The man behind me kept shouting, "Have you no shame? Five meters from the bull and waving the muleta like a dirty shirt. God, has Spain's manhood come to this! Think of Joselito—think of your family! Get control of yourself, man, for the love of God, for the love of Spain!"

Even when the bull swerved suddenly and José was hurled five feet into the air, the crowd didn't pause in its clamor. He didn't even get tossed well, for he came down sprawling on the bull's back, and his plight looked more ludicrous than dangerous. He slipped down to the ground awkwardly, and his banderillero lured the bull away. José lurched to his feet, his beautiful jacket ripped up the side, Joselito's sash hanging down in back like a ridiculous tail, but one could see he wasn't hurt. He picked up the muleta and the sword and went wearily back to the bull and the fresh insults of the crowd.

He tried desperately now to unfurl his fancy passes, but at each heavy lunge of the bull his arms and feet mutinied. The cushions began to rain down in the arena. I wondered how José was going to leave the ring alive. Not because of the bull. It isn't very hard to kill a bull if you don't care how you do it, and José managed to hack the

225

brave animal down to an ugly death. But when it came time to leave the plaza he had to have an escort of six police and two Guardia Civil. The other fighters got inside the convoy too, afraid that the frenzied mob would mistake one of them for José.

It took me some time to work my way through the crowds to José's house. When I walked upstairs I found him lying motionless in the big brass bed with a sheet over his naked body, staring up at the ceiling, his swarthy face still pale, his unseeing eyes wide and moist. His mother was on the same little chair, in the shadows of the corner. His sword boy was running a bath and his banderillero was taking the torn costume off the chair and putting it on a hanger. There was no one else there. José didn't look at me as I entered, but neither did he turn away; it was as though I hadn't come in.

I felt I should say something so, as I sat down, I cleared my throat and said, "Were you hurt at all?"

José kept staring at the ceiling and his banderillero said, "No," in a hard tone and too loud, "he wasn't hurt."

After a few minutes I started to go. But then I heard the front door slam and someone pounded up the stairs. It was his uncle, El Caracol.

El Gallo (left) and Barnaby Conrad
before the big fight.
El Gallo was Joselito's brother,
and hence José's uncle.

The man's big body filled the doorway, and the terrible goiter quivered on the side of his red face as he whispered, "Look—look, is this a verónica?"

He slung his raincoat off his shoulders, and, stepping into the room, he waved it around him in an absurd gesture. "Does this look like a verónica?" His legs danced away from an imaginary bull as he flapped the raincoat. "And this," he did a new grotesque maneuver, "whoever told you this was a natural?" His frame shook with emotion as he cavorted. "I only tell you this because I love you, José. Stay with your farming, never fight again! I only tell you because I love you, José!"

Great sobs burst from his throat as he turned and lurched down the stairs.

José stared after him a moment with his big eyes, swallowing hard and trembling. When he heard the door slam, he gave an agonized moan and slowly pulled the sheet up over his head. I got up and left without saying anything.

I didn't see El Gallo for two weeks, and then only by chance on an off street. He looked detached and old. I thought of avoiding the subject, but then I came out bluntly and asked how José was.

El Gallo tapped his forehead sorrowfully. "Not right." He sighed. "I'm afraid the poor boy's not quite right. That day—after all that—you know what he did? He took all of those pictures of Joselito, all of them —invaluable—he took them down off the wall and smashed them. Anyone who would do that is not right."

I didn't say anything, and the old man shuffled off, muttering.

José and his sister Gabriela
on the day of José's fight.

Fastening the pigtail.

Praying before the fight.

Portugal

15. Portugal

BULLFIGHTING IN PORTUGAL HAS LITTLE IN COMMON WITH REAL BULLFIGHTING. Although the country has been watching corridas, or "touradas" as they call them, since 1790, and although it has fifteen arenas of varying sizes and several ranches raising respectable fighting bulls, the spectacle simply is not the same as in Spain and hasn't become part of the way of life of the Portuguese people the way it has with the Spanish.

The most important difference, of course, is that the bulls are not killed and there are no picadors. It has always struck me as the height of some kind of hypocrisy that they place real banderillas in the bull, then shun the sword thrust, take the bull out of the ring, and poleax it in the corrals as though it were a beef steer. It is also highly unfair (though that is a word that has little place in tauromachy), since the bull's best chance to collect the man is at the Moment of Truth, and that opportunity has been removed.

Not so long ago Manoel Dos Santos, the only really fine matador to be produced by Portugal, was fighting in his home city and drew a marvelous bull. He put up one of the greatest faenas of his life, and when it came time for the climax he somehow found himself with the sword in his hand, he was running at the bull, it was running at him, and a second later the bull was dead on the sand. It was the sensation of Lisbon; Dos Santos was brought to trial, and after pleading innocent "by reason of temporary insanity" he was exonerated.

Lisbon's ring, Campo Pequenho, was built in 1892, holds eight thousand

231

spectators, and despite the unorthodoxy of la fiesta brava in Portugal, the top names in the bullfighting world appear there every year. Although the Portuguese like to feature an atavistic abomination known as "os forcados," wherein a dozen men wrestle a bull to a standstill, the country's real contribution to tauromachy is el rejoneo, or Portuguese Style. This is a beautiful exhibition by a horseman on a highly trained mount, whose function is completely the opposite of a picador's; the rejoneador tries at all times to keep his horse from even being scratched by the bull's horns, while at the same time executing difficult maneuvers like placing short banderillas with both hands, guiding the horse with knee pressure only. The guiding principle behind Portuguese Style is that the horse must be more afraid of the man astride him than of the terrifying sight of the charging bull. It must have complete confidence in the judgment of the man, totally abandoning its natural instincts of self-preservation, or rather trusting more in the man's instincts than in its own. To bring a horse to this state of training is a high, specialized art.

Parar, mandar, and *templar* are the three precepts upon which fighting on foot is based. These could be translated roughly: to hold one's ground, to control the bull, and to execute the passes slowly and suavely. The three tenets of fighting on horseback are: *clavar de alto a bajo, al estribo,* and *que salga la cabalgadura ilesa.* The first means that the banderillas or rejones should be held perpendicular at the moment of placing, the second that the placing should be made when the bull is head-on to the man's stirrup, the third that the horse should come out of every encounter unscathed.

The Marqués de Marialva is considered the true founder of rejoneo, bringing the spectacle into prominence around the end of the eighteenth century. Other great names up to the present are Ruy da Cámara, Nuncio, Simão da Veiga, the Spaniards Antonio Cañero and Alvaro Domecq, and the half-American girl Conchita Cintrón. The finest rejoneador in the world now, and perhaps the greatest who ever lived, is Angel Peralta, a young Spaniard. Ex-matador Carlos Arruza has taken up the art, has been doing it for only one year, but gives promise of being Peralta's greatest rival.

Most Americans going to their first bullfights enjoy an exhibition of rejoneo more than anything else. It is much easier to grasp the point of it all, the danger is more obvious, and the methods of escape from danger more apparent than the many intricate subtleties of fighting on foot.

However, though I have great admiration for the skill involved in rejoneo, I do not really like it and do not think it belongs on the program with formal corridas. When I want to see horsemanship or equestrian

232

tricks I go to a horse show or a circus or a rodeo, not to a plaza de toros.

Rejoneo is relatively safe for the man, as is the fighting on foot as practiced in Portugal, since the bull's horns have the tips removed—"afeitado"—
"shaved," as they call it. But in spite of this, one top matador was killed by
a shaved bull in 1947. Kenneth Tynan in *Bull Fever* reports it this way:

> All of Spain mourned Manolete, and with some members of his pro-
> fession his mischance became a morbid preoccupation. On September
> 14th, just over two weeks after the disaster of Linares, the Mexican
> bullfighter, José González López, known as *Carnicerito de Mexico*, was
> gored in the Portuguese bullring of Villa Vicosa. He was forty years
> old, competent with the cape and muleta and an acknowledged maes-
> tro with the banderillas. His second bull, a difficult manso, came
> treacherously to the faena, and, after submitting to two valiant statuary
> passes, caught Carnicerito high up in the right leg, severing the femoral
> artery. As he was being carried to the hospital, half a mile away, he
> said:
>
> "Don't leave me. Take care of me. My cornada is like Manolete's."
>
> He was convinced that he had been chosen to re-live Manolete's
> anguish, and nothing would dislodge the idea from his mind. He
> mouthed Manolete's words:
>
> "I can't feel anything in my legs, doctor . . ."
>
> And later:
>
> "I can't see you, Don Luis . . ."
>
> At half-past six next morning he called for extreme unction. Two
> hours later he began to sink, and Conchita Cintrón, the *rejoneadora*,
> bent over to decipher his last words.
>
> "Watch me," he said, "I am dying like Manolete." *

Although Portugal has produced some fine bulls, notably those from
Infante da Cámara and the terrifying Palha breed, it boasts of only three
Spanish-style matadors in its history, and these in the last decade: Manoel
Dos Santos, his cousin Antonio Dos Santos, and Diamantino Vizeu. Nevertheless, the country has been the first proving ground for three of the
greatest matadors of history: Belmonte, Joselito, and Carlos Arruza. Here's
how Arruza tells of his Lisbon experience in his autobiography, *My Life as
a Matador:*

* It's interesting to read Hemingway's note about Carnicerito in *Death in the Afternoon*, published in 1932, fifteen years before this happening: ". . . a Mexican Indian belonging to the
gutful-wonder school who eats them alive and while very brave, a good banderillero and a
capable and very emotional performer, will not be with us very long if he takes the same
chances with real bulls that he does with the young ones."

We were approximately a year and a half making the whistle-stop circuits, until 1938, when I managed to fight two novilladas in Mexico City. I didn't attract any attention by my small-town style, which by now had become very ingrained in me. Though young still, I was already getting old in the profession without the slightest indication of my becoming a *figura* in the bull world. At barely eighteen years of age, I was already better known in all of the Republic than any of the other novilleros. These others, by their very newness, pleased the public more than I did.

My situation was precarious. I certainly wasn't going ahead in bull-fighting, and on the other hand I didn't have any desire or aptitude to study or take up work of any other type. With my burning desire to bullfight I would have flopped at any other endeavor. In that period I got very little sleep worrying about what to do.

Once again the big bull season started, and with it came complete inactivity. All we could do was to sit around our café in front of our banquets of coffee and bread and perform thrilling verbal bullfights to each other.

One day right in the midst of a great faena of mine, Manolo slapped his hand down on the table, "Portugal!"

"What?"

"We'll go to Portugal! There's no war on there and we'd be a novelty!"

"I hear the bulls are enormous and difficult."

"The Arruza brothers can handle any animals."

"All right—we'll go!"

We arrived in Lisbon knowing absolutely no one.

"Now what do we do?" I asked Manolo as we wandered around the strange city. "Here we are with no money and no contracts to fight."

"Someone told me all the bull people hang out around the Café Suizo. We'll see what's doing there."

On the way to the café we saw gaudy posters announcing that the coming Sunday there would be a corrida in which that marvelous Portuguese-style bullfighter called Nuncio was going to take part along with two young Spanish novilleros.

In the Café Suizo, a counterpart to our beloved Tupinamba back home, we sat and elegantly drank coffee for hours, hoping to make contact with the people connected with bullfighting. Our wallets were well stocked with dozens of photos of us in action, and we passed them from table to table as calling cards, trying to look nonchalant, experienced, and highly successful. With the few pesos we still had we kept inviting people around us to join us in a *cafezinho*.

"This is getting expensive," I whispered to Manolo after paying for a round for a large group. "We don't have much left."

"We have to make a big impression," Manolo whispered back. "We have to show them who the Arruza brothers are."

No one seemed a bit impressed with the Arruza brothers, but they kept drinking off us.

And then we caught this bit of dialogue between two men at our table:

"Understand the impresario's stuck."

"So I gather. No toreros."

"Couldn't get visas—Spanish War."

We glanced at each other. We got up casually, said good-by to our new acquaintances, strolled nonchalantly out of the café, and then streaked for the impresario's office. We got in to see him without too much trouble, and dumping our load of photos on his desk we said, "You have to put us on, señor, we will be great and make you a lot of money! Please put us on!"

He was a very decent man, and he listened with great patience to the torrent. He studied the photos carefully. Then he sat back in his chair and said, "I don't doubt that you're very fine toreros, but I—and

you must forgive my lack of awareness—I quite frankly have never heard of you. The plaza of Campo Pequenho, the greatest in Portugal, cannot risk introducing two, excuse the expression, two unknowns, so could you, if it wouldn't be too much bother, before I decide, could you just give me a little sample of the kind of toreros you are?"

We nodded numbly.

"Then be at the bullring in half an hour—and ready to perform."

Imagine how we left that office. Everything now was going to depend on what we might do with this bull that he was going to test us with. What ranch would it be from? Would it charge well? How big would it be? For thirty minutes we sweated. What a rough go it was, to fight like this without any warning and without being prepared or dressed right. On this was our whole future career to depend? We tried to cheer each other up, giving each other all kinds of advice and trying to plan how we'd work it. We decided that we would do it the way we did it when we were kids and first threw ourselves into the ring back in Mexico. "Manolo, you fight for a while and then I'll go out, and then we'll flip for who'll kill."

Finally, very fearful that things would not turn out well, we arrived at the bullring with its empty stands. "Ready?" the impresario said to us. "Ready, señor," Manolo said bravely, "whenever you please." We went into the ring. We prepared our capes and muleta, got ourselves into that who-cares-about-living-anyway frame of mind one needs just before a corrida, and then gave him the sign that we were ready.

"Let loose the bull!" I called.

"What bull?" asked the man.

Then we found out that our enemy was to be ourselves. All the impresario wanted to see was us fighting *de salón!* He explained to us that he just wished to see us swing the capes and go through the motions of placing banderillas. If we did it well, that was enough for him.

My God! And just for this we had gone through a half-hour of anguish!

At fighting *de salón* and at playing a brave fighting bull nobody in the world could beat us. We had behind us the wonderful experience of the bullfighting school of Solís, and you can't imagine the tremendous performances we put up, Manolo and I, that afternoon. When the bull is your brother, how can you lose?

"Well, señores," said the impresario afterward, "you are quite splendid. I just hope the presence of rather large bulls won't dim the brilliance of your performances tomorrow."

236

Above: Carlos Arruza
placing a *rejón*
in the Portuguese
style.

Below: The bull is dead,
and even the sand sweepers
stop to watch as
Peralta makes his horse
leap triumphantly.

That afternoon the whole Café Suizo knew that we were fighting the next day. The afternoon papers came out with our names announced on the program, the posters went up on the billboards shortly, and the whole thing was getting so important it scared us. It had all happened so fast!

In the morning we went to see the bulls. They were not only the biggest animals we'd ever fought, they were the biggest we'd ever seen. When we got there they had one of the monsters in a squeeze chute, and they were preparing to saw off the points of the horns.

"Say, what are you doing?" Manolo called down to the men.

"This is Portugal," one answered. "No picadors. We always take the points off."

"These aren't your Mexican calves," said another. "And we'd hate to see young blood all over our pretty sand."

Then to my astonishment Manolo ordered, "Don't touch this animal's horns and don't touch any of the others!"

The men looked up at us. "Are you crazy?" But Manolo's tone made them put down the saw.

Manolo tried to look casual. "I don't believe in taking advantage of the animals."

The men snorted at this arrogance. "Sonny, you're going to wish to God we'd cut these babies' advantages off right close to the head before this afternoon's over! But if that's the way you want it, that's the way it'll be."

As we left I whispered to Manolo, "But they're cathedrals, those animals! What'd you go and do that for?"

"We've just got to be good, Carlitos," Manolo said, determined but a little pale. "Think how fine it will be if we get through this well."

"Think how fine it will be if we get through it at all," I answered.

"Look, buck up," he said. "We're the Arruza brothers!"

"That's right," I said gloomily. "I forgot—we can handle anything."

Word of our act—or rather Manolo's—spread like wildfire through the city, and now in the streets people began to look at us with a touch of respect. "Are they crazy?" they asked. Yes, we were crazy. Crazy to do so well that we'd be another step closer to being full matadors instead of just unknown novilleros.

I was white when I saw my first bull of the afternoon slam out of the toril. It looked so terribly big and its horns were so sharp. Damn Manolo and his sportsmanship! I waited so long and let the banderillero cape it so much that the crowd began to catcall. "Where's the matador?" they demanded.

"Carlos, it's a dream bull!" said Manolo, shaking me. "Just act as though it were small—just do everything you'd do if it were a calf!"

I pulled myself together and went out there. It was a little hard to imagine that this animal whose shoulders were up to mine was a calf, but I kept saying to myself: "This is just a bull—a little bull like any other—and you can handle him, boy."

After two passes I saw that Manolo was right—the bull charged as though it were on rails, and my confidence came rushing back to me; the size really didn't matter too much, if you put it out of your mind. I gave out with my entire repertoire, and the crowd appreciated every pass much more than usual because they knew the bull had those sharp horns intact, something they'd never seen in Portugal. Naturally, without any picadors to slow the animal down, it was almost too much bull to handle, but the audience realized this and understood. At one point in the fight I wanted to leave the animal, to walk away and catch my breath after so many passes, but the bull wouldn't let me. He just kept charging and wheeling and charging and charging with this great power and strength. We stayed out there in the center of the ring, in the center of the world, in what seemed like one continual prolonged pass, the bull and I drunk with what we were doing.

Then suddenly—in the middle of a spinning molinete pass—I felt the

animal's bulk swerving into me instead of hurtling on by. And then in the next instant I felt myself flung into the air. I felt the tip of the right horn jab into my flesh, but I grabbed the horn at the base and pushed myself off of it and away from the bull's lethal head. When I hit the ground I was momentarily stunned. I saw the animal lunging at me again. Then the red flash of a cape came between me and the horns, and I realized that Manolo was luring the animal away. I scrambled to my feet and saw that I had a slight wound on my thigh. The sight of the blood running down my leg made me furious, and I snatched up my muleta and went back to passing the bull closer than before.

In Portugal they don't kill the bulls, they only imitate the sword thrust using a banderilla, but they execute the maneuver in exactly the same way. I lined the bull up, profiled, and went through the motions of a perfect sword thrust, and that was the topper. The crowd was completely an insane asylum now, and they made me take lap after lap around the ring, me with a big lump in my throat. I neither saw nor felt anything, not even the wound in my leg. It was a great triumph. On my second bull the success came through the banderillas, which is one of the most popular acts of the bullfight in Portugal, and one with which the bullfighter who knows how to do it well can perform all season on the strength of that alone. I placed the banderillas so well that on this one bull they made me place seven pairs instead of the usual three! The crowd was a howling group of madmen. I will never forget that afternoon, no matter how many years go by. These were other faces, another type of public, other surroundings, and there was frenzy in the stands. . . . The program for the coming Sunday was formed around us, and many a Sunday after that during the next two years. We returned to Mexico, but never with the luck that we had in Lisbon. My record of good fights there, more than anything I did in Mexico, finally put me in a position to "take the alternative"—to become a full matador.

France

16. France

LIKE PORTUGAL, FRANCE IS AN OFFSHOOT IN LA FIESTA BRAVA. BULLS ARE fought there, and have been for about a hundred years, and in an average year there will be approximately thirty corridas held with top performers from Spain and Mexico. But still there is a feeling of ersatz about it all. The principal plazas are Arles, Dax, Nimes, Bayonne, and Béziers. Those of Nimes and Arles are ancient Roman amphitheaters, the setting couldn't be more perfect, and they are worth seeing whether there is a bullfight on or not. Every once in a while, Paris decides to have an exhibition bullfight, but these are mock affairs held in some hippodrome, generally at night, and the bulls are not killed.

As in Portugal, it is against the law to kill bulls in an arena in France, and there is a five-thousand-franc fine for doing so. Therefore, with splendid Gallic cynicism, most of the plazas simply pay the fine to the officials automatically, hold the corrida as planned, and everyone is happy but the S.P.C.A.

The poor S.P.C.A. has met its master in the Latins, I'm afraid. The Spaniards do not take delight in cruelty to animals—they simply do not see it. They just don't quite grasp the basic idea behind treating animals more or less as one treats humans. They tell the story of how American S.P.C.A. leaders came to Madrid and protested the treatment of animals in general on the Iberian Peninsula. The Spanish officials listened to all the arguments, and with the usual Spanish desire to please they agreed to help in any way possible.

243

"We need to raise money badly," said the S.P.C.A., "so how can we best do it?"

The Spanish officials thought deeply for a few moments. "I have it," said one finally. "We will give a giant benefit bullfight!"

As the other Spaniards chorused their approval, the S.P.C.A. slunk dispiritedly away, realizing the utter futility of trying to penetrate this ingrained mentality.

Bullfighting is cruel, in France or any place else, and there is no doubt about it. One simply has to make up one's own mind as to whether the beauty that is sometimes created in the arena is worth the cruelty. Bullfighting exists, and as long as it does, I intend to enjoy the nobler aspects of it and put up with the less noble ones. However, I can honestly say that if elimination of all bullfighting from this world depended on a single vote of mine, I would unhesitatingly cast that vote. At the same time I would like to eliminate rodeos, cockfights, the trapping of fur-bearing animals, the shooting of birds and deer, fox hunting, and zoos. And especially, the noble, genteel, uncriticized sport of steeplechasing! I recently read this comment by E. V. Durling in his daily column:

> In the 1921 Grand National Steeplechase at Liverpool, England, thirty-five horses started and thirty-four fell! Only the winner, Shaun Spadah, negotiated all the jumps successfully. The jumps on the Aintree course where the Grand National is run are much too high for the safety of the horses. At each jump during the Grand National there is stationed a man with a pistol to destroy any unfortunate horse that might break a leg while jumping. As currently conducted the Grand National is, from the standpoint of cruelty to animals, worse than bullfighting.

Probably more horses are killed every year in England this way than are killed in all the bullrings of the world, since the peto protective mattress is required for every picador's mount and has been for twenty-five years.

If we all became vegetarians and eliminated the abattoirs of the world, then the bullrings would certainly be heinous things. But one should ask himself this question: If a bull had the choice between going to the slaughterhouse to be clubbed on the head or engaging in a hot-blooded twenty-minute contest, which would he be more likely to choose?

Leslie Charteris, in a fine introduction to the Belmonte autobiography, has this to say in favor of the second choice:

> Certainly it must be admitted that the bull is wounded during the fight, with the pics and banderillas; but these are straightforward

244

wounds with clean, sharp steel, which anyone who has been stabbed or cut knows are not excruciatingly painful, at least until afterwards, and for the bull there is no afterwards. Everyone also knows that men do not feel pain very much when their blood is hot—for instance, when they are wounded in a fight—and I see no reason why bulls should be considered more sensitive than human beings. But certainly bulls are killed and possibly suffer a little more pain in dying than they would suffer in a scientific slaughterhouse; and certainly horses are often disembowelled, even if they are broken-down horses with very little more life left in them; these are the cold facts of bullfighting. The point to consider is whether the artistic result justifies the abuse of the material, and that is a question which cannot be judged entirely on its own merits, because the art of the torero has no real parallel. The most one can say is, Let us imagine that violins were so fragile that they could only be used for one concert, and that in order to make a violin it was necessary to subject some animal to considerable pain: how many people would think that all this was justified if they could hear Kreisler play? I believe that there would be a large number of music lovers who would vote for Kreisler. The artistic argument is one which cannot be applied to any blood sport in which animals suffer and are killed; but the Anglo-Saxon temperament can understand and approve of killing and inflicting pain in the name of "sport" and "healthy exercise," while it is quite incapable of admitting the same thing on the justification of art or scientific research.

One thing you can count on: not just Charteris, but everyone, has an opinion on bullfighting, one way or the other, and I find it interesting to note the many variations. In the last pages of *Death in the Afternoon* Hemingway describes seventeen different reactions of people seeing their first bullfight, and it makes for fascinating reading. Washington Irving wrote candidly of bullfights, "I did not know what a blood thirsty man I was until I saw them at Madrid on my first visit. The first was very spirited, the second dull, the third spirited again, and afterward I hardly ever missed." In a later letter, Irving denounced bullfighting, or rather he severely reprimanded a lady friend for enjoying such a base spectacle.

Seldom do you read a dispassionate, objective denunciation of bullfighting. Usually people write about it at the top of their voices, choleric, emotional, swinging wild, the way D. H. Lawrence does in his novel, *The Plumed Serpent*.

Without doubt the finest dissection of bullfighting that I have read is the following article, which appeared in the periodical *Discovery 4*. Of course,

This remarkable series of photographs,
taken by Tex McCrary, shows the reactions
of several people watching an accident in
the bullring. Above, the veteran matador Dominguín warns Jinx
Falkenburg McCrary that the young bullfighter in the arena is taking
the bull from a bad angle and that he will be tossed. What happened
next is recorded by the camera and the ring action is mirrored in
Mary Martin's face.

Jinx gasps as she waits for
Dominguín's prediction to occur;
Dominguín smiles smugly with the
surety of what must happen;
Mary Martin thinks everything is
fine; her husband, Richard Halliday,
shows no change of expression.

Dominguín leans back, knowing
that this is the time when the
young torero is in real trouble,
and even Mary Martin can see that
something is wrong.

The inevitable happens. Dominguín bites his lip; Mary Martin screams; but there is no change of expression from Halliday.

Dominguín reacts, for he is not so cynical that he has forgotten how it feels to get a horn in the thigh. Mary is stunned; no change of expression from Halliday.

As they carry the boy out to the infirmary, the full impact of the tragedy hits Jinx and Dominguín.

I am theoretically on the other side of the fence as to the evaluation of the spectacle, but one can not help conceding most of the author's points and admiring his calm, unmuddied thinking.

THE ONLY BEAST
Reflections on Not Attending the Bullfights
by Lysander Kemp

The fascination of the bullfight is very great. I must admit that at the beginning, in order to be honest. I have not attended a bullfight, and will not, but I have read what I could come by on the subject, and visited a bullfight museum, and even bought a complete *corrida* in miniature, beautifully fashioned from painted clay and wire by a Mexican craftsman in Tlaquepaque, with the toreros and banderilleros and mounted picadores and all, and a dead bull being dragged out by a team of three mules. So, I admit its fascination, and to a point I can understand why its popularity has been growing in the United States, both as a literary topic and as a spectacle to be seen on a visit to Spain or Mexico.

At the same time, I believe the sport to be nearly indefensible, and I wish to submit a minority opinion contrary to that of its many gringo enthusiasts.

The apologies for it—the "explanations"—take many forms: it is a real-life drama, it is a ballet, it is a great tradition with a splendid set of rituals and a noble history. But I think Ernest Hemingway, in his classic book on the subject, set down its basic attraction in the first word of his title: *Death in the Afternoon.* We are mortal, death frightens but fascinates us, and when we buy a ticket to the arena we know we are buying a ticket to see death in action, certainly the death of several bulls, possibly the death of a man. Homer Casteel, in *The Running of the Bulls,* tells us that when the great Manolete was asked why he did not move away from a bull that was obviously going to gore him, he replied that the public had not paid to see him run. Casteel offers this approvingly, and of course it is quite true that the public had not paid to see Manolete run, it had paid to see death—to see *his* death if they were lucky (and one day they were). Blasco Ibáñez said it perfectly: The only beast in the Plaza de Toros is the crowd.

Bullfighting is not legal in the United States, and is not likely to be made so. However, *The Running of the Bulls* is only one of several recent and popular books on the sport, and Hollywood has produced at least two bullfight pictures in the last two or three years. In addition, an increasing number of Americans have seen the real thing in Spain, in Mexico City, or elsewhere in Mexico, for the great majority of tourists attend at least once, with the tourist's peculiar compulsion which demands that nothing be missed. You will find aficionados even in so unlikely a city as Buffalo, New York. Buffalo is a long way from the Rio Grande, and it is about as Spanish or Spanish-American as Vladivostok, but I have argued there with at least three knowing and violent enthusiasts, and when I was leaving for a sabbatical in Mexico a good dozen friends and acquaintances remarked that they envied me, not so much because I was escaping part of a northern winter but because now I could see a bullfight. When I said I had no intention whatsoever of seeing a bullfight, they were astonished.

The most persuasive apologists (in the United States—I would not argue with a Spaniard or Mexican, because I think he would find my arguments incomprehensible) are those who have actually seen, understood and enjoyed good bullfights. If you remark to them that you dislike the sport they ask, almost automatically, if you have ever *seen* a bullfight. If you reply, as I must, that you have not, they present what I consider their most destructive argument: "How do you know you'd dislike it, if you've never seen one?" The question is simple enough and it is asked without much thought, and I wish it could be answered with equal simplicity and thoughtlessness. But, after all, I *don't* know —and I am not so absolutely sure of myself, so utterly sure of my ability to predict my reaction to a new experience, that I can assert a bullfight would only disgust me. Instead, I have to be honest and admit that in the beauty and excitement of it I might lose my head and howl with the crowd. I think not, but I might, for Hemingway says this has happened and I believe him. So, my answer to the question is that I don't know and don't want to know. In other words, if there is an appetite for blood and violent death lying dormant in me, I think it is healthier to let it lie.

Beyond this, I think the two most persuasive arguments are the aesthetic and the emotional—one praising the beauty of the bullfight, the other its excitement. The second is usually kept in reserve, in order to be rushed in as a substitute when the other falters.

The aesthetic argument, which I have heard most eloquently put, is that a good bullfight is a kind of spectacular ballet, and makes very much the same kind of appeal. There is your *corps de ballet:* your picadores, monosabios, banderilleros. There is your Nijinsky: the matador himself. And there is . . . well, not your ballerina, but perhaps your ogre: the bull. Each "dancer" in the classical ballet of the bullfight has his traditional ritualized movements, the matador most of all, and a great deal of lyrical prose (some good and much bad) has been written about the passes—the verónicas and mariposas and gaoneras and others—executed by a good matador with a good bull. Here for example is Hemingway: "It is impossible to believe the emotional and spiritual intensity, and pure, classic beauty that can be produced by a man, an animal, and a piece of scarlet serge draped over a stick." Since I have not seen a bullfight I can only take his word for it that it is not possible to believe these things.

The aesthetic argument does not mention blood and death, or it dismisses them as incidentals. But if you should take the argument literally—take the "art" of bullfighting as a literal equivalent of the art of ballet—perhaps you will want to suggest that if the appeal is aesthetic, then there is no good reason for the matador (the word means "killer") to kill or even wound the bull, and no good reason for the bull to be so dangerous. Why not remove the horns of the bull, or at least put "buttons" on them after the manner of buttoned foils? And why not deprive the matador of his sword? This would reduce the likelihood of harm to either party to a minimum, and would not seriously impair the aesthetics of the performance.

At this point, unless you are overwhelmed by technical reasons why it is supposedly not possible to do this, you will find that the grounds of the argument have suddenly shifted. The bullfight is no longer a ballet with a merely aesthetic appeal: it is a dramatic spectacle which differs from theatre in that this is not make-believe but the real thing. A living creature will be killed, really and truly killed, spilling not ketchup but real blood (yum-yum). Probably it will be the villain, the bull, who dies, but just possibly it will be the hero. And if, you are told, it were not for the third principal member of the cast, who is Death, then there would be no drama, only a charade. "That is, only a ballet," you remark, but you are out of order, you are now to consider the gripping real-life drama of it all. Here is *Time* on the subject, as quoted by Homer Casteel (the reference is to the death by goring of Manolete): "Throughout the Spanish world plain people felt they had lost one who had given them not joy, but a bitter glorious excitement, a pageant of death, and courage, death's enemy . . ." Apparently this is meant to describe the bullfight as what Hemingway calls a tragedy or as what I have heard called a "moral entertainment." This is Hemingway again: "So far, about morals, I know only that what is moral is what you feel good after and what is immoral is what you feel bad after and judged by these moral standards, which I do not defend, the bullfight is very moral to me because I feel very fine while it is going on and have a feeling of life and death and mortality

254

and immortality, and after it is over I feel very sad but very fine."

It seems to me, however, that the bullfight is not a tragedy (even if the matador is killed) nor a drama (even though it is in a sense "dramatic") nor a moral entertainment (though it is not necessarily immoral either). True, the matador (and the bull too) must be brave, but bravery is moral only when the circumstances which occasion it are moral also. Combat between an armed man and a wild animal—the bulls are raised as wild animals, and in theory they see a dismounted man only once before the time they are to be fought—is not a moral occasion when performed for an audience for money, however beautiful and exciting the performance may be, for the simple reason that there is no initial moral obligation for the man to enter the arena in the first place. When Hemingway writes of a nervous and ignorant bullfighter who was severely gored, and who was shown no sympathy afterwards by the aficionados, he asks: "Why did he insist on being a bullfighter?" This is to say that there is no moral obligation, simply a matter of choice at the outset, and he could have chosen not to become a matador, to become a waiter or a grocer instead, without dishonoring himself, without the question of honor having arisen at all.

On the other hand, consider Shakespeare's *Hamlet:* the crucial choice is again the initial choice, but here it is wholly in moral terms. Hamlet can choose to turn his back on the "unweeded garden" of Elsinore without taking any action, or he can accept the obligation and combat evil as best he can. The bravery of Hamlet is not only physical but moral, and if we paraphrase Hemingway's question and ask, "Why did he insist on being a hero?" the answer is that he was a morally brave man. In contrast, the bravery of the matador is that of Harry Hotspur, of the trapeze artist, of the man who rides over Niagara Falls in a barrel of his own design. This is not to deny that very great professional courage and professional honor are necessary in the bullring, only to say that the display of it is not a moral entertainment but a paid spectacle.

The apologists usually avoid the "humanitarian" objections to the sport, or else dismiss them. Hemingway simply says that some people are horrified by the suffering of the horses and the bulls and that some are not, and leaves it pretty much at that, merely remarking that for the true aficionado the brief suffering of the animals is a minor detail, lost in the splendor of the whole. This will not satisfy the S.P.C.A. (and does not satisfy me), but it is honest enough, and certainly preferable to another sort of argument (from Rodney Bright's *Toros With-*

255

out Tears): "There are elements of cruelty in it . . . but so are there in *paté de foie gras,* in fox- or stag-hunting, in fur coats, and in zoological gardens where tamed and shabby tigers are condemned to spend years confined in cramping cages, until death comes to release them from the prying eyes of humanity. The bull spends the first four years of its life literally living on the fat of the land, and the last fifteen minutes of it in mortal combat. Do many other animals which come into contact with human beings have such a high percentage of good luck?" Well, now, I agree with Oscar Wilde that fox-hunting is "the pursuit of the uneatable by the unspeakable," I agree that fur-trapping which causes suffering is indefensible, I agree that animals should not be caged if it can be shown that such confinement causes them to suffer, and I cannot understand how one form of cruelty is excused by a list of other forms of cruelty that are inexcusable.

Even so, this argument is preferable to still another I once heard propounded quite seriously: that the bull dies a beautiful death, and *knows* he is dying beautifully. It is a temptation to argue back that the bull dies, not beautifully, but in a baffled and pathetic rage, unable to comprehend why he has been tortured so by the pics and banderillas, and why his great strength is so helplessly draining away. The real answer, I think, is that claiming the bulls know they die beautifully is like claiming the milk one sells has come from contented cows. Perhaps it has, but a cow's apparent contentedness, for all anyone except a cow can say, could equally well be drooling idiocy or plain pepless boredom.

However, I cannot wholly sympathize with those who base their objections to the bullfight solely on the fact that a few animals must suffer. The suffering is deplorable, but the harm to the human beings who watch it is even more deplorable. It is not good, it is not healthy, even though it may in some sense be "normal" or "natural," to enjoy the sight of suffering and death, or to ignore or tolerate it for the sake of enjoying other emotions. It has been argued that in all of us there is an appetite for raw violence, and if we are deprived of satisfying it vicariously, in some such innocent form as the bullfight, we end up by satisfying it directly, in rioting, beating up our wives or neighbors, or, at the extreme, lynching Negroes or shoveling Jews into ovens.

This is half-true. The appetite exists, and to a point it does need to be satisfied and will somehow find satisfaction as do our other appetites. But it can be satisfied less grossly than in the Plaza de Toros. One of the functions of civilization is to direct the expression of our desires, by early training and social pressures, so that, ideally, we will

256

receive the minimum harm and the maximum value and pleasure from that expression. If we satisfied hunger directly, like animals, we would gulp down the first edibles we could find, till our bellies were full, and would scarcely taste what we were eating. Instead, we have the apparently silly rites of table etiquette—*and* we have that minor triumph of civilization, the properly made strawberry shortcake. And we rise from the table with our bellies full. We have accomplished what the animal accomplishes, but we have enjoyed a richer experience. The same is true of an appetite for violence. When it exists it must be fed, but in a civilized society it can be directed so that it usually feeds harmlessly: we offer it the equivalent of strawberry shortcake (in movies, TV, sporting events) and insist that it be eaten according to Emily Post. At the bullfight arena you are invited to eat with your fingers as fast as you can.

There are still other apologies for the bullfight, and if this were intended as a practical manual for those who wish to debate with aficionados I should have to discuss them. However, I wish only to mention two others, because I think they are interesting if nothing else.

The first is the Freudian interpretation, and it defines the bullfight as a depiction of the human mind with its three divisions, the id, the ego, and the super-ego. The bull portrays the id, man's subconscious, instinctive, "animal" nature; the matador of course portrays the ego; and the approving or disapproving audience is the super-ego. I know no way of replying to such a statement, except perhaps by smiling.

The second, and much more ambitious, is the historical-symbolic interpretation, which is related to the Freudian but is fancier. It traces the sport back into the mists of pre-Christian times, equates it with the Greek Mystery Plays, and asserts that the rituals of the bullfight are a kind of school which teaches man to conquer his lower nature. "Each stage of the fight"—I am quoting *Toro Without Tears,* a more serious piece of writing than its title suggests—"can . . . be given a symbolic meaning, starting even with the prior enclosure of the bull in a dark place which symbolises man's ignorance. The entry into the ring represents esoteric school, where he is first given free rein to express his characteristics and tendencies. . . . The next two stages of the picador and banderilleros symbolise the first direct attack on the ignorant side of man's nature, which leave the bull in a state of bewilderment and humility and prepare him for the final domination by the matador who represents man's higher nature. The final stage leading up to the 'moment of truth' as it is still symbolically called"—that is, the actual killing of the bull—"represents the gradual complete

257

domination by man of his ignorant passions, and can be achieved only by his own hand." I am smiling again, but this is considerably more interesting. I will only point out the fact (conveniently not mentioned in *Toros Without Tears*) that an especially brave bull, one the matador cannot kill, may be led from the ring to the cheers of the crowd and later released to the fields alive, reflecting glory on the ranch which provided him.

At the beginning, I remarked that the bullfight is presently growing in popularity in the United States. I wish, since I mentioned it, that I could account for it, in some profound generalization about Western Civilization if possible. For example, the bullfight might be considered as a version of the ancient Roman Circus, to produce a most deeply direful forecast of our impending decline and fall. I regret to say, however, that I believe the new popularity of the bullfight is caused only by the increasing tourist business in Spain and Mexico. Bull-fights are one of the sights to be seen. I am distressed only by the fact that so many tourists attend them unprepared, not understanding that there are serious aspects to it, and not caring. They go to be able to say they attended, perhaps to find a few thrills and to participate in a little local sentimentality.

In the city of Guadalajara, which is Mexico's second city, there was a small commercial museum called the Museo Taurino. It was a kind of traveling museum, and after a considerable stay it has since moved on. As the bullring offers violence in action, the Museo offered the aftermath of violence: it was a monument to death. I wish to describe it briefly by way of conclusion.

First you passed the hawker dressed in a matador's costume, bought your one-peso ticket, and entered. The Museo was one long room, and every available scrap of wall-space was hung with a bullfight memento, often a *memento mori*—there were photographs of the late great bullfighters, framed letters, handbills of memorable fights, excellent posters, a few drawings and paintings. Much of the collection was from Spain, but part of it was Mexican. Then there were items of equipment—swords, capes, various parts of various trajes de luces, which are the glittering gold-embroidered suits of the matadors. And there were the stuffed heads of the bulls that killed Manuel Granero and the great Gallito.

This collection of souvenirs was fairly interesting, here and there, but most of it was almost meaningless to anybody who had not followed the bullfights closely for years. The real attractions were the waxworks, all life-sized. The first was a set of three, showing the three

258

stages in the killing of Manuel Granero. The first two in the set showed him lifted up onto the bull's head and shoulders, ungored. He looked a trifle surprised. The third showed him on his back in the sand of the bullring, with the bull's horn entering his eye-socket. The amount of blood depicted was eminently satisfactory. Next there was a single scene showing the goring of Gallito, who received a horn in the abdomen. Finally there was the goring of Manolete, who received a horn in the thigh which presumably severed the femoral artery (I am guessing—he may have died from infection rather than loss of blood). In the last two tableaux there was unhappily little blood in sight, except on the shoulders of the bulls where the pics and banderillas had entered. In all the tableaux the bulls were well modeled and much more lifelike than the matadors. Perhaps this was appropriate, since in the represented actions the matadors were on the verge of possessing no life whatsoever.

The masterpiece of the collection was in a little cubicle at the far end. The cubicle had been gotten up as a hospital room, there was a white hospital bed in it, and in the bed was the dead Manolete. The sheet had been turned down across his chest at the armpits, his arms were raised, and his hands held up a crucifix so massive that, in the actual situation of which this was a replica, the arms must have been allowed to reach an advanced state of rigor mortis in order to support it. But you scarcely noticed this detail, because of the face. It was a long, thin, arrogant face, and the sculptor fashioned it in such a way that it looked not merely dead but extremely dead, very very arrogantly dead, much deader than you ever dreamed dead could be. The image was shocking, that dead yellowish-white waxen face against the dead-white pillow. You were almost afraid to breathe the air in that small room. You stared, and you departed.

That was the last of the exhibitions. When I saw this last morbid item, and then stepped outside into the clean sunlight of a Mexican afternoon, I felt like a Lazarus returned from the dead. I had seen death in the afternoon and I, for one, had not liked it.

Mexico

17. Mexico

On the fourth of march, 1519, hernán cortés landed on mexican soil, and less than seven years later the first bullfight was held in the capital of the country. Since those times Mexico has become the world's most important taurine center, other than Spain.

The "formal" season in Mexico is in the winter, the opposite of Spain, and the novilladas are held in late spring and summer. The capital has two arenas that are larger than Madrid's: El Toreo, holding twenty-five thousand people, and the newer La México, a colossal cement funnel that crams in more than fifty thousand. Lately they have taken to the practice of having fights in both arenas on the same day—a lamentable innovation, it strikes me, especially when you pick the wrong plaza and read in the newspapers the next day about the great faenas that took place in the other.

The greatest faena I ever witnessed in El Toreo was in December of 1956 at the first Guadalupana Feria. It showed what aficionados must go through to see that ideal, that perfect fight of which Patricia Hetter speaks in the chapter on Málaga; for of the thirty-six bulls that I saw killed in six days, only once was the ideal approached, and that was when Antonio Ordóñez immortalized the bull Cascabel in a superb performance.

The greatest in La México—certainly the most dramatic—was Luis Procuna's extraordinary affair on February 15, 1953. He had put up a characteristically disastrous exhibition on both his bulls, and I had left the arena in disgust. As I went down the passageway I heard the reverberations of a tremendous "olé!" Guessing what had happened, I ran back to find that Procuna had bought the substitute bull. The highly capable American girl bullfighting critic, True Bowen, reported the affair the next day in the *Mexico City Daily News:*

Luis Procuna Made History Sunday

On Sunday there were brave bulls and there were brave men. Carlos Arruza, the best; Manolo Dos Santos, the valiant Portuguese; and Luis Procuna, "the character." Three men. And bulls of Zacatepec. One of them was great. Polvorito was this bull's name, and he was an extra bull given to the Plaza because Luis Procuna was angry. The matador had fought two bulls, one manso—tame—but with a certain nobility, the other showing bravery but going into a querencia or natural retreat by the corral door, prepared to fight and die there. Procuna killed with a descabello without first having entered in the prescribed manner,* and the Judge of the Plaza fined him a thousand pesos. Fines are nothing new to Procuna, but he was angry and most of the people were in agreement with him, so he gave the present of the extra bull and dedicated it, sarcastically, to the Judge.

Procuna had the reputation of being a once-great who was about through. He does ridiculous things, sometimes stupid things, often thoughtless things. In some corridas he wants to keep his feet together and fulfill his talent, and in most corridas he just can't do it. Maybe once in a season, or in five seasons, he gets a bull he likes well enough to do real work with. Sunday he got his bull . . . and it was better than a one-a-season kind. Polvorito was a real fighting bull; it came out bravely and it died bravely, and in between was the magic and the passion and the enormous beauty of the fiesta. There have been many great faenas performed in the Plaza Mexico, and Procuna's will rank near the top. He did things that even he has never done before—it was the greatest moment in a career that has had as many boos as cheers.

Polvorito was a black, beautiful, powerful bull. It was Luis, silver and white and shining, who was the sparkling figure doing everything that a man can do with a great bull and achieving a glory he will probably never reach again. But it was the bull who made Procuna's triumph possible, charging and recharging and charging again until it seemed that man and bull were in continuous motion, winding around each other and becoming part of each other. The man . . . standing

---

* An extraordinary and cowardly maneuver since the descabello is intended only as a coup de grace after the matador has entered to kill several times and the bull is unable to charge fairly.

264

with his stomach and chest sticking forward, with his cheeks puffed out, looking like a caricature of himself. And the bull always looking like what it was: a great animal, a brave beast with as much nobility as had the man . . .

The facts will live on in record books, but the hysteria and the insurmountable triumph exists in our minds along with the cries of "To-rer-o!," along with the sombreros hurtling through the air into the ring until the sand was barely visible, along with the fluttering of white handkerchiefs that made the Plaza look snowbound . . . all this will blend in to that glimpse of Luis Procuna, "the character," riding uncomfortably on the shoulders of hundreds of men and boys, his face radiant and confident and somehow transfigured because he had killed one of the bravest bulls the Plaza Mexico has seen in years . . . and in killing it had matched it in honor and in bravery. For the moment Procuna, the man who was through, has ascended to the platform of the gods.

A triumph like this one of Procuna's is what every boy in Mexico dreams of. But to find oneself in a position to fight in La México or El Toreo a man must go through an unbelievably rough apprenticeship. It helps explain why there are only about thirty top matadors in the world in spite of the rewards. "Bullfighting is a pile of riches guarded by a pair of sharp horns," toreros say. Many want the money and the fast cars and the easy women and the adulation, but few have the guts to go through with what they must go through. Unquestionably, the finest account of a young Mexican torero's hell is Luis Spota's powerful and shocking novel, *Más Cornadas Da el Hambre* (translated under the title *The Wounds of Hunger*).

In English, I have never read a better picture of a young aspirant's struggle than Bill Ballantine's fine piece in *True* magazine a few years ago. It is called "The Brave Kids," and it reeks of Mexico City. The greatest Mexican toreros of modern times have been Gaona, Armillita, Balderas, Garza, Ortiz, Solórzano, Silverio, and Arruza. In this vivid picture of one minor Mexican novillero you will find something of all these men who are now immortals in the history of tauromachy:

The first novilleros I met were Rufino Gallito and his friend Sixto González. I had gone to Plaza Mexico on a weekday morning to see what a bullring is like without its slather of Sunday maniacs. The gatekeeper didn't stop me; I guess he thought I was with the Hollywood movie outfit shooting scenes in the bullring that week.

Inside the walls of the huge amphitheater it was awfully quiet and

265

very windy. From the main entrance a long ramp sloped down to the bullring's backstage area, well below street level. Down there, sombreroed workmen were bringing in next Sunday's bulls, gingerly shifting them from heavy, piano-box-size wooden crates, which had metal sides made of old patent-medicine signs, into a narrow chute leading to a sturdy stockade of timber and concrete. "Like handling wild lions," said one of the men. The bulls were being lured down this one-way road by the clanking cowbell of a "Judas steer."

In a broad corridor running partly around the curved backside wall of the seat tiers were torero dressing rooms, smelly and dingy, like most locker rooms; a beautifully equipped surgery; a chapel with Persian rugs and gaudy, sacred trappings; a horse corral for the picadors' bony nags; and a semi-open-air butchery, where the dead bulls are cut up for sale in poor-district butcher shops (most popular cut—testicles).

I got to the bullring itself through the long tunnel in which the toreros form their grand-entry parade. The nearly-noon sun seemed impossibly bright on this big, flat disc with its perimeter of garish signs. The 48,000 empty concrete seats leaned back to the sky.

When my eyes adjusted to the glare, I saw six or seven pairs of Mexican boys scattered on the flat-packed sand, posturing and maneuvering like bulls and matadors.

One boy of each pair held a set of bull's horns mounted on a stick and charged the other, who received these rushes with slow, suave flourishes of a large rose-colored cape lined with yellow—both colors badly sun-faded, the capes bedraggled and worn.

A kid about 14 was leaning against the ring barrier. His sombrero made about the only piece of shade in the whole arena. He told me the boys were novilleros. Many people, their own families in particular, call them vagos (bums) for novilleros consider any gainful employment, except bullfighting, beneath their notice. He said that the main reason the boys get into bullfighting is the lush life of the matador. While it holds little promise of a ripe old age, it does offer mighty sweet returns while you last.

A matador leads the kind of rich, full life for which most Mexicans can only supplicate the Blessed Virgin or the National Lottery. A first-class matador can pick up, in one Sunday afternoon at the bullring, twenty-five to sixty thousand pesos. That's about three to seven thousand American dollars—a nice piece of change anywhere.

A matador's life is nice in other ways, too. He never wants for girls; those tight pants really get them. It's also comforting to own a fancy

266

convertible or two and a cattle ranch with maybe an imported marble bathtub—or two. And it's good to be bowed into the plushest cabarets, the fanciest restaurants and the stuffiest banks.

We were watching a pair just over the barrier whose performance differed from the others. One boy had a sword and a piece of scarlet cloth, smaller than the rose capes and folded over a short stick. His partner was lunging at him, pushing a queer contrivance—a real bulls' head attached to a frame mounted on a single bicycle wheel. The kid at the barrier said this was called the carretilla.

When the kids charged they grunted and snorted in imitation of a bull, and the would-be matador cajoled, coaxed and soothed, just as if he were facing the real thing.

All the boys appeared to be under 20. They were brown and lean, most of them bare to the waist. Some wore drawstring swimming trunks, others had turned-up pantlegs.

The two with the contraption stopped after a while to rest and came over to investigate me. I got a better look at the carretilla. There was a metal tube (rainspout diameter) slanting toward the ground just behind the bull head. It was filled with coarse straw, its top covered over by a chunk of maguey plant. The tube was for taking the sword thrust into the simulated bull's shoulders, the thick plant leaf giving the right fleshy feel.

The kid with the sword said he was Rufino Gallito, the Idol of Temascaltepec, killer of fifty-three bulls (fifty-five come Sunday) and this was his friend, Sixto González, the Phenomenon of Bullfighting. Rufino had to reach for his English a little and I had to thumb my Spanish-English-English-Spanish a lot, but we got along.

He let me lift the heavy sword, and I knew then how tough it would be to get it up over real horns and make a killing plunge into one certain spot in the shoulder of a 1,000–pound angry bull.

Sixto kept egging Rufino to get back to practice, so we didn't talk much. But I did learn that a kid becomes a novillero by his own say-so the minute he seriously picks up cape and sword, and that the boys play a great deal of *jai alai* to get strong wrists for good cape work, sharpen their eye and increase their wind.

Rufino said there weren't many good places in the city to practice any more; his favorite, for instance, a vacant lot on the street Niño Perdido, was now a bus terminal. An appropriately named street, I thought, for kid bullfighters—Niño Perdido, The Lost Child.

The boys stepped off to do some fancy cape work, calling to me after each figure, its name: "Ayudado" . . . "Manoletina" . . . "Afaro-

267

lado." Rufino was trying to get the cape to wrap gracefully around his chunky Mexican hips in the Molinete, when a man appeared high up in the seats and called down to the boys through cupped hands.

I didn't catch, but Rufino said everyone had to leave the ring now; the movie company (la pelicula *Los Toros Bravos*) had arrived to work some more. This afternoon, he and all these other boys would be actors, playing the parts of monosabios (wise-monkeys). Hollywood pesos had induced these proud aspirants to matador to play the lowliest role of the bullring. Monosabios shovel up after the horses and bulls, and man the mule teams that drag out the deaders.

An elderly Mexican, new-saddle color, was passing out the mono-sabio uniforms in a narrow, concrete room near the corral. Rufino said he was Simón, the famous monosabio who throws himself down over gored matadors to protect them from further damage.

The outfits were pretty beat up—faded red jackets, dirty white pants, peaked caps that even a burleycue doorman would shy at.

Rufino smiled wryly at his misfit suit. He said, "Some traje de luces." Which is what the spangled costume of the torero is called—suit of lights.

As I walked up the ramp to leave the Plaza, sound trucks and costume vans lumbered down. At the gate, I looked back, and down beyond the bull pens, thick black cables were being snaked out, shimmering reflectors set up and someone was handing out box lunches.

A couple of days later I found out what really tough going novilleros have. An American friend, who knew I was interested in the kids, had me meet Señor Alfredo Pierce, Executive Secretary to Dr. Alfonso Gaona, Empresa (Impresario) of Plaza México.

The downtown headquarters of Mexico's most colorful spectacle are in a long, extremely drab one-story building, one room deep, with a dirty, gray-cement face. Only a row of ticket windows, opening to the sidewalk, keeps it from looking like any run-down machine shop.

I found Señor Pierce in the Empresa's office. It was as colorful as the outside had been dull. A couple of huge bull heads, mounted like hunting trophies, hung on one wall. There was a slew of colorful bull-fight posters, one gigantic aerial photo of Plaza México on a Sunday (it looked like a soup bowl full of fleas) and many large, framed photos of famous matadors. In the space left between them hung small wooden plaques on which were mounted the severed ears of bulls. Each plaque carried a metal plate engraved with the story of the bull's defeat.

Señor Pierce couldn't have been more accommodating.

"You have come to the right place, señor," he said to me. "This boy here," indicating a slim youth, busy answering two telephones alternately, at a desk just outside the door, "he was a very good novillero until the bulls got his leg one afternoon. They had to cut it off when he was gorged." He had a habit of saying "gorged" when he meant "gored."

The boy had long sideburns, combed-back black hair and a jiblike Spanish nose. Through a doorway behind him, I could see the back-sides of the ticket sellers, busy behind their wickets. The public sale for next Sunday had begun at 9:30 that morning. Some of the people clamoring out on the sidewalk had been there since dawn; some had waited all night.

"Paquito, bring your map," called Señor Pierce in Spanish. "Show this gentleman the places you have fought the bull." The boy turned over his jangling phones to another chap and came in, one leg swinging stiffly.

Pierce helped unfold the map, which covered most of a desktop. Shyly, in Spanish, the boy with one leg began to trace the career that a horn cut short. Señor Pierce translated.

"He says he started at what are called ferias—fairs, village festivals; like for the village saint day. Besides the bullfights, there are cock-fights, bareback horse races, dancing, music. They throw up a corral fence around the village square and hold the bullfights there. Peoples that can't get into the bleachers sit on the top rail of the fence. Other peoples hang on ladders leaned against the cathedral; the good climbers squat up among the bells in the towers.

"Sometime there are only six bulls for all six days of the feria. One is killed each day; the rest fight again next day. Is bad for the boys: the bulls get wise and wicked, fighting without being killed. When a bull fight for three, four days the same boys, he learns a lot, gets treacherous. And many time a bad bull who gorged a boy in last year's feria is brought back to fight again. And in the hinterlands there may be just a bottle of iodine instead of a doctor, or there may be nothing at all."

Paco pointed to a tiny dot on the map. "Here, in that town," continued Pierce, "he says six boys fought six days the same bulls and got only sixteen pesos each boy—that's less than two dollars apiece. Novil-leros, they all have it very tough; even fight cebús, the bad bulls from the Argentine, very dangerous, and what we call cross-eyed bulls (bizcos) that have one horn up, one down."

Paco was talking now about a town down near the Guatemalan bor-

der. "In that place below Tehuantepec," said Pierce to me, "five boys fight *each* one, five bulls—for a total pay, for the whole bunch, of fourteen hundred pesos. That's twenty-five bulls at six and a half bucks a bull. And the boys even pay all their own expenses." Paco's finger was on another dot. "In that town he fight espontáneo," Pierce went on. "You know what that is? Is when a boy jump into the ring from the audience and fight the bull. For that he went to jail. And in *that* town he pay two hundred pesos (about twenty-three fifty) toward the cost of the bull that he kill. And there . . . he fight the bull in a swimming pool. Yes. Bullring is down inside a dry swimming pool. Very hard to get out of if bull turns on you. And, at Otumba there, his proudest moment, the first time he ever dress as matador, was spoiled. They wouldn't let him fight the bull at all; only place the banderillas."

I asked Señor Pierce if he thought the small rings deliberately exploited the boys. "No," he said. "They only pay so little because they have so little. Village peoples can't pay much for seats—thirty-five cents sombra (in the shade), maybe, twenty-five cents sol."

"It all sounds plenty rough to me," I said.

"It is plenty rough," agreed Señor Pierce. He shrugged. "But the mania—it gets in the blood."

Paco went back to his work. Pierce and I talked some more about the novillero business.

It's not as harum-scarum as it seems on first look. A boy cannot become a professional matador simply by killing a lot of bulls. There are rules and regulations, a definite pattern to be followed. There is even a union.

Roughly, this is the way the thing works. When a kid gets good enough, the novillero union takes notice and invites him to join up. Then, if the boy can bring to the union committee certified official programs proving he has had five fights which employed picadors or fifteen without, he gets in the union.

After that, he goes on fighting in the sticks and waits for his bid to come to Plaza Mexico and be a real matador. This bid can come only to novillero union members and from only one man, the Empresa of Plaza Mexico. Some novilleros wait two, three, five years for the bid; some have waited ten, twelve; some never get it at all.

"But how does the Empresa find out about these kids?" I asked Señor Pierce.

"There are many ways for the new boy to come to Dr. Gaona's notice. If he gets good write-ups in the press when he fight at small-time rings; one week he gets an ear, next time two ears, another time even the tail . . ." Señor Pierce was referring to the custom of honoring a matador for exceptional performance by awarding the severed ears and tail of the vanquished bull, in some cases even the hoof (seldom done in Mexico).

Then there is the big novillero season at Plaza Mexico, the novilladas (learner's fights), starting at formal season's end in April and running through rainy season until November.

And there are private trial corridas at Plaza Mexico too, when rejected bulls, with horn points cut off, are used against likely novilleros. Dr. Gaona watches these trials and the novilladas for new talent.

"And there's Rancho del Charro," Pierce added, "a small ring here in town, run as a private club with some fights open to the public. At times a boy gets to perform there in a benefit; no pay, of course, but everybody important see him."

When the bid comes, a novillero must go through a ceremony known as the alternativa, before he can meet a bull as a full matador. This alternativa is given only two places in the world, Mexico City and Madrid.

The alternativa ceremony is very brief, held in ring center. The bull is kept at bay by other toreros and is always an interested observer. The sponsor makes a pretty little speech, embraces the boy and gives him a muleta (the scarlet cloth) and sword for the kill. The boy's seniority as matador dates from this moment.

The new matador, under union regulations, gets an established price of 1,000 pesos (about $117) for this first fight. What he gets after that depends on how good his manager is.

The next morning after my visit with Paco and Pierce, I was walking on Bolívar Street, along which are the favorite hangouts of Mexico City's bullfighters, when Rufino Gallito hailed me. He was leaning on the front of a sad-looking Chinese restaurant, identified in crooked neon as El Cantonés.

The Idol of Temascaltepec looked so natty I hardly recognized him. He was wearing a splendid pair of alligator shoes (not expensive in Mexico) and an ornately tooled suede jacket hung with long leather fringe, a la Daniel Boone.

Rufino said his traje de luces was in for repair (no horn rips, just split seams) and he was downtown to fetch it. When I offered to buy a beer at the cantina, Rufino said he was in training, but he would buy me a papaya cooler, then take me to lunch. I hoped he didn't have El Cantonés in mind. I didn't think I would enjoy the daily special, chop suey de res (head of cattle). Rufino said the boys all ate here because

it was cheap, but they liked to hang around the Tupinamba across the street, where all the real matadors ate.

The Tupinamba didn't look elegant, but still I didn't think Rufino could afford lunch there, so I suggested we just have coffee. It was a good idea; the house specialty is thick, black *café espresso*, which is delightful.

The restaurant is quite large, an extremely plain, dismal room, harshly lighted by rows of fluorescent tubing on a pressed-metal ceiling. It has the feel of a better-class skid-row hash house.

The only women I saw were several fleshy, uncomely waitresses uniformed in black. Hung over the counter running down one side, and jammed around white-top tables which fill the rest of the room, were knots of men in drab business suits. It was hard to associate this lackluster mob with bullfighting. If they hadn't been so noisy and argumentative—there was a constant hum like flies over a manure pile —they might have been shoe clerks or shopkeepers. But Rufino assured me these men were all toreros. He spoke to several, addressing them respectfully as "Matador" never as "Señor" or by name.

We didn't stay long at Tupinamba. The Idol, anxious to regain his identity I supposed, hustled me down the street to a pastry shop called the Flor de Mexico.

I hardly expected to find bullfighters here. But Rufino said the well-pressed young men sipping sodas and spooning sundaes at marble-topped tables inside were very high type novilleros. I wondered what the bulls would think.

Rufino treated me to a *tres marías*, which turned out to be a triple scoop sundae in the national colors—strawberry, vanilla and pistachio.

After this orgy, we went several blocks down Bolívar to No. 89, the tailor shop of Ignacio Ysunza, to pick up Rufino's traje de luces. Ysunza's place is on a high second floor and overlooks a grubby little park, where a crude wall painting of a bull identifies the men's side of the public lavatory.

Ysunza, slightly hunched and gnome-like, was spangling and embroidering with two assistants in a room almost as dark as a cave. It was lighted by a couple of bare hanging bulbs and what daylight got through an open door from a small balcony.

It was apparent that bullfighters were Ysunza's main custom. Faded relics of many deaths-in-the-afternoon all but covered the walls—photos, programs, heralds and posters.

There was a dandy chromolitho (put out by a beer company) of the death of Manolete. It showed him laid out in a high-style coffin, and rearing over him spewing blood was a more muscular bull than ever existed, a veritable bovine Sandow.

And there was a picture of Ysunza in street clothes standing calmly in a bullring on a kitchen chair as a bull charged past. (A virtuoso piece. Man stands still enough, bull thinks he is a statue.) "It was easy," said the tailor. "I was only fifty-six then."

Rufino said Ysunza is the best matador tailor in all Mexico; there are three families besides him who cater to the bullfighting set. The finest outfits come from the house of Antonio Manfredi in Sevilla, Spain. But only top-notch matadors can afford them since first fittings must be made over there.

In Mexico, a first-class tailor-made traje de luces costs around $400; same quality in the States would run $3,000 and take at least a year to make. Ysunza has turned one out in fifteen days.

The novilleros who haven't their own costume rent from Ysunza. Rufino said he owned his, of course.

His ripped seams hadn't been mended yet (Ysunza said *mañana* for sure) so we left with the Idol of Temascaltepec grumbling a little into his hairless chest. But, by the time I said *"adiós"* to him, he had brightened enough to invite me to lunch at his home Sunday, so I could see him dress as a matador. He was going to perform at Temascaltepec in a benefit bullfight sponsored by the electricians' union for the parish church.

The next morning, as I left the dining room after breakfast, a bell-hop said that two gentlemen were waiting to see me over by the elevator. It was Rufino and another boy. They were trying to make themselves inconspicuous behind a portly lady tourist, and the Mexican desk clerk had a fishy eye on them.

"Buenos días, mister," said the Idol. "This is my manager." Then, after an awkward pause, Rufino blurted, "Señor, I have need of ninety pesos to get my vestido, my traje de luces for the fight tomorrow."

It all made sense now—papaya cooler, *café espresso, tres marías,* invite to lunch. I was just being buttered up for the bite.

The bellhop and I went into a hurried conference. He said, "Señor, that's a lot of money in Mexico and you will never see it again." I thought so too, but the Idol of Temascaltepec won. *"Muchas gracias, señor,"* said the manager. Incidentally, the bellhop was right.

Rufino had said to come early Sunday because his cousin was driving them all to the bullfight right after lunch. I got to the house, only a couple of bull tosses from Plaza México, just before noon. It was a narrow one-story, plain as a shoebox; one of a long row spaced along a sun-baked street like baby teeth, a skinny gap of courtyard between each one.

In this narrow cement space at Rufino's a very small boy with a wooden sword was learning to be a matador. An older boy made a credible bull, holding his index and middle fingers together for horns.

"How old's the kid?" I asked Rufino.

"Him? Sebastián? He's five year." I wasn't surprised.

Rufino's father had just returned from the Plaza where he goes every Sunday morning to study the day's bulls, and to watch the noonday drawing that decides which bulls each matador fights that afternoon. He was in the front room with Sixto, tacking up (for my benefit, I thought) a florid Spanish poster. The two of them had just done a masterful job of dubbing Rufino's name onto matched parts of two other posters, so that it looked as if he had been a star performer at Plaza Mexico in a corrida featuring Piedras Negras bulls, a really first-class breed which I doubt Rufino had faced yet at this point in his career.

Papa presented me with his business card, which said in old-English type that Gabriel Gallito was a "Carpenter, Cabinet Maker, Wood-carver, and Varnisher in General, a Specialist in Furniture Carving and Cabinets for Radio."

Rufino's sister sliced me a thin moon of papaya, tuned in some flamenco on the radio (a heap of wires and tubes without a cabinet) then left the room to the men.

Papa brought an example of his work, a hand-carved prayer bench, and a cigar box of photos, mostly snaps of his son in action with various now-deceased bulls. In the rummage were a couple of dog-eared ones of Papa himself as matador. Under cover of the photos, Rufino and Sixto tacked up homemade placards displaying their pictures, names and titles.

On a slablike bed a kid of Rufino's age was laying out all the things the budding matador would use in his fight that afternoon. He was the mozo de espadas, sword handler, combination valet-propman. The most intriguing item was a little black pigtail to attach to Rufino's own hair in back.

A small photo of Rufino, propped against a jar of pink-paper roses on a bedside table, was the focal point of a shrine which climbed the wall to a Virgin of Guadalupe under glass near the ceiling.

"Excuse me, mister," Rufino said. "I go make my 'meada de miedo,'" and went outside to the lavatory. When I asked Papa Gallito what this meant, he laughed and said Rufino was making a joke; real matadors call the last time they urinate before a bullfight the "leak of fear." Papa told me another expression about a matador's fear on bullfight day: "los huevos le llegan hasta la garganta"—literally, "the eggs (Mexican slang for testicles) have climbed into the throat."

Rufino came back, took off his Sunday suit and modestly closed the front shutter for a trice as he slipped from his shorts into swimming trunks. As it takes a professional matador several hours to dress, I was struck by Rufino's speed and casualness. He didn't bother with the long, tight underdrawers into which matadors have themselves sewn. He simply pulled on his spangled knee pants, and his mozo made them snug as possible by suspending Rufino above the floor on a thick roll of towel through his crotch, jouncing him a little as Rufino strained at the pants top. For knee padding the boys used strips of folded newspaper. The whole dressing operation took less than half an hour, and Rufino looked almost as resplendent as anything to be seen at Plaza Mexico.

Several friends had drifted in while Rufino made ready and there were eleven of us at lunch, Rufino's mother at the head of the table. He sat with us but didn't eat; a bullfighter must remember that there may be late-afternoon surgery. One bite would probably have split his tight seams again anyway.

Lunch was sturdy and plain. Spoons for the soup were the only tableware. The *frijoles* had to be attacked with rolled-up *tortillas*; likewise, a potent blackish sauce lurking in what I think was a bird-bath. The main course was meat—small slices, highly seasoned (could have been horse, goat or beef) served with fried potatoes and chopped lettuce.

After lunch, the cousin arrived in a squarish Buick sedan, which must have been right elegant in Papa's day. It was faded gray with tasseled portieres at the windows, was lined with velvet and had bud vases inside. It looked like a hearse.

Rufino knelt before the little shrine in the front room, while his mother gave him her last blessing and lighted the vigil candles, which would burn until his return.

In the courtyard, Rufino and his father locked in a last embrace. And soon the mother, sister, the 5-year-old potential and I stood at the gate, watching the fabulous automobile disappearing down the street with the toreros behind a veil of dust.

Rufino was a brave kid. I hoped that if he was "gorged" at Temascaltepec there would be something more than iodine.

The Border Towns

Many Americans have seen their first, and often last, corrida de toros in one of the several towns along the North American–Mexican border, such as Tijuana, Mexicali, Nogales, Matamoros, or Ciudad Juárez. These arenas start their seasons in the spring and put on fights sporadically until about mid-October.

Are they real fights, people ask, just like Spain's? Actually, all fights in Mexico are like the ones in Spain except for such minor formalities as not playing "The Virgin of the Macarena" in Spain and as taking laps around the ring counterclockwise in Mexico. But there are more subtle differences between Spanish and Mexican bullfighting, such as the fact that the Mexican tends to be more varied and florid with the cape, more importance is given to the matador's placing his own banderillas, the bulls of Spain and Mexico are very different, and so forth. In the same way there are subtle differences in Mexico between the border fights and ones in Mexico City and the interior. The ritual is exactly the same, they use bulls from good ranches, and the matadors are often the best in the world. But there are differences in the atmosphere. Somehow the corrida is not enhanced by a voice over a loud-speaker saying in English, "And now Antonio Velázquez takes his turn at making the *quite* with chicuelinas, which means Chicuelo's "maneuver."

I once heard the broadcaster giving a tense, Clem McCarthy type, blow-by-blow description of the matador as he "crossed" with the bull: "There he is, he's moving forward, forward—now he's reversing his field . . ." I kept expecting the matador to fade back for a pass.

I am constantly amazed that, in spite of this atmosphere and the second-rate bulls and the frequent performances by female bullfighters, there are often great fights at Tijuana. Arruza, Silveti, Capetillo, and Armillita have put up some of their greatest performances there, and even Manolete fought in Tijuana the year before he died (at fifty dollars per shady side barrera). The same can be said for the other border towns. For the real aficionado, knowing the men who are to perform and the bulls they are to take on, the day of a fight along the border can be as exciting as one in Sevilla.

The audiences are made up largely of Americans, mostly curious and unknowing ones who have come to see "this fellow Ahrootzah I've read about" or to see a fight just because they want to see if it's as bad as Aunt Prunella described it. I remember one pink-slacked, heart-bottomed, mink-stoled blonde standing up and shouting, over and over, "Come on bull!"

However, there are also a few well-read, voluble, and regular "aficionadil-los" who really work at their afición; Los Angeles, San Diego, and Tucson have several bullfighting clubs which boast of hundreds of Americans on their membership lists. One, the Club Olé of San Diego, has regular monthly meetings with lectures and films, and even publishes a little newspaper in English.

A big corrida in Tijuana is a frenetic affair, with hundreds of Americans driving down from Los Angeles and San Diego and jamming up at the bars at Caesar's and the Foreign Club, where the kings for the day are Gilbert Roland, Antonio Moreno, Budd Boetticher, and Ruben Padilla. There is nothing in all the bull world comparable to it. It is American BIG GAME day applied to la fiesta brava, and as such it is frightening.

Herb Caen, the consistently witty columnist of the San Francisco *Examiner,* joined me in one of these forays recently, and out of it came one of his classic columns. It was entitled "Death of an Atomic Pig," and it nobly captured some of the frenzy and wackiness of Tijuana of a Sunday afternoon in fall:

Six bulls and four bees died slowly in the Mexican border town of Tijuana last Sunday. The bulls died in the Plaza de Toros. The bees died, in what must have been a state of high confusion, some 8,000 feet aloft—in a Mainliner airplane. But more about THEM later.

Tijuana was far from sleepy that day. True, a few Mexicans were dozing here and there under their sombreros—on orders from the Tijuana Chamber of Commerce, to keep things "authentic"—but elsewhere, things were definitely at fever pitch. About 101 degrees.

For on Sunday, Carlos Arruza, the greatest living matador, was launching a brand new career in the bull ring—as a rejoneador. That is, he will now fight bulls on horseback, weakening them with rejones (long lances) and then dismounting to make the kill. You gather, of

278

course, that it is Arruza who is on horseback. Not the bull. The bull walks to death, as always.

To observe this memorable event, the drybacks poured into Tijuana Sunday in near record numbers. They came from San Diego, in their pedal pushers and sportshirts. From Hollywood, with their movie cameras and their low necklines. From Mexico City, with their knowing looks and flashy women.

And they even came from San Francisco, in their Ivy League suits and button-down shoes, led by the noblest aficionado of them all, Señor Barnaby Conrad, official biographer of Carlos Arruza and the man who has sold bullfighting to almost everyone except the S.P.C.A. And me.

On Tijuana's main drag—and I use the word advisedly—the carnival spirit was already approaching the bacchanalian. The sidewalks were jammed with tourists, inviting disaster by stuffing themselves with stuffed *tacos* sold by sidewalk vendors. Little girls walked up and down selling "chewn gom." Hawkers implored you to have your picture taken in tiny carts drawn by burros painted with black stripes to make them look like zebras.

Everywhere the atmosphere of Old Mexico was heavy, even rancid, in the air. At the Waikiki Club. At the Alt Heidelberg, whose sign reads "Mex-German Dishes." And especially at Caesar's, where the bar was loaded with gringos getting loaded.

The talk was of nothing but Arruza and the fight. "Carlos has been sick all night," breathlessly exclaimed a ravishing blonde friend. "He only had two hours' sleep."

We trooped up to the matador's quarters in Room 18 at the Foreign Club Hotel. The great man looked a little peaked, and the dramatic vertical wrinkles in his sunken cheeks stood out sharply. He chatted pleasantly, but a large bottle of Kaopectate on a nearby table spoke mutely of his woes.

You see? It doesn't happen only to tourists.

The fights began at 3 p.m. in Tijuana's rickety, splintering old arena.* Arruza, despite his inner grief, looked dashing on his Portuguese-trained stallion, and although the bull (a smallish 800–pounder) almost caught him twice on the far turn, he dispatched it with consummate grace, to the "Olés!" of the mob of 8,000. As he strode around the ring, women threw their shoes at him. Also scarfs and handbags (all of which he threw back). And one girl tossed him her brassiere—an empty gesture if I ever saw one.

* Recently replaced with a steel arena holding 10,800 people.—B.C.

After the fights, we wandered along the crowded main street, and in a little novelty shop, we found the perfect souvenir of our mad day in Alt Mexico. Puercos Atómicos—atomic pigs! These are pecan shells, artfully carved and decorated to look like tiny pigs. Their wooden ears, eyes and tail move constantly and mysteriously—"because," said the salesgirl, "they have Mexican jumping beans inside." We bought out the shop, at 50¢ per atomic pig.

But alas. Once on the plane across the border, the atomic pigs became lifeless, immobile. The tiny ears no longer wiggled so intriguingly. The tiny tail was once more just a stick. The tiny eyes no longer jiggled around like Eddie Cantor's.

As the plane roared aloft, Señor Conrad pondered this problem. Then the man who has faced many a bull in the ring came to grips with the problem of the pig. "We'll have to break one open," he said gravely, "and see what's inside."

He broke off the wooden snout—and out of the pig crawled a bee. Then three other bees fell out and dropped to the floor of the Mainliner, quite dead. While Señor Conrad watched in awed disbelief, the first bee slowly spread its wings and buzzed through the ship, while passengers screamed, children cried, and the stewardess ran up and down the aisle, in cold pursuit.

The bee, like the bulls of a few hours earlier, struggled gallantly to keep going, and then suddenly fell lifeless to the floor. We saluted the brave bee, and then sat silent, contemplating the strange land of Mexico—where bulls die in the afternoon, and bees wiggle the ears of atomic pigs.

Guadalajara, Morelia, and Monterrey

These rings are probably the most important ones in Mexico after the two in the capital city. They hold about half as many spectators as El Toreo, but the best toreros of Latin America and Spain appear there every year. Of the three, Guadalajara is the most important and has the most charm.

I always think of Monterrey as the place where the greatest American bullfighter took his alternative. Sidney Franklin? No, the lesser known but greater Harper Lee. Many people consider him the finest non-Latin ever to try the "art of Cúchares." He was born in Texas in 1884, but his parents moved to Guadalajara when he was quite young. He became a civil engineer but soon left the profession when "el gusanillo de la afición"—the bullfighting worm—got into his brain. He fought in many Mexican cities

Harper Lee.

with considerable success before graduating to full matador in 1910. Harper was very brave, had a large repertory, and placed his own banderillas. A terrible wound prevented him from confirming the alternative in Spain, and he retired from the ring prematurely. He went to work for an oil company in the United States and died in Texas in 1941 at the age of fifty-seven. He was not a truly great matador, but he was a highly competent one, and that is quite miraculous considering his background and nationality.

It is rare when a dedicated Spanish boy, with all the opportunities and atmosphere and afición, makes the grade in the bull world. It is virtually impossible for an American to make it. Take the recent Spanish article by Don Atonio, in the bullfighting bible, the weekly *El Ruedo;* reviewing a performance of Porter Tuck, a serious, dedicated, proper Massachusetts youth who is billed incredibly as "El Rubio de Bostón"—The Blond from Boston:

281

I believe my advice is sane and definitive: Porter Tuck should retire from the ring and dedicate his energies to a less rigorous job than bullfighting. Right at the start he has against him the fact that he has no Spanish blood in his veins, and it is that seed which gives one an innate feeling for the fiesta, for elegant disdain in the presence of danger, for the graceful gesture in the face of death. In Spain itself only the regions of Andalucía, Castilla, Valencia, Aragón, and Cataluña have given great bullfighters to history; there are a few from other regions, but these are the exceptions which prove the rule. Spanish blood made possible such Latin American greats as Gaona, Arruza, Armillita, and Girón. A North American such as Sidney Franklin or Porter Tuck can learn bullfighting as a job, by rote, through hard study and practising. But they are totally incapable of producing art in the bullring.

What about this Sidney Franklin, I am continually asked. Was he great—as great as he claims he was in his autobiography, as great as Hemingway says he was in *Death in the Afternoon?* I must answer that I really don't know. It is an eternal argument. I never saw Sidney fight in a real corrida, though I know him very well and have for years. However, I did see him in a festival fight in San Roque, near Alegeciras, in 1944, and though he looked painfully rusty and out of condition with the cape and the muleta, he killed superbly and was granted both ears. No one knows Sidney's age (any more than they know anything else for sure about him), but he must have been considerably over forty at the time. I cannot possibly judge how Sidney was in his prime. Most Spaniards will tell you, "Frahng-cleen was brave, but cold and not graceful." But when you pin them down, they didn't actually see "Frahng-cleen" perform, they just heard from someone else—who probably also didn't see him perform. After all, there weren't a great many opportunities to see Franklin, in spite of the impression that Hemingway gives, since in all he has fought only twenty-three fights in Spain in his career. His first was in Sevilla on June 9, 1929, in which I know for a fact that he did extraordinarily well. He fought thirteen more novilladas that year, three of them in Madrid. The next year he fought only nine, in one of which he was badly gored. It was a terrible wound in the rectum, requiring many operations over a period of several years. Meanwhile he made *The Kid from Spain* with Eddie Cantor and fought occasionally in Mexico. He never fought again in Spain until 1945, when he took the alternative in Madrid, surely the oldest novillero in the history of the spectacle to be graduated to a full matador.

Sidney, who now manages a cafeteria in Morón de la Frontera, sixty

282

kilometers from Sevilla, is one of the great characters abroad in the world today, and everyone who knows him has tales to spin about him and an evaluation of his prowess in the ring. Here are some random opinions:—

Ex-matador Chucho Solórzano: "Sidney knows his job—and well. He is not an artist but he is brave as a lion and he is a craftsman."

Juan Belmonte, reminiscing one day: "I only saw him once. That was in Lisbon. Though not accustomed to placing the sticks, he tried a cambio with the banderillas and he cambiar'd too soon and the bull cambiar'd also but then it un-cambiar'd upon seeing that it had been tricked, and it hit him in the stomach and knocked him out. He came to in the infirmary but the presidente wouldn't let him return to the ring 'por inepto'—because of ineptness! I believe Franklin hates me because he thinks I was the one who wouldn't let him come out since I was sitting in the presidente's box as a guest. But it wasn't I who restrained him 'por inepto,' although I admit the expression amuses me. I have never heard of such a ruling being made before or since in all my years of bullfighting." He laughs and savors the phrase: "Por inepto!"

Sidney Franklin
and the author
before the former's
festival fight
in San Roque.

(In rebuttal Sidney said to me: "Belmonte saw me a lot more than that once! He used to follow me around in '29 and '30 and sneak into the plazas incognito to catch my act and learn all the new stuff I was pulling off." It must be confessed that modesty is not one of Sidney's most glaring short-comings.)

Hemingway, writing of Franklin in *Death in the Afternoon:* "He is a better, more scientific, more intelligent, and more finished matador than all but about six of the full matadors in Spain today."

The late painter of bulls, Roberto Domingo: "He was cold and uninteresting in the ring and wouldn't have gone anywhere had he not been an American and hence a curiosity. However, he is very simpático."

Manuel "Bienvenida," ex-matador: "I tell you, after his debut in Sevilla we walked out of that arena with our jaws down to here. I remember saying, 'This boy will finish with everyone fighting today, my sons included, if he keeps going this way.' Luckily for us, he never was able really to repeat his Sevilla triumph."

José Mario Cossío, in his monumental work, *Los Toros,* says: "He was valiant, he manipulated both cape and muleta with grace and he killed quickly and well, though with little style."

Mexican critic Sanchez Gavito, *Don Inda:* "He had quite a marvelous verónica, was fair with the muleta, good with the sword. I would put him in the same category with Argentina's Rovira on one of the latter's best days."

So much for the hearsay. The fact remains that Sidney Franklin is the only North American and non-Latin to ever take the alternative in Spain and to become a full matador. This is indisputable. No other American, except Harper Lee, has been taken seriously in professional bullfighting in Spain or Latin America. Several have tried, and at present there are a few "novilleritos gringos" around trying. I hear such names as Harry Whitney and Porter Tuck and John Fulton Short, but these seem to be lucky to fight two or three novilladas a season (as opposed to the 115 that Litri as a novillero was able to rack up in one year). One occasionally sees American "matadors" in this country appearing in newsreels and on line-guessing television programs, but a cursory investigation proves that no one has ever heard of them in the bull world, a world where everyone works at knowing everything about everyone else. There have been a few outstanding American "aficionados prácticos"—that is, amateur matadors who know bulls and like to fight them but don't need the money enough to have to go professional and perform when they don't feel like it. Among them is movie director Budd Boetticher. I myself was, and am, an aficionado práctico; in other words, I still fight when I can find a tubercular enough bull. Al-

284

though I had planned to go professional at one time, it is far pleasanter to listen to the easy speculations of how great one *could* have been than to get out there and try to prove it.

Actually, in the professional line the American girls seem to have outdone the men. Conchita Cintrón is the daughter of an American mother and a Puerto Rican father, and she is the best torera of all time. Betty Ford and Patricia McCormick, no matter how they are rated, work hard at their craft, are learning and gaining respect, and perform five times as often as any present American males. In the distaff department only the skilled and attractive Juanita Aparicio of Mexico is better than these two.

These modern girls have no monopoly because of their sex; ever since Cretan days, girls have been around la fiesta getting underfoot. The first mention of a specific female torera, according to Cossío, the bullfighters' Boswell, is back in 1654. One of Goya's etchings represents the "manly courage" of "La Pajuelera" as she performed in the Zaragoza arena. Even a nun, Doña María de Gaucín, supposedly left a convent to become a torera. According to Havelock Ellis *(The Soul of Spain)*, "She was distinguished not only for her courage but also for her beauty and virtue, and after a few years, during which she attained renown throughout Spain, she peacefully returned to the practice of religion in her convent, without, it appears, any reproaches from her sisters, who enjoyed the reflected fame of her exploits in the bullring."

My own favorite female bullfighter of all time was "La Reverte." She came into prominence around the turn of the century and fought with considerable success for seven years, at the end of which time the Spanish government decreed that it was illegal and immoral for women to fight bulls. Whereupon La Reverte took off his wig and tried to continue in the profession as the man he really had been all along. They nearly lynched him, and though he stayed in bullfighting he was a ruined man.

Peru

18. Peru

Francisco pizarro founded the city of lima, peru, on january 18, 1535, and five years later the first corrida was held there. It featured three "toros de Maranga," and according to historians the star rejoneador was Pizarro himself (although some suggest it was his brother Hernando).

Ever since those times, Lima has been the center of bullfighting in South America. La Plaza de Acho was built in 1765, the first real bullring in the New World. Today there is a relatively new bullring in the city, the Plaza of Chacra Rios, which holds eighteen thousand people as compared to Acho's thirteen thousand, but it has had a disastrous history; the aficionados appear to want to see bulls fought in Acho, and only in Acho.

The aficionados of Lima are some of the finest in the world. They also have the best "gentleman toreros" of any country; aficionados prácticos like Roca Rey, Fernando Graña, and Gabriel Tizón can and do compete with the professionals who come to Lima every year. I think the reason that they are so good is that they practice on half-breed animals from the hills that are as wily and rugged as any I've come across, whereas the Spanish "señoritos" are spoiled by the general excellence and predictability of the bulls in Spain; I've paid a couple of visits to the distinguished Dr. Pancho Graña, the beloved "médico de los toreros," after bouts with those bulls.

Graña is a name closely identified with Peruvian bullfighting for years. Among other things, the Grañas own "Huando," which, along with La Viña and Fernandini, produces the best fighting bulls in Peru. I remember being up in Manolete's room at the Country Club as he dressed before his first fight in South America in 1946. He looked pale and kept pacing up and

289

The author doing a
manoletina in the
practice ring
in Lima.

down. Fernando Graña was there also, and it was a big day for him, since this was to be the "debut" of the bulls from his ranch.

"He's very nervous," I remarked to Manolete. "Afraid they won't turn out right."

Manolete stopped pacing, and he looked at me with that good, sad smile of his. "You know," he said, "I could tell you about someone who is more afraid."

Neither had much reason to be nervous, as it turned out. But the next day a strange thing happened in Acho. Manolete came up behind a bull to take it away from the horse it was charging. It was reluctant to pull away, and the matador slapped his cape across its stern to distract it. Without leaving the horse, the bull disdainfully kicked out its back leg and caught Manolete high on the thigh. The torero went down in great pain and was carried out of the ring completely *hors de combat*. I have never seen this occur to any other matador before or since.

I recently received a letter from César Graña, a sociologist at the University of California, which gives a rambling but graphic picture of bullfighting in Peru, especially in its golden age, and I shall publish it here just as he wrote it:

> Now you realize that it is impossible for an aficionado not to take advantage of whatever the opportunity to unload on his fellows all sorts of personal and, of course, unique reminiscences. So you will have to put up with some of mine.
>
> It occurred to me the other day that a good many Peruvian bullfighters have been colored. The two Peruvian "Facultades" (how many people have used this nickname?!), Germán León in the 19th century, and Pedro Castro in recent years, were both Negroes. So was the great local figure of the latter part of the 19th century, Angel Váldez "El Maestro." I once saw a picture of him. He was a full-blooded Negro and quite a big man. To judge from pictures it wasn't altogether unusual for large men to be in the ring at that time. I think that Matías Lara "Larita" must have been the last of the hefty ones. The banderillero "Fosforito," killed in Acho, was a Negro too. And so is the present day Santa Cruz, of course. "Fosforito" wasn't gored. The bull simply stepped on his head. From the pictures I have seen of the practitioners of the Peruvian "suerte nacional" [caping on horseback], they too were colored. The best of them, Juan Gualberto Asín, was a pure-blooded Negro.
>
> The Italians are another group. Carlos Sussoni, Alejandro Montani, the old banderillero Juan Giani "El Rubio" and the only good Peruvian

291

picadores, the brothers Juan and Humberto Murro, were all Italian. Of Italian ancestry, that is.

I talked the other night, you may remember, about El Toro del Miedo (this became the "historic" name; what the bull's real name was no one seems to remember though, of course, he had one), a titanic Asín, the biggest and, I think, the most beautiful animal I ever saw. I forget everything else about the corrida, but I remember everything about the bull, and still get excited thinking about it. "El Gallo" and "Chicuelo" were on the cartel; I forget who else. The Toro del Miedo came out of the chiqueros walking, looked around and jogged calmly to the médios, stopped and brought up its head in an awesome "en-campanado" gesture. He stood there while the crowd kept silent and nothing happened. Finally Mariano Carrato waved a very tentative cape from what seemed like a safe distance. Instantly the bull shot towards him with tremendous swiftness and Carrato had just enough time to drop his cape and leap out of danger. No one else came out. Ignoring all questions of "vergüenza" and "pundonor" Chicuelo signaled to the judge that he had no intention of facing the bull. While a storm raged in the tendidos, the Toro del Miedo inspected the ruedo at will, shaking a horn here and there at a bit of capote shown to him through a crack in the burladero. This was one time in which the bull was completely the victor. I don't want to sound like a professional old timer but one of the hardest things to accept in modern bullfighting, with the decreased size of the animals, is the loss of that almost superstitious and certainly primitive awe which the old bull seemed to inspire. The great British historian, Gilbert Murray, says speaking of ancient animal cults in his *Five Stages of Greek Religion:*

"We modern town-dwellers have almost forgotten what a real bull is like. For so many centuries we have tamed him and penned him in, and utterly deposed him from his place as lord of the forest. The bull was the chief of magic or sacred animals in Greece, chief because of his enormous strength, his size, his rage, in fine, as anthropologists call it, his *mana;* that primitive word which comprises force, vitality, prestige, holiness, and power of magic. . . ."

I suppose the fascination of the old "suerte de varas" was related to this; making the destructive power of the animal unsparingly clear. I first saw a horse gutted when I was a very young child and, though my heart was leaping, I couldn't take my eyes away. My most entrancing and terrible memory of the pica, however, is that of a very clean job of knifing through the chest. The bull charged the horse front-wise, burying his right horn into the left side of the horse's chest. Then the

292

bull stepped back without knocking the horse down and you could see a neat round hole where the horn had been. Out of it shot a full, round jet of blood. The horse stood there, motionless, legs wide apart, until, his blood emptied out, he dropped to the ground, dead. Two more recollections of the "tercio de varas." One of the two great Peruvian ganaderías of the twenties was El Olivar, a Parladé breed. Its debut was a fearsome success. Before the corrida was half-way through twelve horses had been killed, all that was available. Montani, the horse concessionaire (and father of the present-day matador) had to buy horses off the coaches waiting for customers outside the ring so that the corrida could continue. I also remember hearing for years about a legendary "*quite*" of Juan Belmonte. The bull had killed two horses, leaving them lying side by side with a narrow space between. Noticing this Juan brought the bull near the horses and then, standing between them suicidally, he "cited" and gave him four incredible verónicas and the media.

Belmonte's temporadas, particularly the second one, constitute, I suppose, the Golden Age of Lima bullfighting. The great historic "faena" of the period between the wars, however, was not Belmonte's

but "El Gallo's." Rafael literally stopped the show. President Leguía was in Acho that day and after the "faena" he ordered the corrida stopped, sent people out for champagne and asked Rafael to the presidential box for a toast. Part of the legend is that the crowd, stimulated beyond its normal powers of perception, failed to notice an almost equally miraculous "faena" done by "Chicuelo" with the next bull. My memory brings back a picture of "El Gallo" clicking glasses with Leguía and a sense of boundless, overpowering excitement.

The most impressive all-around feat that I recall was Manolo Bienvenida's "despedida de novillero" after which he went to Spain and took his alternativa without going through a novillero campaign there. He was then sixteen years old. He killed seven full-grown Olivar bulls (one as a gift). He and the picadores were the only men in the ruedo during the last three bulls. He gave no more than eight estocadas all told and cut six ears and five tails.

The wildest man I ever saw was Juan Silveti, "El Tigre de Guanajuato." I don't remember seeing him do his "desplante" to end all "desplantes"—a knee touching the bull's snout and a horn between the teeth—but I do remember that he was a monster of courage and vulgarity. Everything with him was complete, blind gamble, but as all these suicidal morons have to be, he was lucky. I once saw a bull carry him about fifty yards dangling from a horn with a torn shirt as the only damage.

The most frustrating of the great men was, in my opinion, Marcial Lalanda. He was amazingly resourceful and brainy and "largo" as they come. But everything he did was somehow disfigured by a kind of innate poor taste. You have heard it said that the closest thing to Joselito in the recent period was Manolo Mejías, "Bienvenida," and I believe that's true. His repertory was encyclopaedic. I even saw him do the old "galleo del bú" once; cape over the shoulders, zigzagging in front of the bull. He was almost a nostalgic bullfighter for he had been schooled in all the niceties and "gallardías" of the old manner such as finishing a "rebolera" by pulling off the "divisa" or taking his "montera" off at the end of a "remate" and touching the bull between the horns with it. Like Joselito he was the finished product of a family entirely dedicated to bullfighting. He was the epitome of the Sevilla school, always "alegre," always brilliant, but never shallow.

One of the eternal quibbles in bullfighting is the question of "banderillas al cambio" and "banderillas al quiebro." I remember debating this question twenty years or more ago. Hemingway says there's only "al cambio" and he's wrong. Cossío says that the two are the same

294

Aparicio performing a *pase de pecho*.

and—heresy!—he's wrong too. The great critic Uno al Sesgo cleared up this point very conclusively in his *El Arte De Ver Los Toros*. There is no such thing as banderillas "al cambio" for "cambio" means to show the bull the "salida" on one side and then *change* and give it to him on the other side. This can only be done with capote or muleta. There used to be a "cambio capote al brazo" with the cape folded over the arm. You would cite showing the "salida" on the right and then, half-way through the charge, pivot and make him come out on the left. The "cambio" with the muleta was done by holding the folded muleta on one side and then, as the bull charged, you would pivot in the same way while allowing the muleta to unfurl. Julio Aparicio, I think, has revived this in recent years. The "larga de rodillas" performed today is a "cambio." The old larga was done by citing the bull full-face with the capote partially spread out on the ground. Then, as the bull went by you would throw the cape over the right shoulder. "El Gallo" would start it the same way but allowing the bull to drift to his left and whipping the capote over the left shoulder in the "afarolado" effect. The "de rodillas" larga is, however, a full "cambio" in that you make the bull reverse his field in mid-charge and used to be called "larga cambiada." Obviously in the banderillas you do not and cannot make the bull do this.

I wonder whether you ever saw the Peruvian "capeo a caballo," that caping of bulls on horseback of olden times. I saw it once when it was revived for the fourth centennial of the foundation of Lima in 1935. It looked difficult because Peruvian high-stepping horses are not fast, but it wasn't interesting; rather awkward and messy, in fact.

I shall finish with a couple of odds and ends. As you know, the greatest descabello specialist was Vicente Barrera. He had a thread-needle eye for it, and he abused it. It was a case of over-specialization rather than lack of nerve, for he had plenty of guts and I once saw him perform the most frightening act of blind courage that I can recollect. He had drawn a large and wretchedly dangerous animal and the members of "la porra" up in the sunny section came down on top of him viciously for the "discretion" of his opening passes. Barrera grew furious and luring the bull out into the center of the ring he did four perfect chicuelinas. As he finished the last one he knelt down with his back to the bull and disdainfully slung the cape away from him. Then he began moving backwards toward the bull; and, incredibly enough, the bull, instead of charging the helplessly exposed man, began to back up also. Clear across the ring they went like this, with the crowd yelling, "No, no, no!" It was all quite fantastic.

296

Finally, an illustration of Belmonte's "dominio." In former days Acho did not have a regular circular barrera; only spaced burladeros, two planks at an angle with side and center entrances. The first row of the tendidos stood directly over the ruedo. The seats were just row-long benches without separate arm rests. You could cram three or four thousand people in over the theoretical capacity by having them stand up in the spaces between rows as well as on the seats. Sometimes the tendidos were a solid swelling, rippling sea of people. I have actually seen first row spectators spewed by the pressure right out into the ruedo as a piece of wet soap will squirt out of one's fist. One Sunday, during Belmonte's second season, the railing simply gave way and at least a hundred people spilled into the ruedo about twenty feet from where Belmonte was doing a "faena." A feast of human flesh lay there before the bull for the asking. The end of the story is brief; the bull never paid the human heap a second's thought. He obediently, almost docilely, followed Belmonte's magic muleta as he led it safely away to another part of the ring.

Venezuela

19. Venezuela

ALTHOUGH THERE HAS BEEN HALF-HEARTED BULLFIGHTING IN VENEZUELA SINCE
around 1776, the spectacle didn't really begin to take hold until the beginning of this century. It is still quite a way from being the taurine center
that Peru is, but it is making strides. The first major plaza was the Nuevo
Circo, which was built in Caracas in 1919, capacity eleven thousand, and
which is still the largest in the country.

However, it is Maracay that the Venezuelan aficionados hold most dear,
for here, about an hour and a half's drive from Caracas, is a splendid replica
of Sevilla's famous and beautiful Maestranza. Built in 1935, it is a perfect
setting for great fights, and more and more they are beginning to take place
there. Manolete and Arruza have fought "mano a mano" in Venezuela, but
undoubtedly the greatest mano a mano in the country's history took place
in March of 1956. Longtime Mexican aficionado Rafael Delgado Lozano
wrote it up expertly in an article titled "Mano a Mano" in 1956 for *Sports
Illustrated*, which, along with *True* and *Holiday* magazines, has consistently
published the best articles on bullfighting in the United States. The article
makes exciting reading, and since it demonstrates how seriously the Vene-
zuelans have come to take la fiesta brava, it is well worth reprinting here.

Over twisting mountain roads, 60 miles from the capital city of
Caracas, lies the lovely little Venezuelan city of Maracay. It is not easy
to reach, not even easy to find on your map. Yet one day last week
Maracay was the focus of the Spanish-speaking world—and of men
everywhere who are drawn to the encounter of the matador and the
fighting bull.

For in the world today two matadors stand together as the greatest. Never until last week had they matched their talents directly against one another in hand-to-hand (mano a mano) competition. Last week Spain's Luis Miguel Dominguín, 30, and Latin America's César Girón, 22, had an appointment in Maracay.

Their ages and temperaments whetted expectations. Dominguín was born, as Spanish-speaking people say, to silken diapers. He is the son of a famous Spanish family of matadors and bullring impresarios. When he retired, a multimillionaire, three years ago, he was the world's acknowledged Número Uno. César Girón's diapers were old flour sacks. The son of a Venezuelan carpenter, he began life hawking peanuts on the streets of Caracas. But after Dominguín retired, Girón fought his way to the very top.

I had come from Mexico, two thousand miles away, to watch them decide which, now that Dominguín has returned to the ring, is Número Uno. And, like everybody else within the confines of Maracay, I had come to watch for a ghost, the ghost of Manolete, the greatest bullfighter of them all.

Nine years ago Manolete was alive, 30 years old and the king of the plazas. The pushing young rival then was the 21-year-old Dominguín. In one bullfight after another, pressed by Dominguín, Manolete carried the fighting closer and closer to the bull's horns, anxiously trying to re-prove something that had been proved a long while before, that he was forever the best. Then one afternoon at Linares, Spain, with Dominguín in the same ring, Manolete came too close to the horns. Next morning, hopelessly bleeding from wounds in his groin, Manolete died, and cast the Spanish world into long mourning.

The hand to hand between Dominguín and Girón would have packed the plazas of Madrid, Barcelona and Mexico City with crowds up to 50,000. But, thanks to Venezuela's prosperity, the test fell to Maracay, and its little 8,000-seat Moorish jewel of a plaza, patterned after Seville's Plaza de la Maestranza. By charging $13 for the poorest seats and $75 for the best, Maracay was able to guarantee $30,000 each to Dominguín and Girón.

Tension built up as the Sunday of the fights approached. People waited for hours in the lobby of his hotel for brief glimpses of Dominguín, tall and imperious, as he glided off in a big black Cadillac to hunting parties on the ranches of old friends or returned in the evening for sleep. Sipping sherry with friends, Dominguín addressed himself to why he had returned to the ring. Money was the main reason; he used a lot of it. But there was something else too—the gusano, the

302

worm that gets inside a man and brings him back again and again to the bulls. "As a matter of fact—" he smiled—"I never really lost sight of the bull's face. On my ranch I've fought them. I never really retired. You'll see."

César Girón, meanwhile, awaited the day in a house jammed with his relations, 11 of his brothers and sisters, two cousins and his parents. He spent long hours in hard training, up every morning at 7, a swim, then a game of frontón tennis and a couple of miles of roadwork. After breakfast he stood for hours in front of a mirror, practicing his passes. He complained that though he has adopted Maracay, the city has not properly adopted him. "They boo me here," he said. "I had to go to Spain to be somebody."

They are very different, these two. Girón smashed through to success and pulled his whole family out of the gutter. He has a poor man's love of possessions. He talks for hours about his television set, his deep freezer, his Mercedes, Hispano-Suiza, Fiat and Buick. At a gas station he is immediately out of the car to talk with the attendant about the exact pressure that must go into his tires, the exact oil for the engine. He is jovial, shouts cheery "How art thou, my loves?" to girls who giggle or scream at him from passing cars. Dominguín would die first. He does not shout at girls. Women come to him, and if they are worthy of it he kisses their hands. He has not the slightest interest in what makes his car run. If it stalled, he would walk away without a glance backward. It is the difference, people agree, in their diapers years ago.

They are strange figures, dwellers in a land where death can come any Sunday afternoon after 4 and they lead lives straight out of grand opera. Dominguín was scarcely 24 when the Duke of Pino-Hermoso in great agitation called on Generalísimo Francisco Franco to save his daughter from the wiles of the bullfighter who was, the Duke agreed, charming but a commoner. The generalísimo waggled a warning finger at Luis Miguel. For months Ava Gardner, who has a great feeling for bullfighters, followed Dominguín from one corrida to the next, later switching her allegiance to Girón. Meanwhile, when Dominguín's marriage to Lucia Bose, the Italian movie actress, was announced, Miroslava Stern, a Mexican movie star, committed suicide with a picture of Dominguín in her hands.

But in their lives Sunday always comes. On Saturday Dominguín went to the estate of a Venezuelan friend, don Alfredo Acero, outside Maracay. There on Sunday morning he went to Mass in the family chapel and then, stripped to swimming trunks and slippers, lounged

303

On following pages: Girón and Dominguín at Maracay.

around the house. Toward noon he went out for a swim in a stream on the Acero estate. It was full of neighborhood youngsters who flocked around for a scar-by-scar examination of the matador's body. Dominguín obliged by describing in detail just how and where and from what bull he had received each wound, then got his revenge by ducking as many of the kids as he could get his hands on.

Till well past noon Dominguín was calm, relaxed. His brother, Dominguito, once a bullfighter himself, came in from the sorting where the bulls had been divided between Dominguín and Girón. The two brothers kissed in greeting and Dominguito said, "You have a chestnut and two blacks." Dominguín shrugged and talked of something else. Not far away Girón was spending his morning in bed, joking with his brothers and sending them for more and more orange juice. Both men wanted people around them and light talk. Each bellowed if by chance he was left alone for a second or two.

At 2 o'clock the tension stiffened in both camps. Noises died down. A man singing on the lawn near Dominguín's window was harshly hushed. Almost unconsciously people began to whisper, and the matadors themselves, suddenly silent and strained, began the long and elaborate process of dressing for the fight. Dominguín stripped himself naked and started pulling on and working smooth his rose-colored stockings. His valet handed him long white underwear pants, rather like the affairs worn by girls in the Nineties. Dominguín pulled them on and tied tight the ribbons just above his knees. Next came the taleguilla, the outer pants, skin-tight, all but iron-stiff and heavily embroidered in silver and black. Dominguín worked himself deeper and deeper into the pants, the valet first pulling fore, then rushing around to pull aft, then bending to smooth the cloth in a glove fit to the skin.

The only talk in the room came in grunts from Luis Miguel. "Too loose," he said. "Smooth those wrinkles." The valet began helping him into his shirt, heavily laced and starched like a coat. Suddenly Luis Miguel exploded in exclamation.

A wrinkle wouldn't smooth down. He ripped the shirt off his back, tore it into two pieces and snapped, "Bring me another." The valet flushed red and looked as if he might suffocate. But Dominguín, calm again, continued dressing. He spent long minutes getting his thin black necktie just to his liking, and then a tinkling sound filled the room. The host, don Alfredo Acero, walked in carrying a decanter of cognac and a trayful of coffee in demitasse. Now Luis Miguel was pacing, sometimes pounding the palm of one hand with the fist of the other. He sipped coffee and cognac, walked to the window and checked the wind, the bullfighter's worst enemy. Wind fluttering a cape can cause the matador to lose control of his bull, and increases the chance for a serious goring. Luis Miguel sipped coffee and cognac again and returned to the window. He had eaten nothing all day, lest the surgeons might later have to open his stomach.

The valet called him back to a chair and began to wind up a lock of hair at the back of his head to which he would attach the anadido, the bullfighter's false pigtail. Once it was in place Dominguín jumped up and walked to a dresser on which he had arranged, row on row, more than 50 religious articles, pictures of saints, crucifixes, rosary beads, medals. Places of honor went to the Virgin of Macarena, patroness of bullfighters, and to Jesús of the Great Power, patron of the city of Seville and of bullfighters. The valet turned, signaled with his eyes, and the little group that had been watching Luis Miguel dress walked out leaving him to pray alone.

A few minutes later Dominguín rode to the ring. There was a long moment of extra anxiety. More than 1,000 people, some brandishing $50 and $75 tickets, were in pandemonium outside the bullring, unable to get in. Twice the great doors of the plaza were opened to admit Dominguín's car and twice they swung shut before he could enter, lest the crowd rush the entranceway. Dominguín waited in the car, biting his lips, until a way could be cleared.

Inside, the crowd overflowed the seats and spilled dangerously into the narrow circular alleyway that surrounds the fighting area. If a bull cleared the fence, as bulls often do, there might be a slaughter. After a worried conference with Girón, Luis Miguel, as the senior matador, warned the official judge that he and Girón could not be responsible for accidents. Then Dominguín turned to the two teams of helpers who were standing, hats respectfully off, in a little group. "You will try to keep the bulls away from the fence," he ordered. A murmured "Sí, matador" went up from the group. Outside, the band blared the first brassy notes of "Under Andalusian Skies," the two-step that by tradition opens bullfights the world over.*

Dominguín in black and silver, Girón in lemon-green and gold, strutted across the ring at the head of their squads of helpers, afoot and on horseback, both looking stern and withdrawn. Between them and a step or two to the rear walked a third bullfighter, Carmelo Torres of Mexico. He was the extra sword who, if both great matadors were disabled, must kill whatever bulls remained. They bowed in salute to

---

* In Latin America "La Vírgen de la Macarena" is played just before the parade; for the actual procession: "Cielo Andaluz."—B.C.

the judge, tossed their dress capes to friends in the seats, who spread them out fanwise on the railings.

The crowd roared again and Dominguín saw the first of his three bulls, Castañoso, the Chestnut One, flash into the sun, head up and looking for trouble. That was the moment for which Castañoso and all the other bulls who were to fight this afternoon had been born four years ago on don Manuel Labastida's Santo Domingo hacienda in San Luis Potosí, Mexico. He was ready for it. Running full tilt around the ring, the big tossing muscle atop his neck hunched tight, he probed the air with his horns in short slashing motions. Every skyward jab was a challenge, a signal, "Here I am. Who dares come against me?" To Dominguín's left a helper dragged his work cape along the ground, and Castañoso charged, charged straight.

His face suddenly all alight, Dominguín walked into the ring shouting, "Enough! Enough! Let him alone. Let me have him." He stood for a second or two, his work cape held high in his hands, biting his teeth into its collar in the traditional gesture, a classic picture, a memory for the fans to treasure. Then he took tight and wide hold, lowered the cape and called, "Mira, torito"—look, little bull, look, look. Castañoso whirled and charged, his feet spitting sand behind him. Moving the cape slightly, shifting his feet by quarter inches, Luis Miguel centered him as he came and received him with the great fanlike swirling pass, done low and slow, that is called the verónica, basic to all cape work. It wrenched the first olé from the crowd.

The bull turned and charged again, and now Luis Miguel was cooing at it like a pigeon in passion, "Ha-ha-ha-ha, toro. Ha-ha-ha-ha, toro." Seven times in seven straight verónicas, each one closer and tighter, Luis Miguel drew the bull past him. Then he brought the charging animal to a stop, turned his back and walked away from it. The crowd sent hats sailing into the ring. His head thrown back, Luis Miguel shot a quick insolent glance at Girón as if to say, "Did you like them, young sir?" Girón stared back, his face showing nothing more than a polite interest.

Moments later Dominguín and Girón came briefly into direct competition, each in his turn trying to outdo the other in elegance in drawing the bull away after he had charged the picador's horse and been pic-ed. Luis Miguel, moving with a dancer's grace, drew the bull to him with three magnificent pirouettes (chicuelinas), with the bull following a cape flaring out from his hips. He stopped the bull's charges with the cape wrapped around his body. The crowd screamed approval. When it was his turn to divert Castañoso, Girón chose a series

309

of verónicas. They were able verónicas, fine verónicas, and they were applauded. But after Luis Miguel's performance of the same pass earlier, they seemed flat and uninspired. Girón walked thoughtfully back to the circular alleyway, leaving Luis Miguel alone with the bull.

Dominguín placed his own banderillas, a task Spanish bullfighters usually delegate to a helper, and the crowd, pleased, cheered him for it. With the first pair he met the charging bull on an oblique line, in a spectacular shock, but the barbed sticks were not well placed. He played with the second pair, showing them to the bull, forcing him to follow in short zigzagging charges. Then he put them in well.

You could feel the happiness in the plaza as Luis Miguel took sword and the small red cloth muleta in his right hand for the final phase of the fight. The bull had been well handled, was untired, still full of strength and valor. Luis Miguel walked in front of the bull, planted his feet on the ground and took him through eight passes, head and horns up, one after the other. He transferred the cloth to his left hand and put the bull through three superb passes (naturales), close, very beautiful and very dangerous. The crowd went wild. Luis Miguel walked away, let the bull rest a moment, then returned and sent him through four more left-hand passes. Still full of fight and power, the bull raced himself to his knees in one dash for the slow, graceful cloth. The crowd's olés came in short, explosive bursts. Luis Miguel took the bull four times again on the left side, then eight on the right side and then dropped to both knees for three breathtaking passes (molinetes) in which he three times drew the bull completely around him. By now the crowd was screaming, "Maestro! Maestro!"

Like all the rest in Maracay that day, Luis Miguel remembered Manolete. He rested his bull a few seconds, then called it through a set of six decorative and dangerous passes developed by Manolete himself. In it (the manoletina) the bullfighter stands in front of his own muleta in high good faith that the bull will keep its eye on the muleta and not on the exposed body of the bullfighter.

Then Luis Miguel killed. His final pass had squared the bull off, brought its feet together so that the shoulder bones on top were apart. Luis Miguel sighted down his sword, went up on his toes and moved in directly over the horns to thrust in the sword halfway to its hilt. Manolete had been in just such a position, over the horns, when the dying Miura bull Islero hooked upward suddenly and eviscerated his enemy. But now it was only Castañoso who died.

The crowd roared approval. Hats and coats came flying into the ring in tribute. From the judge's box came permission to cut two ears off the dead bull and to parade twice around the ring, taking the applause of the crowd.

Then it was time for Girón's first bull, a black named Indiano. Now and then it seemed that Girón might match the heights of Luis Miguel. He received ovations for a chanting, side-to-side, swinging march in which he led the bull away from the mounted picador, for a pair of well-placed banderillas and for a series of pendulum passes with the muleta, swinging it to take the bull first across his chest, then across his back. But he was booed for a prolonged series of awkward testing passes and for a grotesque kill. He drove his sword into the base of the bull's neck and out its side. Desperately trying to retrieve his sword, he chased the dying, retreating bull this way and that, until suddenly Luis Miguel, nearer and more opportune, rushed to his aid, pulled out the sword and handed it to Girón.

Girón was hardly happy—but the thanks he offered Luis Miguel were genuine. Dominguín had saved him from what might have been a prolonged and ludicrous situation. It was a friendly act.

Dominguín came to his second bull, a black named Saleroso, determined to show Girón once and for all who was best. With the muleta he took the bull six times by his right side, six times by the left, then six times more on the left. The bull, which had been charging straight, began to hook with his left horn. Luis Miguel ignored it and went into a series of ornamental manoletinas, his body forward of the cloth muleta.

It was on the fourth that the ghost of Manolete himself suddenly darkened the sun. In the blink of an eye the bull hooked Luis Miguel under a leg and sent him pinwheeling into the air in what bullfight fans call the church-bell turn. He was still in the sky when the bull's horns reached him a second time, ripping his pants and opening a long and bloody scratch across his belly. For just a moment, it was 1947, and Linares. Hoarse shouts and screams rose from the seats. "The bull has him!" men cried. "He's had it!" Women shrilled, "Take him out! Take him out of there! He's hurt!"

In the ring Luis Miguel had hardly hit the ground when his brother Dominguito, in civilian clothes, and Girón were with him, Girón to take the bull away in a series of fast passes, Dominguito to help his brother up. Hurt and dazed by the bull's blows and the heavy fall on head and shoulders, Luis Miguel climbed to his feet furiously angry. He was screaming himself—"Out, everybody, out of the ring! Give me the muleta and get out."

His tattered clothes flapping about him, staggering a little, Luis

312

Miguel went back to his bull. He passed him three times more, and killed him. Then he limped off to the infirmary for examination and rest.

The bullfight went on. Girón killed a stubborn, uncooperative bull and returned to the alleyway cursing the bull and cursing the crowd which refused to understand his problems. Wearing white trousers borrowed from a bullring attendant, Luis Miguel killed his third bull. Girón paced the alleyway, paying very little attention. His afternoon seemed lost. Dominguín had won two ears, endless ovations and, through his accident, the sympathy of the crowd. Despite skillful bull-fighting, Girón had won little applause and large boos.

Suddenly Bellotero, his last bull of the afternoon, roared into the ring. At the sight of him, Girón's eyes began to sparkle. The bull was aggressive, full of fight and it charged straight. Here was opportunity. Transformed, radiating confidence and grace, César Girón went out to meet it.

It was then that I saw something about Girón which was not apparent in his corridas in Mexico. He is still, basically, the methodical dominator of bulls, following one mechanically skillful pass with another in foreordained order. But there is a good deal of the angels in his soul too. When he catches fire, as he never has in a Mexican plaza, he runs his bulls with passion.

And now he was afire in Maracay. He pulled the crowd out of their seats with the first slow, stately verónica and held them there, exploding olés, as he passed the bull four times more. Saving the bull's strength for his muleta, he would permit only two lancings by the picadors.

He opened his muleta work with three magnificent passes, drawing the bull head and horns high. He switched the cloth and took the bull past seven times left-handed, then took him five more times on the right in one set, then moved the bull to another part of the arena and took him by five times more. Now the crowd was chanting, "Heeee-rón! Heeee-rón! Heeee-rón!" Girón stopped and looked up at them with a small boy's grin.

Now everything was working for him. He dropped to his knees and passed the bull in six head-high rushes. Hats, coats, women's shoes were being tossed into the ring and—as of that moment—he had won two ears and a tail.

But his kill flawed it. Twice he went in over the horns and twice his sword hit bone and failed to sink into the bull. On the third try he succeeded.

314

From the judge's box came the verdict: one ear. Girón, riding the shoulders of the crowd, stared up at the judge in angry disbelief. Then he slid down, disappeared momentarily into the crowd, and a moment later was lifted triumphantly aloft again shaking what he believed to be his due: both ears and the tail. He lifted one finger, the bullfighter's traditional boast of, "I am Number One," and shook it at the judge's box.

Some were shouting, "Not the tail, not the tail," but most did not care. It had been a great afternoon. Dominguín and Girón were both Number One.

A couple of hours after they were carried triumphantly from the plaza I met Girón at a lakeside resort. He was drinking Coca-Cola. He said: "It was a great afternoon. Dominguín was superb and I was superb."

Not far away Luis Miguel nursed his wounds. He was drinking an excellent wine. He said: "It was a great corrida. Girón was great and I was great." I agree. I must agree.

Colombia

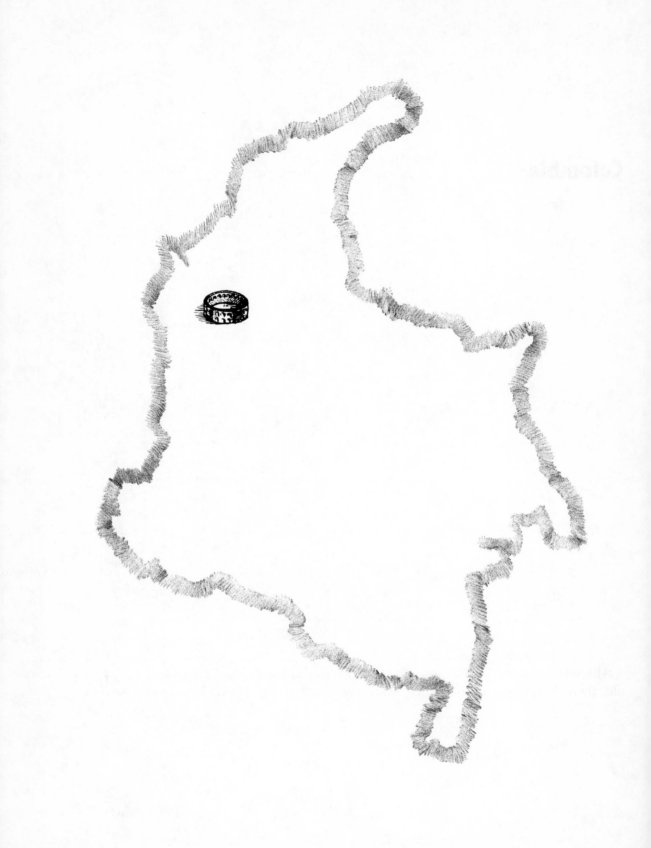

20. Colombia

As in the case of Venezuela, bullfighting in one form or another has been around in Colombia for centuries, but only relatively recently has it really caught on. Colombia's spotty taurine history doesn't actually begin until 1918 with the arrival of Manuel Mejías "Bienvenida." The performances of the talented Spaniard seemed to spark the afición of Bogotá, and four years later they brought over Rafael "El Gallo" for a series of corridas. Afterward the afición seemed to fade away for many years. Domingo Ortega revived it in 1938, and he was the sustaining spark until the advent of Manolete and Arruza in 1946. This was the high point of Colombian bullfighting, and people still talk of that temporada lovingly, despite the later appearances of such stars as Silverio, Dominguín, Procuna, and Solórzano.

Besides the Plaza de Santa María in Bogotá, which holds thirteen thousand people, there are also respectable plazas in the cities of Medellín, Cali, and Cartagena. While Venezuela can boast of its highly talented Girón brothers and Peru can at least point to Alejandro Montani, Rovira, and Conchita Cintrón (who took Peruvian citizenship), Colombia has never produced a first-class matador.

Although most top toreros now include Colombia in their season's schedule, there have been no important matadors killed there. However, one almost died in Bogotá in 1950, and if he had it would have been the greatest ring tragedy since the deaths of Joselito and Manolete. Carlos Arruza tells about it in *My Life as a Matador*:

319

We went on to Colombia, and in Bogotá one of those strange things linked with superstition happened. I've always had an aversion to purple uniforms, since two of my bad gorings were when wearing that color. But for my comeback they had sent me three new expensive suits of light from Spain and one of them was purple and gold.

"Throw it away," I said when I saw it.

"Do you realize what that cost?" said Gago, thinking like a manager. "Besides it isn't really purple—it's more sunset violet."

"It looks purple to me."

"No," said the always persuasive Gago. "It's the light. It's not purple, I guarantee you. I would say this was more El Greco rose."

Andrés Gago could talk anybody into anything, and in a short time he had me believing that this material wasn't even close to purple in the color spectrum and that all superstition was silly. As my fat and loyal banderillero, Cerrillo, helped me into the still newly stiff costume I said, "Once and for all I'm going to prove that this superstition business is childish. What could a color have to do with success or failure?"

Just before making the parade into the ring, I said to Cerrillo, "I wish it were seven o'clock and we were all having dinner."

He laughed and said, "Forget it; everything'll be fine."

And everything did start out fine. I did pretty well with the cape and the banderillas, and the applause made me forget the color of my suit. On the last pair I went out in the center of the ring where the

bull was, and decided to place the banderillas from a very short distance. Suddenly, without warning, the bull charged before I was ready. I lunged off to the side, and placed the sticks right where they should go. But as I did, I felt a searing pain, and the red-hot poker of his horn ripped into the flesh of my right thigh. He slammed me back, and I crashed down against the fence. I was stunned. He whirled on me, hooked me again, and tossed me so high and with such force that I was thrown over the five-foot fence and into the alleyway. Staggering to my feet, I looked down and saw that my entire thigh had been perforated by the horn. It was a pretty little gash, and I saw my life pumping out of it in red gushes. They picked me up and rushed me to the infirmary as fast as they could, and then my real troubles began.

"Where the hell's the doctor?" said Cerrillo, as they took me in and laid me on the operating table.

In a few moments the doctor arrived and bent over me to see what was wrong.

"Well, well," he mumbled. "Li'l accident?"

I realized that he was dead drunk.

"Bad," he stared blearily at the wound and shook his head. "Gonna 'nesthetize you."

"That won't be necessary," I managed to gasp out. "Just breathe on me a few more times!"

"Gotta put you to sleep," said the doctor.

"Like hell you are," said Cerrillo, pushing him away. Then he called an ambulance. While we were waiting, Cerrillo himself bandaged up the wound and frantically tried to stop the bleeding. He tried making several jokes but his good, fat face looked worried.

Once in the ambulance I heard Cerrillo say, "Take us to the best hospital—and drive like the devil—this man's bleeding to death!"

We arrived at a large fancy building soon and parked in the emergency entrance. Nobody was there.

"Don't worry, Carlos," said Cerrillo. "I'll find somebody."

Cerrillo, still in his suit of lights, raced through the corridors and finally collared two orderlies. They took me out of the ambulance, and put me on a guerney, but they refused to take me into the operating room until I had made a down payment!

Two men in bullfighting costumes aren't likely to have money in their pockets, even if suits of lights had pockets. Cerrillo exploded, but they wouldn't budge. He ran to a phone and got the impresario of the bullring to talk to the people in the hospital, and with the money guaranteed, they wheeled me into the operating room and put me on the table.

"Send the doctor in immediately!" Cerrillo ordered.

I was flooding the table with blood.

"Ah, that's the thing," said one of the orderlies. "There is no doctor."

"No doctor!" Cerrillo roared.

The men shrugged. "Sunday."

At this point I was very weak, the wound was going cold, and the pain was terrible.

Cerrillo, bathed in sweat, patted my shoulder. "Don't worry, Carlos, I'll do something."

He ran out into the hall. After what seemed like an eternity he came back with a young man by the arm. "I got a doctor!" he said triumphantly.

"I'm not a doctor!" the youth protested. "I'm only a medical student."

"You're a doctor," said Cerrillo, "and you're going to operate!"

The student looked at my torn thigh. He shook his head firmly. "I've never operated on anything like this. I wouldn't dare. I wouldn't know how to begin, much less finish."

Then Cerrillo suddenly grew grim, and his jaw set the way I'd seen it do so many times when the going would get tough in the bullring. He took the startled student by the shoulders and shook him hard.

322

"Listen, sonny!" he hissed, "wash up and get on your rubber gloves—we're operating!"

He grabbed a doctor's face mask and tied it around his own head, and then when the student was ready, he said, "All right—give him a local and then take your scalpel and cut along there!"

The young man shook his head and swallowed. But Cerrillo repeated the order so fiercely and looked so menacing that he had to do as he was told.

Horn-wound surgery is a highly complicated specialty, and of course Cerrillo had seen a great deal of it, but still it is a minor miracle that things turned out the way they did. The unwilling student refused to make a move unless Cerrillo directed it. Cerrillo showed him where to cut, how to look for the trajectories that the splintered end of the horn had made in the flesh, how to open up the tissues, how to sterilize every part of the wound, and in general did everything that a top horn-wound surgeon would have done. I remember every detail of the operation, and I can assure you that the most scared of the three of us was not I nor the venerable director of the proceedings, but rather the student, who trembled, stuttered, and sweated throughout the whole performance.

It wasn't until the next day that I finally saw a real doctor—and a good one. With amazement he checked over the operation that Dr. Cerrillo had performed, called it a perfect job, and congratulated him heartily.*

---

* It might have been perfect on the inside, but I've seen the outside. The scar it left looks remarkably like a hieroglyphic on the door leading to Tutankhamen's tomb.—B.C.

I think that now you can appreciate part of the great affection I hold for Javier Cerrillo, and also you'll understand why, although I don't like to believe in superstitions, I've never worn another purple uniform.

These, then, are the gates of fear. There are others, many others—Palma de Mallorca, Oran, Central America, Ecuador, and even Manila, to name a few.

But they have a long way to go to acquire the histories and atmosphere of the ones mentioned in this book. Perhaps some day, far in the future, someone will write a history of the bullfighting in those arenas.

That is, if bullfighting arenas and bullfighting still exist. I somehow think it will survive. People need heroes, need conflict, need violence, need bravery, need pageantry, need triumph. There is something universal in bullfighting that touches all of us; for, as Steinbeck says, bullfighting is a lonely, formal, anguished microcosm of what happens to every man, sometimes even in an office, strangled by the glue on the envelopes.

The gates will swing as long as men have courage enough to stand the sight of what comes out of them, which I believe will be a long time indeed.

CALENDAR

BULLFIGHTS IN LATIN AMERICA ARE NOT DEPENDABLY SCHEDULED AS THEY ARE
in Spain and France. If one so desired, one could travel around Spain
and France and see a bullfight every day of the eight months' season. Here
are the more prominent traditional *corridas* in those countries:

March

SPAIN *Castellón de la Plana:* A fight on St. Mary Magdalene's Day.
      Valencia: Four or five fights at the Festival of the Fallas (March
      19).

April

SPAIN *Madrid, Barcelona, Sevilla, Zaragoza, Murcia:* Several Easter fights.
      Sevilla Fair: Five or six fights after the eighteenth.

FRANCE *Arles:* An Easter fight.

May

SPAIN *Madrid:* Ten fights in the San Isidro week (May 15).
Talavera de la Reina: A fight on the sixteenth.
Aranjuez: A fight on San Fernando's Day (May 30).
Alicante: A fight, usually on the first Sunday in the month.
Jerez de la Frontera: Two fights at the time of the Fair.
Ronda: An important fight or *novillada.*
Cordoba: Two or three fights at the time of the Fair.
Teruel: A fight on the thirtieth.

FRANCE *Céret, Nîmes,* and *Vic-Fezensac:* Fights on various holidays.

June

SPAIN *Bilbao:* Two fights for the "fiestas of the Liberation."
Toledo: A fight at the Corpus Christi Festival.
Granada: Two fights at the Corpus Christi Festival.
Burgos: Two fights at the San Pedro Festival (June 29).
Badajoz: Two fights at the San Juan Festival (June 24).
Algeciras· Three fights at the Fair time (June 14 to 21).
Alicante: Two fights at the San Juan Festival.

FRANCE *Arles, Bordeaux, Marseilles,* and *Mont de Marsan:* Several fights
on various holidays.

July

SPAIN *Palma de Mallorca:* One fight or two in the month.
Pamplona: Five or six fights at the San Fermin Festival.
Tudela: A fight at the Saint Anne Festival.
Santander: One or two fights in the month.
Valencia: Six or eight fights at Fair time.
La Línea: One or two fights at Fair time.

FRANCE *Arles, Bordeaux, Marseilles, St. Vincent de Tyrosse,* and *Mont de Marsan:* Several fights in the month.

August

SPAIN *Vitoria:* Two fights in the early days of the month.

Coruña: Two fights in the first week of the month.

Huesca: One or two fights at Fair time (August 10).

San Sebastián: Several fights during the month.

Santander: Two or three fights on Sundays.

Bilbao: Five or six fights at Fair time.

Toledo: A fight (August 15).

Almagro: A fight.

Huelva: Several fights and *novilladas* at Fair time.

Málaga: Two fights at Fair time.

Linares: A fight at the end of the month (August 28).

Puerto de Santa María: One or two fights the first two Sundays.

Almería: Two fights at Fair time (August 21 to 29).

FRANCE *Bayonne:* A fight on the day of the Town Fair and another on the fifteenth.

Dax: Two fights at the time of the Town Fair.

September

SPAIN *Valladolid:* Four fights at Fair time.

Barcelona: Four fights at the *La Merced* Festival.

Oviedo: A fight (September 21).

Cuenca: One or two fights (September 3).

Salamanca: Four or five fights at Fair time (September 8 to 21).

Logroño: Three fights at the San Mateo Festival.

Albacete: Three or four fights, starting from the first ten days of the month.

Sevilla: Two or three fights at the San Miguel Festival (September 29).

Cordoba: A fight.

329

FRANCE *Bayonne, Bordeaux, Arles, Céret, Vic-Fezensac,* and *Nîmes:* Several fights in the month.

October

SPAIN *Zaragoza:* Five or six fights at the *Pilar* Festival (October 11 to 18). *Jaén:* Two or three fights at Fair time (October 17).

FRANCE *Béziers:* A fight on the first Sunday in the month.

PICTURE CREDITS

The following paintings, drawings, and photographs are by the author: Paintings on pages 2, 17, 45, 82, 84, 148; drawings on pages 57, 93, 119, 158, 200, 276; and photographs on page 227.

The author wishes to express his gratitude to the following persons and organizations for permission to reproduce drawings and photographs in this book:

Fotografía Arenas, Málaga: Pages 114, 115

Fotografía Arenas, Sevilla, Page 202

Foto Baldomero: Pages 20 (bottom), 29 (top and bottom), 50 (bottom)

Bill Ballantine, illustrations from "The Brave Kids": Pages 265, 269, 272

Boudot-Lamotte: Page 109

Cano: Page 50 (top)

Francisco Coll: Pages 132, 170, 171, 173, 295, 323

Roberto Domingo: Pages 67, 77, 308, 310, 313, 324

J. Galle: Pages 168, 169

Gonsahni: Page 237 (bottom)

Juan Guzman (Black Star): Page 179

Mark Kauffman and *Sports Illustrated:* Pages 304, 305

Ruano Llopis: Pages 59, 64, 111, 142, 182, 183, 186, 187, 190, 191, 192, 213, 234, 235, 238, 239, 240, 259, 285, 293, 320, 321, 325

Tex McCrary: Pages 246, 247, 248, 249, 250, 251

Fotos Mateo, Barcelona: Page 140 (bottom)

Photo Mayo: Page 146

Foto Payá: Page 51 (top)

El Ruedo: Pages 48, 52

Sedley (*Tucson Citizen,* Tucson, Arizona): Page 91

Fotografía Serrano, Sevilla: Pages 20 (top), 29 (center), 204 (bottom), 205

True, The Man's Magazine: Page 210

United Press Association: Page 126

Luis Vidal, Valencia: Page 140 (top)

L. J. Williams, San Diego, California: Page 237 (top)

INDEX